A TRAILS BOOKS GUIDE

CLASSIC WISCONSIN WEEKENDS

MICHAEL BIE

TRAILS BOOKS
Black Earth, Wisconsin

Library of Congress Control Number: 2001097356
ISBN: 1-931599-06-8

Editor: Stan Stoga
Photos: Michael Bie
Designer: Kathie Campbell
Cover Designer: John Huston
Cover Photo: Clint Farlinger

Printed in the United States of America.

07 06 05 04 03 02   6 5 4 3 2 1

Trails Books, a division of Trails Media Group, Inc.
P.O. Box 317 • Black Earth, WI 53515
(800) 236-8088 • e-mail: books@wistrails.com
www.trailsbooks.com

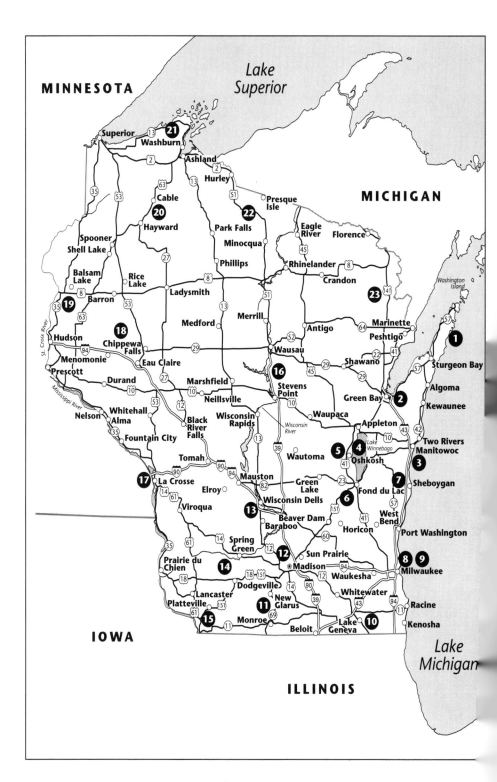

CONTENTS

INTRODUCTION

In trying to get a handle on the concept of a "Classic Wisconsin Weekend" for this book, I started out with the basics: a definition, some facts, the helpful advice of people I asked (friends and strangers), and my own experiences as a lifelong resident and public relations coordinator for AAA Wisconsin.

First the definition. "Classic: a. of recognized value; serving as a standard of excellence; b. traditional, enduring; c. historically memorable; d. authentic, authoritative; e. a typical or perfect example."

Now some facts. Wisconsin encompasses 35 million acres of rolling hills, bluffs, valleys, and farmland, and 1.1 million acres of water, not counting two Great Lakes. Forests cover a remarkable 45 percent of the state. The most recent census showed that its 72 counties were home to 5.2 million residents. There is an average of 97 residents per square mile, ranging from 3,751 people per square mile in Milwaukee County to 8 people per square mile in Iron County.

But this doesn't tell you much.

Three guys wearing lederhosen walk into a bar. The small tavern sits on the corner of a residential neighborhood. The "décor" of the watering hole is nearly nondescript: beer taps on one side, people on the other, and a Green Bay Packer schedule (with the game scores penciled in) hanging on one wall. A card table holds a crock pot loaded with grilled bratwurst swimming in beer and sauerkraut. Next to the crock is an open bag of buns and one condiment bottle, brown mustard. The scene might be of concern to the local health department, if only the authorities knew about it. In fact, it's reasonably certain this place has no business serving food, but no one seems to care. There are few things more tantalizing than a pot of grilled brats (two dollars each), and everybody in this place is partaking. The clientele is dressed in flannel coats, blaze-orange knit hats, and University of Wisconsin sweatshirts, not counting the three guys in lederhosen. It's 10 a.m.

The happy crowd moves outside and dissolves into a sea of people who are lining the street 10–15 deep. As a backdrop, big, beautiful bluffs tower above the scene. The day is gray and cold and damp, warmed only by the autumn colors in the trees. La Crosse's Maple Leaf Parade is about to begin, kicking off another Oktoberfest celebration.

So, then, what is a Classic Wisconsin Weekend? Is it a festival? A place? Food? Some would argue that it's a scene like the one in La Crosse. Another might say it's the solitude found in forests covering nearly half the state. What about a Badger football game? Eagle-watching on the Wisconsin River? Milwaukee's Summerfest?

I dare say the answer is yes: it's all those things and a whole lot more. So I have to confess that the method I used to select 23 Classic Wisconsin Weekends in this book was based on intuition and some good-old Midwestern common sense.

Ultimately, it came down to intangibles . . . the gut feeling that occurs when the morning mist rises through the bluffs along the Great River Road; when the apple-peeling contest in Bayfield's downtown starts, and the Big Top Chautauqua band begins jamming on a makeshift stage; when hopelessly lost on an old logging road in the Nicolet National Forest; when Wisconsin's champion timber athletes are dominating at the Lumberjack World Championships in Hayward; when the tower of a Door County lighthouse reveals the oceanlike expanse of Lake Michigan; when a crowd of 60,000 people rises and sings the National Anthem at Lambeau Field.

Yes, the book certainly deals with beer, bratwurst, cheese, and fish fries, but if this strikes you as too stereotypical, please hear me out. These "Classic Wisconsin Things" are not a necessity for a Classic Wisconsin Weekend, and this book is not a guide to such delicacies (not entirely anyway). But beer, bratwurst, cheese, and fish fries are as integral to Wisconsin culture as the history of the good people who put us on the map. Therefore, I hope, that you can detect the aroma of these foods, along with those of hops, charcoal, baby Swiss, and pan-fried walleye, rising from some pages.

But I've also tried to scratch below the stereotypes, to add depth and maybe even a benign irreverence to the exploits of Monroe's cheese makers, Summerfest's party animals, and Eagle River's snowmobilers, to name a few. Wisconsin doesn't take itself too seriously. It's a characteristic that I hope is conveyed in the book.

To help you get the full sensory treatment from your weekend wanderings about the state, here are a couple of travel tips. Your car radio can provide a memorable soundtrack to your trip. Radio-tradeo, polka, fishing reports—tune into a local radio program and you might be surprised by the atmosphere it creates, even in an automobile. On a pitch-black drive through northern Wisconsin, for example, with temperatures plunging into double-digits below zero, I tuned into WXPR in Rhinelander. The station was playing, by local request, some of the hottest blues music heard north of the Mason-Dixon line. Somehow the odd combination of arctic weather and delta blues worked that freezing night. And Tent Show Radio, recorded live at the Lake Superior Big Top Chautauqua in Bayfield and broadcast on public radio, is always a fitting backdrop for a Classic Wisconsin Weekend.

Likewise local newspapers. If you really want to plunge into a Classic Wisconsin Weekend, buy a copy of the hometown newspaper (it's probably a weekly or a small daily), go to the nearest café for a cup of Joe and a slice of pie, and read about who bagged the buck, who landed the muskie, and who's getting married at the VFW this Saturday (you're invited, by the way). To help you hunt for that elusive radio station or local newspaper in a particular area, I've provided lists at the end of each chapter.

One last thing: I believe guidebooks should be as fun to read as they are practical to use. Have fun reading *Classic Wisconsin Weekends* and, more important, have fun on your weekend travels. It's not a crime. Certainly not in Wisconsin.

DOOR COUNTY
A Springtime Adventure

The DOOR COUNTY PENINSULA, Wisconsin's "thumb," or "tea-spout,"

boasts more coastline than any other county in the nation, 275 miles all told.

With Green Bay on the west side and Lake Michigan on the east, the peninsula

lures thousands of visitors every summer. Perennially a top Wisconsin tourist

destination (the Dells is the other), Door County saw more than 412,000

vehicles visit during a recent July. Most of the cars backed up on Highway 42 in

Egg Harbor, Fish Creek, or Sister Bay bear license plates other than those

adorned with "America's Dairyland." That's fine, Wisconsin will never be

accused of being inhospitable, and there is much to be said for lounging

on Lake Michigan sand dunes, bicycling through Peninsula State Park,

or battling trout and salmon from a charter boat.

MAY'S FESTIVAL OF BLOSSOMS

Knowledgeable travelers, however, believe the classic Door County experience can be found off-season. Autumn offers its share of attractions, both natural (fall colors against deep-blue waters) and man-made (Sister Bay's acclaimed Scandinavian festival). But the fall can also bring more than its share of out-of-town visitors. So, a smart traveler would do well to consider visiting the area in the spring, especially May. That's when Door County celebrates the **Festival of Blossoms**, a month-long rite of spring featuring, among other things, the county's 5,000 acres of apple and cherry orchards in full bloom. It was in the early 1990s when boosters began distributing more than 200,000 daffodil bulbs (now called Doorfodils, no kidding). The daffodils, combined with nature's display in the local orchards, and savvy marketing efforts to lengthen the summer season, helped visitors discover Door County in May. May traffic is up 20 percent since 1993, but it's only half as busy as July. Mission accomplished.

Let's not forget the cherry blossoms, which were not created for marketing. In 1858 Joseph Zettle, a native of Switzerland, established the first commercial orchard on the Door Peninsula. The high yields and quality of his fruit drew interest from the University of Wisconsin, which discovered that the Peninsula was remarkably suited for fruit growing. The commercial production of red cherries began in 1896.

The Festival of Blossoms now includes Sturgeon Bay shipyard tours, Egg Harbor garden walks and Blossom Run, a Blossom Ball, a bass tournament ($60,000 in prizes), the Baileys Harbor craft show, Sister Bay's community celebration, and the traditional Maifest in Jacksonport during Memorial Day weekend. Festival details can be found in a special publication produced by the Door County Chamber of Commerce, (920) 743-4456; to get Door County information online, visit www.doorcountyvacations.com.

LIGHTHOUSE WALKING TOURS

During the festival, the area's ten lighthouses, those icons of rugged individualism and the struggle against the elements, are given center stage. If Door County has more miles of coastline than any other county in the U.S., then it makes perfect sense that Door County has more lighthouses than any other. Door County's earliest lighthouses were built in the middle to late 19th century.

The stories these places tell ... In October 1880, the infamous storm known as the Alpena Gale produced wind and waves that pounded Cana Island, flooding the lower level of the keeper's house and forcing Warren Sanderson and his family upstairs. Then there's Victor Rohn and John Boyce. Out on tiny Pilot Island, Rohn, a hardened Civil War veteran who was keeper from 1866 to 1876, compared it to Libby Prison, the abominable Civil War prison camp. And authorities were quick to note that Assistant Keeper Boyce's suicide in 1880 resulted from lost love—as if seclusion on an isolated, fog-draped island in Lake Michigan was not a contributing factor.

Romance, power, majesty, tragedy—all are accessible during the **Door County Lighthouse Walk** held the third weekend in May. Two lighthouses, Cana Island and Eagle Bluff, are regularly open to the public, but this is the only time during the year that walking tours of the county's three other mainland lighthouses (and boat tours of the four island lighthouses) are offered.

The Lighthouse Walk has become the most popular event of the whole bloomin' month. Tours have been expanded in recent years to accommodate growing demand. Tickets are available from Door County Maritime Museum, (920) 743-5958, www.dcmm.org.

Lighthouse visitors have several options. The basic ticket ($10 adults, $5 ages 5 to 17) allows participants to either walk the grounds and/or tour Sherwood Point and Canal Station in Sturgeon Bay; Range Lights and Cana Island in Bailey's Harbor; and Eagle Bluff in Peninsula State Park.

The **Cana Island Lighthouse** is the most photographed of the bunch—a quaint dwelling nestled against a tall white tower capped by a black lantern. The lantern, 82 feet above the lake, is large enough to contain a watch room. It was the tallest structure in Door County when it was completed in 1869. A natural causeway leads to Cana Island and may require ankle-deep wading depending on the water level, so bring an extra pair of shoes. (Water levels have been so low recently that getting your feet wet is highly unlikely.) During Lighthouse Walk weekend, the keeper's house is open. Shuttles to the causeway depart Bailey's Harbor town hall every 20 minutes; park behind the fire station.

With more miles of shoreline than any other county in the U.S., Door County offers 10 lighthouses, such as the picturesque Cana Island beacon.

Eagle Bluff is probably the most visited lighthouse due to its location in popular Peninsula State Park. The Door County Historical Society restored this beautiful structure in 1960; open all summer and through the third weekend in October.

If you want the real deal—wind, water, mist, lighthouses—call ahead for a place on one of the boat tours available at separate prices. The **Chambers Island** tour is limited to 68 people per trip. Three trips (four hours each) are offered for $30 per person during the weekend. Bring a picnic lunch and plan to hike 1.5 miles to the lighthouse. Good bird watching, too. Call (920) 743-5958. The ship departs from the Fish Creek public dock. Another cruise, aboard the *Yankee Clipper*, offers narrated boat and walking tours of **Plum and Pilot Islands** for $10, making two trips daily, Saturday and Sunday. Call (920) 854-2972.

Finally—the best of the bunch—the *Island Clipper* departs Gills Rock (the very tip of the peninsula), rounds two far-flung islands within eyeshot of Michigan's upper peninsula before docking at **Rock Island** for lunch and a hike to **Potawatomi Lighthouse**, the county's oldest light. The first Potawatomi structure was completed in 1837 and manned by David Corbin, a veteran of the War of 1812. An inspector visited Corbin in 1847 and found him competent but lonely, having only a dog and horse for companions. Corbin was given a 20-day leave with orders to find a wife. No luck. He is buried, alone, in a small overgrown cemetery south of the current light. The present structure was built with island limestone in 1858. The Friends of Rock Island have worked to restore much of the building to its original appearance, including the nine-sided lantern room, and hopes are to reconstruct the oil house, privy, and smokehouse. Perched on top of a rugged 137-foot bluff, Potawatomi is among the best representations of the beauty and seclusion experienced by keepers such as Corbin.

The *Island Clipper* circles past Plum and Pilot Island lighthouses on its return trip. The *Island Clipper* makes only two trips during the weekend. Steve Karges, lighthouse historian, is on board to share stories. Cost $27.50. Call (920) 854-2972.

The tenth lighthouse, the old **Baileys Harbor Light**, also known as "the birdcage," is located on private property and is not part of the Lighthouse Walk.

When the lighthouses were first built, burning whale oil and kerosene lamps required that a keeper live on-site. **Sherwood Point** near Sturgeon Bay was the last manned lighthouse on the Great Lakes, automated in 1983. The Coast Guard is turning over the properties to the federal Bureau of Land Management, which subsequently works with the state DNR to form partnerships with non-profit preservation groups.

Visiting Door County's nine lighthouses in one weekend is impossible. The Maritime Museum recommends that you take "a leisurely trip, by revisiting next year to see those you missed." Sage advice.

While you're at it, stop by the fine **Door County Maritime Museum** in Sturgeon Bay for more lore and cool exhibits. The museum is open seven days a week, year-round. Admission is $6.00 for adults; $3.00 youth 5–17; $15.00 family rate (children 4 and under are free). The state-of-the-art facility contains a replica naval design shop, models, antique outboard motors and engines, a rare 1928 Chris Craft, and requisite old-time photos. Look for the museum at the old steel truss bridge downtown.

Locals Know

Tourism is year-round in Door County, with the months of July and August typically booked solid. But if summer is your season, a lull occurs between Memorial Day and the Fourth of July, affording travelers options for lodging.

CRUISING NORTH ON HIGHWAY 42

For your weekend trip through Door County, your best bet is to begin at what most visitors consider the beginning—**Sturgeon Bay**. Not so much a bay as it is a canal between Green Bay and Lake Michigan, it had been a well-known landmark to Native Americans and early European explorers. The canal was made fit for serious maritime activity thanks to federal funding in the 1880s. With the stepped-up business came shipbuilding, packing, and processing industries. Local cherries and apples have been the most famous exports since the early 20th century.

Sturgeon Bay suffered from economic downturns through the years and was frequently bypassed by tourists making their way up the Door. That would be a mistake today. Thanks in part to the state's Main Street program, the town has

Cave Point is a great place for exploring—especially when low water levels expose the battered rock formations.

regained its footing and compares favorably with any destination in the county.

Take a walk downtown. There are plenty of shops and restaurants. Better yet, venture a block or two off the main drag and have a gander at Palmer Johnson, one of the top luxury ship building companies in the world. You might see some extravagant yachts under construction, the kind of seafaring mansions that exceed 100 feet in length and cost, oh, $15 or $20 million and spare change. Guided tours are offered during Festival of the Blossoms.

Potawatomi State Park has two miles of scenic Green Bay shoreline and wooded campsites for tents and RVs. Also here to enjoy are 6 miles of hiking trails, 13 miles of groomed skiing trails, good snowmobile trails, and an observation tower that offers a spectacular view of water and woods. For more information, call (920) 746-2890. Located on the south side of the Sturgeon Bay channel on Green Bay.

Cruising Door County is one the great Wisconsin traditions, as long as you stop frequently to do some exploring, even if it's just a roadside produce stand. It helps to depart Highways 42 and 57 and crisscross the county along the county roads. (Follow the shorelines!)

Among the popular villages is **Egg Harbor**, which supposedly derives its name from an egg fight that broke out among rambunctious sailors in 1825, or from a nest of duck eggs discovered by an early settler. Take your pick.

Since 1935, visitors to **Peninsula Players Theatre** have enjoyed the latest plays and musicals in the open-air setting. (Bring the bug spray.) America's oldest professional resident summer theater performs late June through mid-October. (No performances on Monday. Call (920) 868-3287; visit the Web site at www.peninsulaplayers.com.) The Peninsula Players Theatre and its box office are located between Fish Creek and Egg Harbor, just off Highway 42. Look for the green highway sign and turn west (toward the bay). It's at the end of Peninsula Players Road, along the scenic shore of Green Bay.

Fish Creek is a bustling village midway up the Door. Fish Creek marks one of the entrances to **Peninsula State Park**, *the* state park as determined by the number of visitors every year. Peninsula is beautiful, no doubt, and it contains all the amenities in addition to stunning scenery: bike routes, forests, Eagle Bluff Lighthouse, a fire tower, beach, amphitheater, and more. Use the golf course located near the north entrance as a landmark to find the park. Take note: being the most popular park means it's the busiest. Nicolet Bay Beach, the park's only beach, reaches capacity easily. Campsites are booked up to 11 months in advance. Don't let its popularity deter you from making a day visit. Climbing the weathered fire tower is an experience that won't be soon forgotten. Nicolet Bay offers watercraft rentals. Bike and moped rentals are found outside the park entrance in Fish Creek. Phone (920) 868-3258.

The **American Folklore Theater**, located inside the park during the summer months, presents plays characterized as "historical yet hysterical." Typical of the offerings is *Lumberjacks in Love*, a hilarious comedy with a local flavor that has kept 'em rolling in aisles. "Plenty of sensible souls would rather listen to their brother-in-law drone for two hours about pork belly futures than suffer through an evening of 'original theatre': and we know just how they feel," reads an AFT promotion. "So we build our shows on the rock of American folk culture: the great tales, the aching melodies, the drawling turns of phrase that have survived generation to generation." During the summer, the seating is outdoors, so bring your bug spray. The productions are presented in the Ephraim or Gibraltor village halls during the fall.

North of the state park is **Ephraim**, settled by a group of Norwegian Moravians in 1853. A number of original buildings may be seen. **Ellison Bay** and **Sister Bay** are the next two villages. Fewer people travel all the way up the Door, especially during the off-season, so there are more opportunities for lodging and solitude in the northern reaches.

ACROSS "DEATH'S DOOR"

Land's end on the Door Peninsula is **Gills Rock**. Here, ferry transportation to **Washington Island** across the ominous strait known as "Death's Door" (originally *Porte des Morts Strait*), is available. Death's Door is the treacherous crossing between Washington Island where lighthouse keepers recorded as many as two shipwrecks per week in the days before steam and navigational equipment. Today it's no sweat on a large modern ferry. Imagine, however, crossing in a birchbark canoe in bad weather!

Chester Thordarson's historic boathouse was constructed entirely from materials found on Rock Island.

Ferries run daily April through October at Northport pier, two miles east of Gills Rock. Phone (920) 847-2546 or (800) 223-2094 for rate information and departure times. Crossing time is thirty minutes. Once there, narrated tram tours are offered, as well as bike and moped rentals, or bring your own bike. Autos are allowed on the island. On Washington Island, it's traditional to stop at **Nelson's Hall Bitters Pub**, longest serving bar in the state, having skirted Prohibition by serving bitters, a 90-proof liquor. The feds believed, correctly, that nobody in his right mind would drink the stuff straight. What does that say about the people living on this isolated island in Lake Michigan who consumed more bitters than anywhere else in the world? Do your duty. Have a shot and sign the book. Located on the island's main road, north of the ferry dock, (920) 847-2496.

For the far-flung experience, take another ferry ride to **Rock Island**. Icelandic native Chester Thordarson once owned the entire island and built an impressive stone boathouse that will outlive us all. The island became a state park in 1962, and it offers Potawatomi Lighthouse, 10 miles of hiking trails, and a small number of backpack campsites. It can be reached by the Karfi ferry from Jackson Harbor on Washington Island, (920) 847-2252. Rock Island is an ideal place for those looking to experience the far edge of the inland sea.

THE LAKE MICHIGAN SIDE

Back on the county's mainland, **Newport State Park** is a pristine semi-wilderness park located along 11 miles of Lake Michigan shoreline. With everybody and his sister going to Peninsula State Park, Newport is a good alternative, if a bit more rugged. Hiking, biking, and cross-country ski trails. Nice sand beach. Good spot for snowshoeing. Camping sites are for backpackers only. Phone (920) 854-2500.

Moving south along the Lake Michigan side, the "quiet side" as locals like to call it, you'll find **Baileys Harbor** and **Jacksonport**, as well as Cave Point, "the Dunes," and Ridges Sanctuary. The **Ridges Sanctuary**, including Toft's Point and the Mud Lake Wildlife Area just east of Baileys Harbor, comprise a series of sand ridges and swales. Made a natural landmark in 1974.

A great beach for hot summer days is **Whitefish Bay Dunes State Park**, Wisconsin's highest sand dunes. The beautiful sandy beach and 11 miles of trails are the highlight of the 847-acre park. Sorry, no campsites. Its scenic beauty and great picnic spots make it a favorite with visitors and locals alike. The trails are known for good biking and hiking in the summer, fall colors, and cross-country skiing. Park trails hook up with trails in the **Cave Point County Park** next door. Low water levels have made Cave Point more accessible and scenic than usual. Call (920) 823-2400.

GOOD EATS

The next best thing to sightseeing in Door County is eating. Fish boils—although standard tourist fare—are well worthwhile for the fresh whitefish served up with potatoes, onions, and melted butter. Pies and preserves made from local cherries and apples are found everywhere. And one local restaurant, Bayou on Third, has been judged by critics to be one of the best in the state.

It's impossible in a single chapter to chronicle the number of eateries (and lodgings) available in Door County. Here's a cursory review, mentioning one or two restaurants of note in or around the popular Door County villages. You'll notice most restaurants are found conveniently on Highway 42 in each village.

In Sturgeon Bay, **Bayou on Third** has emerged as one of the top restaurants in the county if not the state. Its claim to fame are exquisite and affordable Cajun/ Creole entrees from $9 to $14. (50 S. Third Avenue; dinners served at 5 p.m.; (920) 743-3033). Locals favor the venerable **Andre's** on the hill, 23 W. Oak Street (south side of the canal), for solid supper club fare and fish right out of the bay; (920) 743-4179.

In Egg Harbor, **Casey's Inn** is the place, located on the main drag (7855 Highway 42). Serves lunch and full dinners year-round with a panoramic view from the "fashionable North end." Sense of humor too. Call (920) 868-3038 or (888) 588-8238.

Fish Creek has a number of good restaurants, the **C & C Club** is an institution. Steaks, seafood, and house specialties are served daily mid-April until November, and during the holiday season. Open weekends in the off-season; call (920) 868-3412 or 854-4417. **Pelletier's** has cornered the market on fish boils. Family breakfast, lunch, dinner, and fish boil served at 45-minute intervals every night. Reservations required for fish boils. Open May through October, (920) 868-3313. Located in Founder's Square. The **White Gull Inn**, 4225 Main Street, is a popular fine dining setting that includes candlelight dinners some nights. Loads of charm in this historic inn built in 1896. Open year-round. Breakfast 7:30– noon. Lunch served noon-2:30 p.m. Fish boils Wednesday, Friday, Saturday, and Sunday, May through October (Friday only in winter). Reservations requested for evening meals, (920) 868-3517.

Moving north to Ephraim, the Norman Rockwellian **Wilson's** is both a longtime restaurant and tourist attraction serving sandwiches and ice cream— truckloads of ice cream.

In Sister Bay, **Al Johnson** had his famous Swedish restaurant shipped in pieces from Scandinavia in 1948. The goats are local. The restaurant is topped by a layer of sod that is kept trim by goats who graze on the grass, not unlike the tourists below who graze on Swedish meatballs and pancakes. Located on Highway 42 in Sister Bay (920) 854-2626. Reservations not accepted. For the tried and true fish fry in the tried and true setting, head straight for the **Sister Bay Bowl**, where you can get your fix of deep fried fish and cocktails-in-a-tub amidst the cacophony of strikes, spares, and gutter balls. Highway 42 again, (920) 854-2841.

Tiny Ellison Bay is home to **The Viking Grill**, located next door to a must-see-it-to-believe-it, everything-under-the-sun **general store** on Main Street. The

Watching a Door County fish boil—especially the eye-opening "boil over"—is nearly as enjoyable as eating a Door County fish boil.

Viking claims the original fish boil, served mid May through October, indoor and outdoor. Restaurant open 6 a.m. daily, all year. Breakfast, lunch, dinner, and daily specials; (920) 854-2998.

Maxwelton Braes, south of Baileys Harbor on Highway 57, has an 18-hole championship golf course, fine dining restaurant, cocktail lounge, and sports; visit www.maxwelton-braes.com to see their Web site.

READ ALL ABOUT IT

The *Door County Advocate*, Wisconsin's largest twice weekly newspaper, going strong since 1862.

HAVE YOU HEARD?

Still family-owned and priding itself on local programming, WDOR, 93.9 FM and 910 AM, celebrated its fiftieth anniversary in 2001.

Double Take:
Don't Fear The Booyah

When driving through the city of Green Bay or the smaller communities on the way up the Door peninsula, don't be frightened by signs that exclaim "Booyah!!!" This is not an insult or a curse upon your family. And since booyah is usually associated with church picnics, you might assume that "Booyah!!!" means "Devil-Be-Gone!!!" or some other exorcizing expression. Not true, although booyah, a traditional Belgian soup, has been known to possess healing powers not unlike the waters of Lourdes.

Recalling chicken gumbo, this thick concoction is usually cooked in huge vats at church picnics and stirred with canoe paddles. Precious few local establishments offer booyah on their menus; more likely you'll have to wait in line on the church grounds. Get there early and bring a bucket to take home extra servings of what locals consider a delicacy. Belgian pie and trippe (a pork sausage) are delicious traditional foods worthy of sampling as well.

Green Bay and small communities of Brussels, Namur, Rosiere, Luxemburg, and Dykesville comprise the largest concentration of Belgians in the nation. Walloon (French-speaking) Belgians and Flemish immigrants began arriving in the mid-1800s.

As a result, their unique foods and architectural styles can be found today in the region where Brown, Kewaunee, and Door Counties bump together. Unfortunately, many of the settlers' original wooden buildings were lost in the Peshtigo fire. (The same conflagration that consumed part of Oconto County blew across the waters of Green Bay and ignited fires on the Door Peninsula.) But the stone houses survived and can been today, some with detached kitchens that were used to keep heat out of the house during the summer months.

A historical marker detailing Belgian settlements is located on Highway 57 in Namur, near Brussels.

GREEN BAY
The Packers
and a Whole Lot More

It's Bear Week in Titletown. Should you forget, there's a guy driving

around town with a stuffed bear strapped to the grill of his pickup truck,

an arrow through the animal's head for good measure. Friendly horn

honking and thumbs-up signs greet the driver, who smiles and waves like

the flannel-clad king of the homecoming parade.

Ah, the heartwarming traditions of Green Bay, Wisconsin's oldest city,

where steeples and smokestacks define the horizon, where a shot and a beer

and a pickled egg constitute hors d'oeuvres, where the Green Bay Packers

reign supreme—and the disdain for the Chicago Bears is legendary.

When Packer mania swings into high gear, even the trees turn green

and gold, stores move enough team sweatshirts to cloth the hemisphere, church services are packed on Saturday afternoons, football programming dominates the airwaves, and the atmosphere in restaurants and taverns is nothing less than electric. This is where the last publicly owned team in professional sports takes to the Sunday gridiron under slate autumn skies. You want a Classic Wisconsin Weekend? This is it.

> And in the final quarter, the Packers made two touchdowns. They seemed to gain strength instead of lose it, and in their yellow, mud-smeared jerseys, and their breath turning to steam in the chill air, they looked like dragons breathing smoke. —*New York Times*, 1929

Another bear takes a beating in Titletown.

Everybody knows about the state's epic loyalty to the Pack—games have been sold-out since the Eisenhower administration and the number of people on the season-ticket waiting list numbers around 35,000.

Upon completion of Lambeau Field's renovation, scheduled for 2003, the Packers are planning to make 4,000 tickets available on a single-game basis and increase stadium seating capacity by 10,000 fans; hopefully, more people than ever will have a chance to experience a game at venerable Lambeau Field.

But don't let the scarcity of available game tickets keep you away from this unique cultural phenomenon, or, as the locals say, 'come by here once.' Tickets or not, visitors can and should wade into the atmosphere that becomes Green Bay from July to December (not counting playoffs). Pick any home game weekend to get a taste of Packer mania. The Packer-Bear game is one of oldest rivalries in sports, more than 160 nasty confrontations, and counting.

THE MADNESS STARTS EARLY

Forget about that 'frozen tundra' mantra. Green Bay awakes from its off-season slumber when Packers training camp opens in July. So, the greatest opportunities for visitors can be found in summer, before the season ever begins. Training camp opens in mid-July, kicking off a flurry of fan and family friendly activities: Lambeau Field stadium tours, the interactive Packers Experience, Legends of Lombardi Avenue city tours. The crown jewel of Title-town, the Packer Hall of Fame, is open year-round.

Not to mention team practices. When practices are open to the public for a month, an estimated 50,000 to 75,000 people stand under the blazing sun to watch the team conduct *calisthenics*.

Lambeau Field stadium tours take fans on a one-hour pilgrimage through football's equivalent of the Vatican. Skyboxes, the visiting team's dressing room, and the press box are some of the highlights. Most fans simply want to genuflect at the altar of Titletown, the hallowed south end zone. Yes, a small flag marks the spot where Bart went over. Bring a hanky. (After all, this is the place where hundreds of people appear after blizzards, shovels in hand, to clear the snow from aisles, not for $7-per-hour reimbursement, but for the satisfaction of performing back-breaking work inside their temple.) Tours depart from Packer Hall of Fame on a first-come, first-served basis during camp.

Packer training camp generally runs from mid-July to late August. Practices are held mornings and afternoons at roughly 8:45 a.m. and 2:45 p.m., with full pads in the morning, shorts in the afternoon. A randomly selected group of eight players will be available to sign autographs after most morning practices, but you need a ticket to get in line. A limited number of free tickets are distributed by inconspicuous Packer employees before each practice. Get there early—tickets are usually gone 30 minutes before the start of practice.

Watching practice from the fences is a longtime tradition; spectators have their own nickname, 'rail birds.' Bleacher seating can accommodate less than 300 people. Again, get to practice early with a lawn chair if you're looking for a good viewing spot.

One widespread criticism of professional football had been that the rooting spirit, such as colleges furnish, is lacking. Green Bay disproves this. The whole town is a cheering section. Any boy on the street can tell you how many games the Packers have won and who was the hero of each touchdown. —*Milwaukee Journal*, 1929

Another longstanding tradition involves players walking down the long Lambeau Field parking lot to the practice field. Youngsters clamor near the administration building, offering their bicycles to players. The sight of an over-sized pro football player pedaling a child's bike to practice, a proud youngster riding shotgun, is one of the enduring images of Green Bay if not all of professional sports. Rookies 'adopt' a youngster to ride his or her bicycle for the duration of camp. Big-name players usually drive to practice for fear of being mobbed. Practices are closed during the regular season, lest spies from opposing teams try to steal plays. The Bears cheat, you know.

Locals Know

During training camp, the Packers reside at Saint Norbert College in De Pere. A stroll around campus or west De Pere's establishments in the early evening, before team curfew, may yield Packer sightings. If not, it's a pretty walk along the Fox River nevertheless. **Nicky's** and the **Abbey Bar** are longtime haunts.

Running concurrently with training camp, and located conveniently next to the practice field, the **Packers Experience** is an interactive amusement park inside the Brown County Veterans Memorial Arena at the corner of Lombardi and Oneida, next to the practice fields. Visitors can kick field goals, run through tackling dummies, try a simulated leap into Lambeau, or gauge the speed of passes. It's all great family fun. Phone (800) 236-3976. Admission is $7.50, senior citizens, $5. Open 10 a.m.-6 p.m. Mondays through Saturday, noon–5 p.m. Sundays.

For years the **Green Bay Packer Hall of Fame** was the only sports museum dedicated to a single team, and some people feel it surpasses the Pro Football Hall of Fame in Canton, Ohio. The Packer Hall of Fame is not a repository for foam cheese apparel. Vintage memorabilia and equipment, classic photos, and gleaming trophies ensconced in a series of galleries tell the Packer story. (If anything symbolizes the insatiable mania of the Packer fan, it has to be the exhibit of wooden splinters that were surgically removed from Jerry Kramer's stomach.) The multimedia presentation shown in the hall's main theater is a must-see. Three other theaters present season highlights, championship games, or football funnies. And there are enough facts and figures, statistics and trivia to challenge the hardest of hard-core fans. Open 9 a.m.–5 p.m., seven days a week in July and August. Combination tickets with the Packers Experience offered. Call (920) 499-4281.

> Green Bay is a football paradise—a happy hunting ground for players and a seventh heaven for fans. Green Bay, ask anyone on the street, is the home of the greatest football team in the world. —*Milwaukee Journal*, 1929

The **Legends of Lombardi Avenue** is yet another activity that takes in Packer-related landmarks. On an area bus tour you'll see site of the Packers first stadium and Curly Lambeau's boyhood home. If you're lucky, Jay Bengston, son of former Packer head coach Phil Bengston, will be giving the tour and telling personal stories of growing up around legendary coach Vince Lombardi. The two-hour tours depart the Hall of Fame daily through August.

On game day, tailgating assumes an art form. The facts: The Lambeau Field parking lot opens three hours prior to kick-off, enter from Oneida Avenue, cost

$20. Lots of parking available on area lawns for $10 to $20 depending on the locale. Not infrequently do fans tailgate at the stadium without game tickets just to throw back a couple or three barley pops and enjoy the party.

GREEN BAY BEFORE THE PACKERS

Contrary to conventional wisdom, the first journeymen to pass through the area were not punters, but French explorers. Jean Nicolet thought he had found a passage to China when he landed here in 1634, just 14 years after the Pilgrims landed at Plymouth Rock. Nicolet donned silk robes and fired his pistols into the air to greet the natives, who were appalled, naturally, as many people are by the French. A statue of Jean Nicolet stands on Highway 57 north of the city near the clay 'Red Banks' where he landed.

By 1671 *la baye verte* ('the green bay') was a well-known French outpost. Father Claude Allouez built a mission at the first set of rapids on the Fox River, *rapides des peres* ('rapids of the fathers'), at the site of what is now De Pere.

After the French and Indian War in 1763, Britain assumed control of the outpost from the French; after the War of 1812, the United States took possession. Talk about football. Fort Howard was built in 1816 by U.S. troops to protect the strategic location once and for all.

A one-two punch of lumberjacks and Great Lakes sailors created a rough and tumble shipping port rife with drinkin', gamblin', and whorin'. Harbor improvements, a system of eight locks on the Fox River, and rail connections attracted industrial development that rivaled Milwaukee and beckoned European immigrants.

A. E. Cofrin established Fort Howard Paper Company in the early 1900s and the paper boom was underway. Through mergers and acquisitions, Proctor & Gamble, James River, and Georgia Pacific are the paper giants today.

It wasn't until 1919—relatively late in Green Bay's colorful history—that a fateful meeting took place (in a saloon) between erstwhile Notre Dame footballer Curly Lambeau and cigar-chomping George Whitney Calhoun, sports editor of the *Green Bay Press-Gazette*. The result was a sandlot football team outfitted by Lambeau's employer, the Acme Meat Packing Company. You know the rest. Curly's old team still plays on Sunday. While Green Bay is inextricably associated with you-know-what, there are several solid nonfootball attractions that deserve attention.

THE REST OF GREEN BAY

One of Green Bay's premier attractions, the **National Railroad Museum**, is located a mile or two east of Lambeau Field. Designated as the nation's official rail museum by an act of Congress in 1958, the outdoor museum displays a spectacular assemblage of iron horses. More than 75 engines and passenger cars are on display, including the Union Pacific's behemoth Big Boy, the 1950s experimental Rock Island Aerotrain, and General Dwight D. Eisenhower's World War

II staff car. The museum's greatest attribute is the amount of interaction permitted between visitors and museum pieces. Some trains are fully accessible, allowing guests to climb aboard a 1910 Lake Superior & Ishpeming steam engine, sit in the passenger dome of a 1955 Union Pacific streamliner, or walk the aisle of a 1939 café car used on the Chicago, Burlington & Quincy's Silver Streak Zephyr. Also included in the price of admission is a guided train ride around the museum grounds with a visit to a reconstructed hobo camp. For many visitors, it's a first-time experience of riding the rails. A 60-foot observation tower offers nice views. The museum's Hood Depot is home to the Green Bay Area Model Railroaders Club. Bring a picnic lunch to enjoy on the banks of the historic Fox River. The musem, 2285 S. Broadway, is open 9 a.m. to 5 p.m. Monday through Friday. Admission is $6 for adults, $5 for seniors, $4 for children ages 4 to 12 and free for children younger than 3. Phone (920) 437-7623.

The National Railroad Museum, designated as the nation's official railroad museum by Congress, houses a spectacular collection of iron horses.

Free admission is just one great thing about **Bay Beach Amusement Park**. Twenty-cent rides is the other (ten cents had been the rate for decades). Since the early 1900s, locals have flocked to this location on the bay. Although swimming is no longer an option, the park has 19 traditional amusements such as bumper cars, a Ferris wheel, Tilt-A-Whirl, miniature trains, pony rides, and merry-go-round to keep kids of all ages thoroughly amused. A vintage, whitewashed pavilion serves as a thirst-aid station, and it's not hard to envision the ghosts of bygone days swinging to big band music on the dance floor. Pack a lunch (grills and picnic tables are located on the grounds) and enjoy a traditional and *affordable* fun day for the whole family. Bay Beach is open daily June through August, weekends in May and September; (920) 391-3671.

A short walk across the road from Bay Beach Amusement Park is the **Bay Beach Wildlife Sanctuary**, another bargain. Started as a refuge for injured waterfowl in the 1930s, today it contains an education center and six miles of nature trails. The main draw is the residents and seasonal visitors: thousands of quacking ducks and honking geese, and some native animals. The sanctuary is open free of charge year-round. Feeding the birds (corn is sold on the spot) has been a tradition since 1940, although the burgeoning Canada geese population may result in a policy change in the near future. Phone Bay Beach for information.

Opposite the railroad museum on the Fox River's east bank, **Heritage Hill State Park**, 2640 S. Webster Avenue, is a 40-acre living history park where costumed interpreters lead tours of the buildings. Many of the 25 buildings located at Heritage Hill are original structures re-located to the site by river barge. Many structures were built for Heritage Hill. The park is divided into four theme areas: La Baye, representing the early French fur-trading years; Small Town Heritage, depicting the early 19th century; the Fort Howard Area with the original hospital and officers' quarters; and the Agricultural/Ethnic Heritage Area, containing a Belgian farmhouse, stone summer kitchen, cheese factory, and chapel. The park is open Memorial Day to Labor Day and special event weekends; (800) 721-5150.

At the foot of the Ray Nitschke Memorial Bridge is the **Neville Public Museum**. Its most prized possession is the Perrot Ostensorium a priceless silver monstrance given to Father Allouez's mission by the French regime in 1686. A year later, the vessel was buried when hostile Indians burned the mission. The piece was lost for 115 years and discovered by accident in 1802; it's part of Neville's permanent exhibit 'On the Edge of the Inland Sea.' Six galleries are devoted to history, art, and science. Major traveling exhibits are scheduled; phone (920) 448-4460.

The **NEW (North Eastern Wisconsin) Zoo**, features live animal exhibits, trout ponds, and 1,600 acres of trails. It's located about 11 miles northwest of Green Bay, west of Highway 41 on County IR, (920) 434-7841. Open daily, including holidays. Closed January and February. Admission is $1 for children and senior citizens, $2 for adults, $5 for families.

If you want to see the historic Fox River by boat, the *Foxy Lady*, docked at the downtown Holiday Inn, is the only public sightseeing cruise offered, (920) 498-8901. The 70-foot yacht offers sightseeing, lunch, cocktail, sunset, dinner, and moonlight cruises from April 15–October 15. Private cruises available.

The **Green Bay Botanical Gardens**, (920) 490-9457, is designed to highlight each of the four seasons on a 60-acre spread located behind the Northeast Wisconsin Technical College on West Mason Street.

GREEN BAY DINING

Years ago Green Bay was derided by big city sports reporters for having few good options for dining. That's no longer the case. Old mom-and-pop establishments have been joined by ambitious new restaurants. Solid family restaurants are everywhere. Ethnic restaurants have multiplied—there are more than 30 now, from Sicilian to Mongolian to Jamaican. And the bar and grill is ubiquitous; this is Wisconsin after all. First, the old standbys.

Kroll's Restaurant on Ridge Road (across from where 'Lambeau Field' is painted on the side of the stadium) is a local institution. A full menu includes a fine Friday night perch dinner, but it's the sinful burgers that built the place. It's a good thing that paper companies are nearby, because you'll need napkins—lot's of 'em. The chili is served on spaghetti noodles. Check out the autographs of Packer greats and not-so-greats on the wall. An older Kroll's is located on east Main Street. Phone (920) 468-4422.

A diamond in the rough, or more accurately, a diamond in a strip mall, **Chili John's** is an inconspicuous-looking restaurant in an anonymous looking mall on Green Bay's west side. Precisely why you should stop. Lithuanian immigrant John Isaac came to Green Bay with a chili recipe that he had painstakingly concocted for more than seven years. The ingredients are still a secret, except for one. When Isaac borrowed $15 to open a restaurant in 1913 he wrote his wife: 'Come up north and bring the peppers. We'll like Green Bay.'

For decades Chili John's was a favorite among visiting teams when the restaurant was located downtown. (See sidebar.) Minnesota Vikings quarterback Fran Tarkington visited religiously until coach Bud Grant ruled the place off-limits. Grant feared the chili could adversely affect players' health and well-being.

Now located at 519 S. Military, (920) 494-4624, customers can get a taste of Chili John's black 'pungent amalgam' served over spaghetti noodles. Beans optional. The more meat, the more heat. Some people order just the meat sauce —not recommended unless you have aluminum innards. The chili's not so much hot as it is spicy. You'll notice vinegar cruets at each station. Yes, vinegar. Give it a shot. John's chili will grow hair on your kneecaps.

Fine dining and a Fox River view can be found at **Eve's**, 2020 Riverside Drive in Allouez, (920) 435-1571, and two doors down at the **Mariner Supper Club**, 2222 Riverside Drive, (920) 437-7107. For tradition as thick as the steaks, try De Pere's **Union Hotel**, 200 N. Broadway, (920) 336-6131, 80-some years and going strong. **The River's Bend**, (920) 434-1383, and the **Wellington**, (920) 499-2000, are popular west side supper clubs. **Titletown Brewing Company** in the Chicago & Northwestern Railroad depot packs 'em in with generous meal portions and home brew in one of the more impressive depots you'll see in Wisconsin; across from Neville Museum on Dousman, (920) 437-2337.

Black & Tan, 101 Fort Howard Avenue, DePere, (920) 336-4430, is one of the area's new-breed of fine dining. **Bistro Jean Paul's** is another, located at 1244 Main Street, (920) 432-2897.

WHERE'S THE FISH FRY?

Maricque's is the place, hands down, though good fish fries are found everywhere in this overwhelmingly Catholic community on the bay. Owned by a longtime commercial fishing family, Maricque's, 1517 University Avenue, serves fish and fish only on Wednesdays and Fridays. Perch is the plate of choice, but smelt (in season), chub, lawyers, and bluegill are on the menu too. (Menu is a relative term here, a dog-eared table tent is more accurate.) The succulent perch is served on paper plates in single, double, or triple portions, with or without bones, and a thick slice of onion and buttered rye bread on the side. No silverware. No linens. No pretense. The antithesis of every cookie-cutter chain restaurant out there, Maricque's is a real-deal Wisconsin tavern that created a minor stir a few years back when it added french fries to the menu. Fries just get in the way of devouring more perch.

GREEN BAY AFTER DARK

For nightlife, Washington, Main, and Broadway Streets downtown have experienced new life in recent years. A $7 million project restored the past glory of former Bay Theater on Washington Street. The new palace is called the **Meyer Theater**.

Who needs tickets? Some people go to historic Lambeau Field just for the pregame festivities in the parking lot.

Really, just saddle up to any one of the endless number of watering holes in town and state clearly, in the immortal words of one local, "Give me whatever you got the most of and keep 'em coming.'"

Your chili might have noodles in it, your fish fry might be served without utensils, and the little old ladies might want to talk about the linebacking corps, but chalk it up to the quirky traditions of this rollicking old town—and to the greater glory of the Green Bay Packers. Amen.

> Yesterday afternoon, in a drizzling rain, twelve husky young piledrivers calling themselves the Green Bay Packers tore the great Giants line to pieces.
> —*New York Times*, 1929

READ ALL ABOUT IT

The daily *Green Bay Press-Gazette* is widely circulated, but refusing to go quietly into that dark night is the *Green Bay News Chronicle*.

HAVE YOU HEARD?

WNFL, 1440 AM, and WDUZ, 1400 AM, for latest Packer news during your tailgate party.

Double Take: My City Is Gone

The mall and parking lot in downtown Green Bay have the requisite look of such places everywhere—big, blank walls on the outside, two floors of stores and food courts inside. There is nothing exceptional about this place. It's just a mall and a parking lot like every other.

Arguably, there is no city in Wisconsin with a history as rich as Green Bay. The area was discovered in the seventeenth century, not long after the pilgrims landed at Plymouth Rock. Settlers lived under three flags—French, British, and American—with the first plats drawn where this mall sits today. Green Bay—fortress, shipping port, football town.

In the 1960s, like most places in modern times, the city grappled with questions about growth and identity. A plan was laid for downtown redevelopment. Nobody could have imagined the result.

Instead of preserving the historic character of its downtown, Green Bay gutted the very best of its central city, built Port Plaza mall . . . and watched the place struggle for nearly three decades now. Major 'anchor' stores have come and gone. Up to 30 percent of Port Plaza's square footage has been empty at times. Ownership has been passed around like a communicable disease, eventually forcing the city to buy the property and sell to local owners who just might tear some of it down.

Some of the old places still exist. In fact, the original buildings have become the go-to places in the form of restaurants, clubs, and taverns. The night scene has picked up so considerably that it offers a glimpse of what might have been if the balance of the commercial district had not been hammered into rubble.

Across the river, Titletown Brewpub probably saved the beautiful old train depot from the wrecking ball. The Bay Theater has been restored to its original glory. Retailers C. A. Gross's Menswear and Lou's Bootery still hang in there.

Bosse's News is across the street from its original site, which is the mall parking lot.

La Crosse, with more than 110 original buildings, has one of the finest downtowns in the state—a thriving entertainment district. Cedarburg's claim to fame is its old downtown. Communities from Mineral Point to Park Falls, from Sturgeon Bay to Osceola, have preserved their traditional commercial districts and adapted to modern markets. Little De Pere, five miles down the road from Green Bay, learned from its neighbor to the north and saved its distinctive buildings.

Destroy a downtown to save a city. It never made any sense.

ALGOMA TO PORT WASHINGTON
All Fish Great and Small

At least one Classic Weekend in Wisconsin has to involve Lake Michigan. After all, this magnificent body of water forms practically the entire eastern border of the state. And it provides residents and visitors alike with unlimited economic, recreational, social, and cultural opportunities. One of them is the Smelt Extravaganza, held every spring in two counties, 15 communities, and 42 fish fry sites near the Big Pond. Despite those impressive details, this is an unpretentious, understated, slightly wacky weekend where locals celebrate the joys of catching—and devouring—the humble smelt.

And devour they do. Before a recent Smelt Extravaganza, organizers casually informed participating locations (Lorene's Y-Go-By, the Fat Seagull, the Smiling Moose Tavern, among others) that the event would probably sell "an additional ton" of smelt than the year before: a total of three and one-half tons—7,100 pounds. Considering each dressed smelt is about four inches long and weighs next to nothing, that would mean that about 700,000 fish, give or take a couple, were eaten.

But even if your Classic Weekend can't be spent among the springtime smelt, this area of Wisconsin is well worth visiting any other time of the year.

A SMELT PRIMER

According to Webster's dictionary, smelt are "salmonoid fishes that closely resemble the trout in general structure, live along coasts and ascend rivers to spawn or are landlocked, and have delicate oily flesh with a distinctive odor and taste." Don't forget that other important detail: smelt are small, the size of sardines. Unlike sardines, which are packed into a can of motor oil and smell like, well, fish crammed into a can of motor oil, freshwater smelt are dished up fried and slightly crunchy.

When the ice breaks from Lake Michigan coastal regions, the smelt start runnin' and the locals start eatin'. You'd be wise to join them (the locals that is). The season is short-lived. Fresh smelt—a contradiction in terms to people who consider the fish naturally rancid—will be hard to find until the following spring.

Fishing by night, using propane- or battery-powered lanterns, anglers cast their nets into dense schools of smelt, the light reflecting off the smelts' silver backs. Smelters can fill five-pound buckets with ease.

Only one commercial smelt fleet, **Le Clair Brothers** out of Two Rivers, is operating today, a far cry from the days of yore when smelt was commercially harvested up and down the lakeshore, when plates piled high with smelt were served from Kenosha to Marinette and bare-chested men wrestled in rings full of harvested smelt. As much as revisionist history would like to overlook this stain on our culture, yes, smelt wrestling did happen. Our heritage may have faded a bit since then. Fortunately, Smelt Extravaganza grabs tradition by the tail and eats it whole, minus the head.

THE MAIN EVENT

In 1998, a creative Kewaunee and Manitowoc County booster group called "The Lake, The Land" decided to promote the shoreline region through this singular animal: the fish, the smelt. Festivities are kicked off the third weekend in May with Friday night smelt fries at restaurants and taverns throughout the two counties. About 400 people compete in smelt-a-thons held Saturday in Algoma and Sunday in Mishicot; the biathletes compete in a 2-mile run, 15-mile bike ride, and another 2-mile run. The routes are scenic and the Smelt-a-Thon T-shirts are priceless. A 5K run/walk has been added.

Following Saturday's race, the much anticipated crowning of the Smeltmeister takes place at Algoma's lakefront pavilion next to Crescent Beach. A little farther down the shore in Two Rivers, the local Main Street program sponsors a battle of the high school bands.

Smelt Extravaganza is modest, but organizers do a good job of integrating permanent attractions with the weekend event. Algoma's **Shanty Days**, held in August, and Port Washington's **Smelt Fry**, the first weekend after Easter, are two established fish fests along the lakeshore. Throughout the fun and frolic, the traditions of lakeside culture are available in quantity, so eat it up. There's enough for everyone.

Locals Know

From the Wisconsin dictionary of bastardized English: It's pronounced "schmelt," not smelt. In fact, the most important duty—well, okay, it's the only duty bestowed upon the Smeltmeister, the annual potentate of Smelt Extravaganza— is to pronounce the fish "schmelt." The pronunciation is a tip of the hat to German immigrants who settled in the area. Smelt Extravaganza conducted a poll one year to settle the matter. "Schmelt" won hands down over smelt. So that's that.

THERE'S MORE THAN SMELT

Much of Kewaunee County lies on the peninsula shared by Door County, but in the minds of most travelers speeding north it is never considered part of the peninsula experience. That's too bad, because many of the attributes native to Door County can be found in its neighbor to the south, and for that matter, in the counties all along the Lake Michigan shoreline: terrific sport fishing, historic sites, beaches, orchards, county and state parks, festivals, fishing villages, campgrounds, trails—all the while, the harmony of waves washing along shoreline plays in the background.

In other words, taking a detour on the trip north and visiting Kewaunee County is no mere consolation, it may be the reward. The county features Algoma and its namesake town, Kewaunee, two fishing villages located eleven miles apart. Inland, Luxemburg and Casco have some attractions, the most notable being apple and cherry orchards and an 18-hole golf course. Dyckesville, often mistaken as a Door County community, is located in Kewaunee County's northwest tip on Green Bay.

ALGOMA

The self-styled trout and salmon capital of Wisconsin, Algoma fulfills its billing. The state record chinook salmon was caught here. So was the record lake trout weighing in at more than 27 pounds and 49 inches long—a whopper by anyone's count. A recent tournament yielded 20 chinook salmon in excess of 30 pounds. Treat yourself to one of the charters offering expeditions. Contact the chamber at (800) 498-4888 or check the Web site at www.algoma.org for charter info. Other water fun includes canoe and paddleboat rentals available on the Ahnapee River.

The **Ahnapee State Trail** bisects the county on a 31-mile rail-to-trail path between Sturgeon Bay, Algoma, and Casco. Extensions lead into Sturgeon Bay and Algoma. A new rest stop was built at the halfway point in Forestville. The northern leg follows the Ahnapee River.

The award-winning **Crescent Beach Boardwalk**, built by volunteers, was constructed from recycled plastic. Handicapped accessible at both ends, the beach is the place to sunbathe, splash around, or develop your child's sand-castle-construction techniques.

Downtown Algoma, a recent Main Street member, offers guided walking tours of historic buildings. Cost is $2 per person for the hour tour (16 and under free). Call (920) 743-2715 for arrangements. One of the highlights is the venerable **von Stiehl Winery**, the oldest winery in the state and housed in an 1850s building that was once home to the Ahnapee Brewing Company. The winery is famous for wrapping bottles in casts to protect freshly made wine from heat and light while it ages. Located at 115 Navarino Street, next to the river downtown; (800) 955-5208, 30-minute guided tours are offered seven days a week, May 1-October 31. Algoma's Visitor Center is located on Highway 42 on the south end of town.

KEWAUNEE

About 10 miles south of Algoma is another picturesque lakeshore town, Kewaunee. Be sure to go to jail. **The Jail Museum**, located next to the beautiful courthouse in the **Marquette Historic District**, is a real eye-opener. Built in 1876 before the concept of reforming criminals, the cells are oppressive, if not gruesome, five-foot-by-six-foot concrete dungeons. Kewaunee was settled following bogus stories of gold discoveries in area swamps. At least ten shipwrecks are located off Kewaunee's shores due to hidden shoals, making the area popular for diving. Phone (920) 388-4822.

TWO RIVERS

The Ojibwe called the Two Rivers area Neshoto, meaning "twins." Today's natives call it "Trivers." After the rise and fall of lumbering and commercial fishing, Two Rivers evolved into a manufacturing town. Its most famous product, however, was manufactured in 1881, when a soda fountain at 1404 15th Street began selling an addictive combination of ice cream and chocolate sauce. Named for the only day of the week on which it was sold, the ice cream sundae is memorialized at the **Washington House Hotel**. The city's connection to Charlton Heston, famous actor and menace to apes, is also detailed here. (Heston married Two Rivers native Lydia Clarke.) Open 9 a.m.–9 p.m., May through October; 9 a.m.–5 p.m., November–April. Phone (920) 793-2490. Two fine museums located downtown are the **Great Lakes Coast Guard Museum**, 2022 Jackson Street, and the **Rogers Street Fishing Village**, 2102 Jackson Street, (920) 793-5905. Both are open daily mid-May to mid-September; admission $2.

MANITOWOC

In 1847 Captain Joseph Edwards constructed a schooner, Citizen, in Manitowoc, sparking a maritime legacy that has ebbed and flowed like so many waves on the shore. Manitowoc became know as the Clipper City in the second half of the 19th century as it built the very first and last schooners on the Great Lakes, and many in between. Smaller shipyards flourished then disappeared, replaced by the Manitowoc Ship Building Company, which churned out 437 hulls.

These included 28 submarines constructed for the U.S. Navy during World War II. Local workers and engineers, 7,000 strong, developed new construction methods including the side launching of submarines to aid the war effort. The first one was launched in 1942. One Manitowoc-made underwater raider, the USS *Rasher*, sank 99,901 tons of shipping, the second-highest total for an American sub. Four Manitowoc subs were lost, taking 336 officers and enlisted men with them. A detailed history of each sub is found at the museum today; the Burger Boat Company is the only shipyard remaining in Manitowoc.

The city takes its maritime history seriously. Thus the **Wisconsin Maritime Museum**, which chronicles the city's shipbuilding heritage and the life of the 19th-century sailor. Two floors comprise the museum's state-of-the-art galleries. You can walk the streets of a historical Great Lakes port and learn the story of shipbuilding and commerce from sail to steam—right up to today's diesel freighters, pleasure yachts, and work boats. There are seven areas where you can sit and watch movies of maritime activities from yesterday to today. The models are outstanding. One gallery's devoted entirely to model ships—a cool exhibit for children and adults alike. Hardly kit-built, these models were painstakingly handcrafted plank by plank, just like their real-life counterparts. At the submarine exhibit, visitors can work an authentic sub periscope that offers a view of downtown Manitowoc.

The award-wining Crescent Beach Boardwalk in the fishing village of Algoma features sandy shores and this scenic breakwater.

Moored adjacent to the museum is the **USS *Cobia***, a National Historic Landmark, and submarine of the same class as 28 similar ones constructed in Manitowoc during World War II. Tours snake their way through the entire ship, which is ready to go just as she was when she joined the fleet in the 1940s: torpedo room, wardroom, crews quarters, engine room, you'll walk down the narrow aisles and climb through the oval portals between compartments (watch your head and shins!). It's a great learning experience. Groups can arrange to spend the night on board!

Museum and submarine tour rates are $7 adult, $5 child (6 to 12), 5 and under free, $20 family ticket. Group rates are available for 20 or more. Reserve your group tour four weeks in advance. The museum and the Cobia are open seven days a week except holidays. Phone (920) 684-0218. Summer hours 9 a.m.–6 p.m.; rest of the year, 9 a.m.–5 p.m.; the Web site is www.wimaritimemuseum.org.

Built in Sturgeon Bay, the **SS *Badger*** offers the only cross-lake passenger-oriented service on the Great Lakes. A four-hour, 60-mile cruise takes passengers and their vehicles or bicycles across Lake Michigan between Manitowoc and Ludington, Michigan. In addition to saving travelers 400 miles of driving around Lake Michigan, the Badger offers amenities—food, theater, gift shop, and a whole new perspective on the lake—that will make the time pass quickly. Check www.ssbadger.com or call (888) FERRY-4-U.

Pinecrest Historical Village is an impressive collection of 25 historic buildings. Norwegian, Bohemian, and German log houses and a 1870s general store and cheese factory among the sites. Gardens, nature trail, and gift shop on site. Phone (920) 684-5110 (seasonal) and (920) 684-4445 (Manitowoc office).

Rahr-West Art Museum, 610 N. Eighth Street, is located in a 1891 Victorian mansion; 19th-century paintings, Boehm porcelains, and Chinese ivory carvings. Free. Phone (920) 683-4501; email address is rahrwest@manitowoc.org.

THE START OF THE LOWER SHORE: SHEBOYGAN

Farther south along Lake Michigan, you'll find more charming towns that reflect lakeside heritage. One of them is Sheboygan, another erstwhile fishing, shipping, and trade center that anoints itself Bratwurst Capital of America by throwing a sausage orgy every year. It's not the brats that are luring more people to the area, although grilled brats on a hard bun with onions and brown mustard are pretty good reason. The county has experienced an 831 percent increase in inquiries from potential visitors in the last five years. Sheboygan always has had strong attractions in the nearby Road America auto racetrack and the Kettle Moraine Forest. The construction of a marina and arts center and the revitalization of lakefront businesses helped spiff up the city, too.

But nothing helped increase county room tax revenues by 136 percent as much as the emergence of world-class golf courses in the village of Kohler. Blackwolf Run and Whistling Straits boast PGA championship links. Golf magazine readers rated Blackwolf as the best in the U.S. Whistling Straits, set alongside Lake Michigan among sand dunes that are larger than anything this side of the Sahara, is designed to emulate British seaside courses. Phone (920) 457-4446 for more information.

The *Lottie Cooper* shipwreck is a unique outdoor exhibit featuring the remains of a schooner that capsized in 1894 just off the Sheboygan harbor. The hull was discovered during harbor development and mounted at the **Harbor Centre Marina. Deland Lakefront Park** and the marina connect to the **Harbor Centre Riverfront**. A boardwalk winds past restored fishing shanties, a converted warehouse, shops, restaurants, charter fishing services, and a motel.

Sheboygan **Indian Mound Park**, 5000 S. Ninth Street, contains 18 American Indian burial mounds, including five deer and two panthers that are considered to be of unsurpassed quality. This is one of the few state mound groups still intact. Nature trails wind through its 15 acres. The park is open 10 a.m.–10 p.m. daily, free.

The USS *Cobia*, a World War II-era submarine similar to those produced in Manitowoc's shipyards, stands guard at the Wisconsin Maritime Museum. The *Badger* car ferry can be seen in the distance.

The area also boasts a bike trail. **The Old Plank Road Bike Trail** is a paved route over rolling hills between Sheboygan, Kohler, Sheboygan Falls, Plymouth, and Greenbush, 17 miles one way. The trail parallels Highway 23 and no fee is required. The Sheboygan trailhead is located at the west end of Erie Street, a half-mile west of Memorial Mall. Summer headwinds can be a challenge when biking westward. Another multi-use trail in Sheboygan, the **North Point Recreation Trail**, includes a scenic overlook and several sets of stairs leading to the beachfront.

For more information and a trail map, contact the Sheboygan Area Convention and Visitors Bureau, (800) 457-9497.

KOHLER

Laid out according to the plan of an English garden city, the village of Kohler is the mother of all company towns. Incorporated in 1913, Walter Kohler, Sr., hired the best architects of the day to plan the community based on his belief that "employees should have not only wages, but roses as well."

Waelderhaus, located on a bluff overlooking the Sheboygan River, was built as a tribute to the forest of Bregenz, Austria, Kohler's homeland. It is notable for

Sheboygan's lakefront contains the remnants of the schooner *Lottie Cooper*, which foundered in 1894 and was discovered during construction of the Harbor Centre Marina nearly a century later.

its distinctive Alpine design. John Michael Kohler's daughter dedicated the building as a meeting place for the Girl Scouts of Kohler Village. Free, guided tours are given daily at 2, 3, and 4 p.m., except holidays, (920) 452-4079.

The reputation of the **American Club** in the Kohler Village has preceded itself for decades. The only AAA-rated Five Diamond resort in the Midwest, the 232-room American Club is the gemstone of attractions that include **Blackwolf Run** and **Whistling Straits** golf courses, the **Immigrant Room** restaurant (arguably the finest fine dining establishment in the state), **Artspace**, Waelderhaus, and a wildlife preserve. Although the American Club was built as the boarding house for Kohler's immigrant workers, its modern clientele is decidedly more well healed. Phone (920) 457-8000.

Sometimes referred to as the "Toilet Museum" or the "Plunger Palace," **Kohler Design Center** is an impressive 36,000-square-foot, three-level space serving as the showroom for the bathroom fixtures giant. A museum is located in the center as well. Free; open Monday–Friday, 9 a.m.–5 p.m., weekends and holidays, 10 a.m.-4 p.m.; (920) 457-3699.

John Michael Kohler Arts Center, 608 New York Avenue, is ranked in the top five percent of the nation's art centers and museums. Theatrical performances are held, too. Interactive exhibits for children. The complex incorporates the original home of Mr. Kohler, an Italianate villa built in 1882 and listed on the National Register of Historic Places. Free. Call (920) 458-6144 for schedule.

SHEBOYGAN FALLS

A member of the Main Street program, Sheboygan Falls, showcases about a dozen buildings of nearly every architectural style popular in 19th-century Wisconsin. Specialty stores occupy many of the old storefronts. A walking tour will capture much of the town's best features; pick up a free map at the Main Street office, 641 Monroe Street, (920) 467-6200.

Rolling dunes are the draw at **Kohler-Andrae State Park** just south of Sheboygan, an ideal place to spend a summer day on the park's two miles of snow-white sand beaches. A boardwalk takes you across the shifting dunescape to a nature center. In the summer, the water warms enough for swimming and there's plenty of room to throw down a blanket and soak some rays (with sunscreen, of course); (920) 451-4080. The park contains 106 year-round campsites.

PORT WASHINGTON

Port Washington, in Ozaukee County, serves as a perfect end, or beginning, to your lakeside excursion. An idyllic fishing village distinguished by a quaint downtown and pre-Civil War houses, Port Washington is home to Saint Mary's Church, the subject of many a photograph. The 1882 gothic church sits on one of the town's seven hills overlooking the downtown and lake. Charter boats operate from the marina during summer and fall; fishing for trout and salmon (coho and chinook) takes place year-round.

WHERE'S THE FISH FRY?

You can find fish fries at every restaurant and tavern up and down the shore. Take some fresh whitefish, trout, or smoked chub home with you. **Suzie Q Fish Market** in Two Rivers is the place. Phone (920) 793-5240.

The best-known landmark in Port Washington is the **Smith Brothers Fish Shanty Restaurant**, 100 N. Franklin, (262) 284-5592, on the waterfront downtown (at the corner, impossible to miss). The restaurant, Wisconsin's oldest seafood establishment, offers a nice view of Lake Michigan's harbor. The menu features Great Lakes fare (smoked chub, perch, salmon, whitefish, trout). The dining room faces the lake, a carryout counter has a table or two for a quick bite, home brew is featured in the pub, and a screened porch (The Landing) is downright sedating in summer.

The Port Washington Smelt Fry takes place the weekend after Easter as a fundraiser for the Van Ells-Schanern American Legion Post. Call (414) 284-4690. A ton of smelt is served at the Memorial Building in Lake Park.

READ ALL ABOUT IT

The *Algoma Record-Herald, Kewaunee Enterprise, Manitowoc Times Herald, Sheboygan Press,* and *Port Washington Ozaukee Press* keep the lakeshore up to speed.

HAVE YOU HEARD?

WTRW, 1590 AM, for local talk; WHBL, 1330 AM, for news and sports; WCUB, 980 AM , for country; WGLB, 100.1 FM, for the best of the 70s; WBDK, 96.7 FM, for "first class favorites;" WJOK, 1050 AM, local sports.

Double Take: End of the Line for Commercial Fishermen?

The troubles might be described best as lake wars, the counterpart to the range wars that sprang up during settlement of the Old West. Instead of ranchers and cowboys facing off, commercial fishermen are grappling with sport fisherman and the state Department of Natural Resources to practice their trade, a way of life that is fading rapidly.

It all started with a small fish, not smelt, but alewives, which had been commercially harvested for generations for use in pet foods. By just about everyone's account, alewife populations were out of control in the 1960s, their carcasses littering beaches and clogging drains. Pacific trout and salmon, predators, were introduced to combat the problem. Then, in the early 1980s, the alewife population plunged. Commercial fishermen believe that the predatory fish were overstocked by the DNR. The DNR blamed commercial fisherman for over harvesting, warning that game fish were in danger of starving without the alewives. Wisconsin banned alewife fishing in 1988, marking the beginning of the end for commercial fishermen, whose profitability took a severe blow.

The chain of events repeated itself with other types of fish. Each new law, regulation, or quota was stacked against commercial harvesting. In Minnesota and Michigan, the DNR simply bought out the commercial fishermen.

Regardless of whose side you take, one thing is certain: It's impossible for Wisconsin's commercial fisherman to operate without other sources of income. After more than a century of commercial fishing, the current generation will be the last. Experts are giving the industry another 10 years, maybe. Most fish we enjoy on our dinner plates today come from Canadian waters.

LAKE WINNEBAGO
Making the Loop Tour

How can you resist a region that boasts of towns like Appleton, Oshkosh, and Kimberly—places that claim Harry Houdini, bib overalls, and printed paper napkins as their very own? These communities and the others circling Lake Winnebago can offer more than enough attractions to satisfy even the most energetic and easily bored weekender.

From the very start, Native Americans and pioneers recognized the tremendous potential of the Fox River, the water highway that rolls *from* Lake Winnebago and one of the few rivers in the country that flows north. Throughout history, the 14 communities that emerged along the Fox River have demonstrated an entrepreneurial gusto that thrives to this day. In 1793 Kaukauna recorded the first deeded land transaction in the territory for five gallons of rum. In 1892, Appleton became the first city in North America to generate electricity from waterpower. Today, the Paper Valley is not just a nickname. Paper mills and paper-related industries are the economic lifeblood of the region.

With the third largest population in Wisconsin (and the state's fastest-growing region), the valley has earned its share of accolades: a little cosmopolitan area in the heartland; a recreational playground; an ideal place to live, work, and raise a family. It's also great place to spend a classic Wisconsin weekend.

The centerpiece of the area is **Lake Winnebago**, which sometimes seems underappreciated. Maybe it has to do with the fact that Winnebago means "people of strong smelling water." The lake, by far the largest in the state at 10 miles across and 30 miles long, dominates the eastern half of the state map, yet you don't hear it mentioned frequently as a travel destination. For the locals that's probably a good thing, because there's a lot for the people of Oshkosh, Fond du Lac, Pipe (yes, Pipe), and other towns to enjoy for themselves. And do they ever. Summer, winter—thousands can be found boating, sailing, fishing (walleye, perch, white bass) . . . or sitting in ice fishing shanties, spears in hand, like Ishmaels in Packer jackets (see sidebar at the end of this chapter). In short, despite its name, Lake Win-nebago is no stinker.

And neither are the Fox River Valley and Lake Winnebago region, which offer much more than crowded shopping malls along Highway 41 and paper mills along the river. Surprisingly, all the good things of the earth remain.

APPLETON

In keeping with that idea, you may want to begin your tour with the **1,000 Islands Environmental Center**, where you can espy eagles near a paper producer in downtown Kaukauna, just east of Appleton. The never-ending melody of rushing water around the many rocks and islands in the Fox River is just yards away

The Fox River winds it way through "the flats" near downtown Appleton. Some of the original industrial buildings have been converted into modern housing.

from the environmental center on 700 Dodge Street. 1,000 Islands is open Monday through Friday, 8 a.m.–4 p.m., weekends 10 a.m.–3:30 p.m., and easy to find by following the signs posted in town. Admission is free. Phone (920) 766-4733.

Another one of the Fox Valley's natural attractions is the **Gordon Bubolz Nature Preserve** in Appleton, a 782-acre green space offering five trails for year-round outdoor activities. The miles of trails range from the easy half-mile Esker Trail path to a 4.5-mile Wilderness Trail. Each trail can accommodate cross-country skiers during the winter months. Try a pair of snowshoes; rentals are available.

Bubolz features an earth-sheltered nature center with a bookstore and exhibits describing seasonal changes of indigenous plants and animals. Fun family workshops and programs are held at various times throughout the year, including maple syruping and craft making. Picnicking is permitted, too. Just carry out what you bring in. Fishing is popular from two wheelchair-accessible landings. The preserve is open dawn to dusk at no charge. (Donations gratefully accepted.) It is conveniently located at 4815 Lynndale Drive (County A) on Appleton's north side, a short drive north of the junction of Northland Avenue. Open Tuesday–Friday, 8 a.m.–4:30 p.m., Saturday 11 a.m.–4:30 p.m., Sunday 12:30–4:30 p.m. There is a fee for skiing. Phone (920) 731-6041.

Plamann County Park and Children's Farm features farm animals in a park setting seven days a week from mid-May through September. Plamann Park also has a popular, 5-star disc-golf course located at 1375 Broadway. Phone (920) 832-4790.

Memorial Park Arboretum and Gardens, 1313 Northfield, showcases the Frank Lloyd Wright-inspired Scheig Learning Center. The center creates an indoor forest atmosphere with plenty of timber, exposed beams and skylights, and serves as resource center for horticulturalists. Phone (920) 993-1990.

If you're looking for the place to be, there's no doubt about it: the epicenter of Fox Cities activity—and a lot of its nightlife—is Appleton's **College Avenue**, so-named because of its proximity to highly regarded Lawrence University. Weekend visitors mix easily with local residents and students to create an energetic strip in the heart of downtown.

In fact, what was already a prime attraction is aspiring to become the most vibrant downtown north of Madison and Milwaukee with the construction of a $40 million performing arts center scheduled to open by the end of 2002. Located on College Avenue, the arts center will showcase national and regional performers more than 180 nights a year. Another $6.3 million is being put into College Avenue beautification. The project is changing the face of the Fox Valley's largest downtown. Hopes are high that College Avenue will expand its appeal from being a solid local hotspot to a destination with statewide drawing power.

One of the most publicized attractions in Appleton is the **Houdini Historical Center** on College Avenue. Before he became known world over as Harry Houdini, young Ehrich Weiss and his family lived in Appleton. The facility offers a good collection of Houdini memorabilia, including the magician's own posters, lock picks, handcuffs, and straitjackets—and the actual milk can used in Hou-dini's most famous escapes. Sorry, no pictures allowed. Many researchers, including those from the Discovery Channel and the BBC, have used the artifacts and archives at the center.

Looking for something different to do? Check out the bust of "Tailgunner Joe" McCarthy, former U.S. Senator and infamous commie-baiter. Controversy had nagged local officials for years because the larger-than-life bust was originally located in the Outagamie County courthouse as a tribute. In 2001, after 40 years, Joe was moved to the **Outagamie County Museum**, where his legacy can be discussed in its proper historical context. It's the only public recognition you'll find of McCarthy, a Grand Chute native, anywhere. (He's buried in a local cemetery, by the way.)

The Houdini Center and the county museum are housed in a Norman Revival-style 1924 Masonic temple at 330 East College Avenue, (920) 735-8445, downtown. The center is open year-round and offers annual events including summer magic shows and Halloween with Houdini. A walking tour map is available. Open Tuesday–Saturday, 10:00 a.m.–5:00 p.m.; Sunday noon–5:00 p.m. Open Mondays, 10 a.m.–5 p.m. during June, July, and August. Admission is $4; senior citizens $3.50; ages 5–17, $2; family rate $10.

Across the street from the Houdini exhibit, **Lawrence University** is never without a full slate of events, including a speaker series and performing arts. The Memorial Chapel and the Stanbury Theater, both located in the university's

Harry Houdini's spirit is alive and well in Appleton, where the young Ehrich Weiss grew up and took a keen interest in chicanery.

Music-Drama Center, host hundreds of performances throughout the year. The Office of Public Events can provide current information at (920) 832-6585.

Nightlife is also the draw along College Avenue, with more clubs and bars than you can fit into one weekend, but no visit to the Fox Cities would be complete without hoisting one at **Cleo's Brown Beam**, 205 W. College, the tavern where every day is Christmas. Cleo's packs 'em in early and often, so get there early, and often. **Jim's Place** is popular among the younger crowd.

Good restaurants are numerous along the strip: With a tip of the fedora to the legendary football coach, the **Vince Lombardi Steakhouse** continues a tradition of fine dining in the Paper Valley Hotel. Italian is standard fare at **Victoria's**, where the comfortable restaurant dishes up huge portions. Try the eggplant Parmesan. **The Gibson Grill** is a remodeled automotive garage listed on the National Register of Historic Places. **Mongo's**, 231 Franklin, two blocks north of College Avenue, is an eclectic downtown restaurant popular for its buffet of Mongolian stir-fry. **Rueckl's Bar and Restaurant** serves southern and Jamaican-style food, with live blues and jazz on weekends. There are also plenty of other cafes, coffee houses, and shops in the area.

A stroll through the downtown is good alternative to the bars and the price is right. Just south of College Avenue is the **Front Street neighborhood**, located along the Fox River; and north of Lawrence University is the City Park neighborhood, two areas full of stately old homes and shade trees—the kind of real-life Norman Rockwell environment that contributes to Appleton's all-American reputation. The Appleton Street Skyline Bridge offers nice views of the Fox River. Some of the old buildings along the banks have been converted to new uses. A vintage 1858 brewery is the location of the **Appleton Brewing Company**, located between the locks on the Fox River.

Located at 100 W. College Avenue, the Avenue Mall contains the **Fox Cities Children's Museum**, a bright, attractive museum with 18 hand-on exhibits designed to stimulate children—including infants and toddlers—and encourage learning by doing. Within 20,000 square feet are an electromagnetic crane, full-scale fire truck, a giant slide simulating the human heart and much more. The museum holds programs through the week (weekends included) and is a favorite for school field trips, day-care providers, and youth groups who make field trips to learn about science, art, safety, and other cultures; (920) 734-3226.

A city as steeped in history as Appleton has its fair share of longtime businesses. **Conkey's Book Store**, 226 College Avenue, holds more than 80,000 titles and recently remodeled and expanded to include a gift shop and coffee bar. The 100-year old business is located in a century-old landmark building; (920) 735-6223.

For the historically minded, **Hearthstone** lays claims to being the first house in the world powered by hydroelectricity. The large home features hands-on electrical exhibits and working models. Nine fireplaces, detailed woodwork, original light switches—all in a fine Victorian setting at 625 W. Prospect Avenue. Admission is $4 for adults, $2 for children; (920) 730-8204.

Finally, the Fox Cities contribution to the national pastime is the Wisconsin Timber Rattlers, a single-A minor league franchise of the Seattle Mariners. They play at beautiful Goodland Field. The season runs April through September. The entire family will enjoy the goofy programs before, during, and after the games; (920) 733-4152.

THE TWIN CITIES: NEENAH AND MENASHA

Moving south from Appleton, Neenah and Menasha meet at the junction of Nicolet Boulevard and Abby Avenue on the island where Lake Winnebago empties into the Fox River. A good walking tour encompasses an impressive collection of mansions lining the **Wisconsin Avenue Historic District**. The homes were built starting in 1858 and show in no uncertain terms the economic strength of the paper industry. Near the historic district are Riverside Park, with the popular **Kimberly Point Park**, the site of a whitewashed lighthouse; the **Bergstrom Mahler Museum**, containing a world-class collection of glass, and the Menasha marina. Phone (800) 200-MORE or log on www.Foxcities.org.

OSHKOSH

The next stop, Oshkosh, a college town and manufacturing center on the west shore of Lake Winnebago, was doggedly rebuilt from not one, not two, not three, but four devastating fires that would have broken a lesser town. Its sawdust days are long gone, replaced by more than 240 acres of municipal parks and the **University of Wisconsin–Oshkosh**. A swimming beach, marina, and zoo are among the recreational facilities available at **Menominee Park and Zoo**, open daily from May through October. The zoo is home to native Wisconsin animals and a few exotic species. Paddle boats, bumper boats, canoe rentals, and a mini-train. Admission is free. Open May–September, (920) 236-5080 at Hazel and Merritt Streets.

Oshkosh contains six historic districts. The **Main Street District** represents the traditional retail center of the city. The majority of the structures were built following the fire of 1875. Things to do include **boat cruises** from the Pioneer Inn, (920) 233-1980; the **Military Veterans Museum** in the Park Plaza Mall on Pearl Ave, (920) 426-8615; the **Grand Opera House** (an architectural beauty at 100 High Avenue), (920) 424-2355; and parks along the Fox River and Lake Winnebago. **Shapiro Park** hugs the Fox River near the UW campus. The **Paine Art Center and Arboretum** is located on the grounds of an English Tudor-style mansion built by entrepreneur Nathan Paine, onetime owner of the largest sash and door operation in the world. Located at 1410 Algoma Boulevard, across the street from the Oshkosh Public Museum, the grounds are home to six gardens open free of charge. Phone (920) 235-6903. Admission for the art center is $3 for adults; senior discount available. Children under 12 are admitted free.

For eats, the **Granary** has the most character and good food; it's a huge

1883 stone flour granary located at 50 W. Sixth Street, south of the Fox River. **Friar Tucks**, 1651 West South Park, is known for heaping sandwiches.

Butch's Anchor Inn, 225 W. Twentieth Street, is the place for supper club dining in Oshkosh. Prime rib is good, so is the walleye—as you would expect from a place decorated to the gills in nautical paraphernalia. **Jansen's** fish fry has lake perch along with steaks and seafood at 344 Bowen Street.

SHOPPING

Shopping can hardly be characterized as an activity indigenous to Wisconsin. Then again, Appleton supposedly built the first shopping mall *ever*.

The Fox Valley has grown to offer the largest shopping opportunities north of Milwaukee and many weekend visitors are here exclusively to shop. So here goes. **The Prime Outlets** mall in Oshkosh features 55 name-brand outlet stores including Eddie Bauer, Samsonite, Fieldcrest, Cannon, Levi's, Farberware, Easy Spirit, Black & Decker, Lenox, and American Girl. Prime Outlets is conveniently located along Highway 41 across the road from the EAA Air Adventure Museum.

The **Miles Kimball Outlet store**, located at Highways 41and 44 in Aviation Plaza, traces its roots back 66 years when young Mr. Kimball took the plunge into the Christmas card business. Today, Miles Kimball is a leading direct marketer of consumer gifts and household products.

Appleton also has its share of shopping opportunities. The **Fox River Mall** in Appleton has more than 180 stores (and counting) under one roof. And the **Valley Fair Mall**, opened in 1954, lays claims to being the world's first indoor mall. Located at Highway 47 and Calumet Street, the pioneering mall today is just another banal strip of cinemas, stores, and restaurants.

When its time to call it a day, the Fox Cities have no shortage of clean and affordable accommodations to rest your weary feet. Dozens of hotels, motels, inns, and B&Bs are located in and around the valley. The best known are The **Paper Valley Hotel** in Appleton, (920) 733-8000, and **The Pioneer Inn and Marina**, Oshkosh, (800) 683-1980.

FOND DU LAC

French traders called it the "fond," the farther end of Lake Winnebago. In 1835 Wisconsin's first judge and later territorial governor, James D. Doty, laid out the town in hopes of it becoming the state capital. Today mansions of industrial barons line Division Street and a good part of the city's downtown, the **South Main Street Historic District**, comprises structures built in a variety of styles.

The **Fond du Lac Convention and Visitors Bureau**, 19 W. Scott Street, (920) 923-3010, www.fdl.com provides a detailed map of rural Fond du Lac County that takes visitors to farm markets, cheese and sausage shops, hiking and bicycling trails, and parks. A "talking house" tour of some historic homes and sites in the city enables visitors to hear information about 15 stops on the route by tuning to a radio frequency.

One of the sites on the tour is **Saint Paul's Cathedral**, which features an outstanding collection of German and American woodcarving in an English Gothic setting. Open for tours weekdays 9 a.m.–noon and 1–4 p.m., or as arranged. Guided tours $2; 51 W. Division Street, (920) 921-3363 or (920) 922-1833.

Fond du Lac's focal point and identity are linked to **Lakeside Park and Lighthouse**, a 400-acre park. Visitor's can climb the imitation lighthouse for a

The observation deck at Fond du Lac's Lakeside Park provides an exceptional vista of Lake Winnebago.

good view of the lake and marina from an observation deck. The park offers picnic areas, a playground, deer park, petting zoo, ball diamonds, marina, and 24 free boat launch ramps. Rides include a miniature train and an old-fashioned carousel; bumper boats, aqua bikes, and canoes can also be rented. Located at the end of North Main Street, the lighthouse is open April 15–October 15, 8 a.m.–dusk, weather permitting. Park rides/boat rentals are available Memorial Day–Labor Day, Monday–Saturday, 11 a.m.–8:30 p.m.; Sunday 10 a.m.–8:30 p.m., (800) 937-9123.

Viewers of the History Channel may recognize the **Octagon House and Costume Closet**. The house is a Civil War oddity. Designed as an Indian fort and reportedly used on the Underground Railroad, it has nine passageways, including a secret room and tunnel, and is rumored to be haunted. It's located at 276 Linden Street, (920) 922-1608; www.marlenesheirlooms.com. Open Monday, Wednesday, and Friday, 1–5:30 p.m.; adults $8, children $5.

For a look at life in the late 1800s, the **Galloway House and Village** offers a tour of this Victorian mansion and 25 authentic village buildings. The complex, 336 Old Pioneer Road, (920) 922-6390, also features a church, photography studio, town hall, newspaper print shop, and one-room school. Open daily, Memorial Day weekend through Labor Day weekend, 10–5p.m.; the gate closes at 4 p.m. Adults $6.50, students 17 years and under $3.50, preschoolers free.

THE EAST COAST

Highway 151/55 along Lake Winnebago's eastern shore is one of the state's unsung scenic drives. Largely ignored as a tourist route, the road is as scenic as they come with the huge lake and rolling farm fields sloping up from the shore. You'll see picture-perfect barns, round hay bales resting among lush fields, orchards, scenic overlooks, beaches, a series of unincorporated villages (Peebles, Pipe, Calumetville, Brothertown, Quinney, Stockbridge, Sherwood); supper clubs and watering holes with names like Fisherman's Inn, Gobbler's Knob, and Lakeview Motel . . . all the ingredients of a leisurely yet worthwhile road trip if just for the scenery.

The **Little Farmer Orchard**, 10 miles northeast of Fond du Lac along Highway 151, is the place to get fresh apples, cider, pies, or caramel apples; pumpkins and hayrides are available in the fall. Small petting zoo, playground, and hiking trail in the woods. Open August to late November. Phone (920) 921-4784; www.thelittlefarmer.com. In the same area, look for the 80-foot **Columbia Park Tower**, which offers good views of Lake Winnebago and the Niagara Escarpment to the east.

One reason to depart the lakeside and drive to Chilton is the **Ledge View Nature Center** where three caves are open to the public May to mid-November. Cave tours are led by naturalists. The center features three miles of trails, observation tower, live animals, and dioramas, and is open year-round. It's located 23 miles north of Fond du Lac. Take Highway 151 to County G to W2348 Short

Road, Chilton, (920) 849-7094.

Sheer bluffs reminiscent of the type that created Niagara Falls can be seen at **High Cliff State Park**—no coincidence, since High Cliff is the western edge of the Niagara Escarpment, a 1,000-mile wide bowl-like feature created in pre-historic times. (The escarpment's eastern edge is the marked by the famous falls.)

The 250-foot limestone bluffs are the gemstones of the only state park located on Lake Winnebago and have long been a draw for spectacular vistas. This is where the Ho-Chunk chief Red Bird made regular pilgrimages. Today, a 12-foot statue located at the summit honors the chief who understood the meditative power of this awesome natural attraction. High Cliff offers the best view of Wisconsin's largest inland lake, and the Fox River Valley cities can be seen glimmering on the western horizon. If you time your visit just right, the sun will be setting behind the twinkling lights of the Fox Cities.

The park lies across 1,147 acres on the bluffs and contains 112 campsites, an authentic old-time canteen, a nature center, and observation tower. Campsites are wooded and well distributed. Five miles of hiking trails, 10 miles of mountain biking trails, 6 miles of snowmobile trails, 4 miles cross country trails, swimming beach, and marina—no lack of opportunities for outdoor fun. History and geology buffs will enjoy effigy mounds ranging from 28 to 285 feet in length, and a former lime kiln and quarry operation.

More than 500,000 visitors frequent High Cliff State Park every year. Half a million High Cliff fans can't be wrong. It's located off Highway 55 on the northeast edge of Lake Winnebago at N7630 State Park Road. Phone (920) 989-1106.

WHERE'S THE FISH FRY?

When staying in the Appleton area it's worth taking a country drive east to **Van Abel's Supper Club** (and bowling alley, six lanes worth), located on County D in Holland, or Hollandtown to locals. Van Abel's, along with the local church, is Hollandtown; this local institution packs 'em in on Tuesday and Friday nights by serving delicious slabs of pan-fried walleye. Perch is on the menu, too. When was the last time you had rutabaga on the side? Brush up on your ethnicity: the area is rich with Dutch and Irish, making Van Abel's an amiable melting pot where likes of VandeHei, Vandenheuvel, and Vander Zanden laugh it up with Clancy, Duffy, and Burns.

Under the Dome, a sports bar and restaurant located at 116 Main, Neenah, serves the full compliment of lake perch, walleye, haddock, and shrimp with the works. Lighter options are available, too. All of Fond du Lac becomes a giant fish fry when the huge **Walleye Weekend** festivities take place at Lakeside Park in June.

READ ALL ABOUT IT

Befitting a large population center in the state, there are three daily newspapers published in the Fox Valley: the *Appleton Post-Crescent*, *Oshkosh Northwestern*, and *Fond du Lac Reporter*, with the *Post Crescent* having the largest circulation (61,000) by far. It and the Northwestern each publish a Sunday edition. Weekly newspapers found on the quiet side of Lake Winnebago include the *Chilton Times-Journal* and *New Holstein Reporter*.

HAVE YOU HEARD?

WHBY in Appleton, 1150 AM, is the station for news/talk; "the Rockin' Apple," WAPL, 105.7 FM, has been playing Led Zeppelin forever and a day; WOSH, 1490 AM, and KFIZ, 1450 AM, talk radio; KFIZ, 107.1 FM; WFDL, 97.7 FM; and WTCX, 96.1 FM, are "hot adult contemporary" stations in Fond du Lac. Country fans tune in to WPKR, 99.5 FM.

Double Take: Sturgeon Season

An only-in-Wisconsin phenomenon: Every winter Lake Winnebago becomes a shantytown for the brief duration of sturgeon season. Thousands of fishing shanties—some as big as cottages—are towed onto the ice where 15,000 or so fisherman use chain saws to cut three-by-five-foot holes and wait like Ishmaels in Packer jackets for the huge, prehistoric-looking fish to pass within spearing range. Lake Winnebago has the largest concentration of sturgeon in the world.

Sturgeon spearing was handed down through generations of Native Americans. The first official season on Lake Winnebago occurred in 1932. Today, it's one of the few sturgeon seasons held in the world. Roads are plowed on the ice and marked by Christmas trees. Most fishermen never see a sturgeon, so there's plenty of time, inside the shanties, to grill bratwurst on the cook stove and have a nip of brandy. The season lasts a couple days since the harvest is tightly controlled, but what a spectacle it is for those few days. And what a hideous looking fish—a missing link or two from dinosaurs. Sturgeon can live for 60 or more years, reach 6 feet in length, and weigh more than 140 pounds. They are just plain ugly, but what do you expect from fish that have been bottom feeding since long before the last Ice Age?

CHAPTER FIVE

OSHKOSH
The EAA's Airborne Circus

Who needs the Super Bowl, Mardi Gras or Dick Clark's

"Rockin' New Year's Eve," when you've got the annual fly-in of the

Experimental Aircraft Association (EAA) near at hand?

The **EAA AirVenture** is the official title. You probably know a few things
about it already. Every year, tiny Wittman Field in Oshkosh becomes the center
of the aviation universe, the busiest airport on the planet. The statistics bear it
out. Over a typical week, the fly-in will play host to 750,000 people, 12,000
planes, 4,000 volunteers, 1,000 media types, and 700 very cool exhibits.

It's the world's largest recreational aviation event. In fact, the EAA
fly-in may be a victim of its own success. Those of us who are not pilots
(not licensed, anyway) or EAA members might be intimidated by the shear
magnitude of the thing. With so much to see in so little time and with so
many other people with the same purpose in mind, a first-time visitor
has got to have questions. How do I get in? Is there parking?

Is the closest hotel room in Ishpeming? Do I want to go at all?

Experts in the know have some simple, sage advice. Two of the most important tips are to get walking shoes and dress casually. You'll see why later. Also, have a plan. If this is your initial foray to the show or if you're a fly-in veteran, you should treat your visit as if you were entering a large city for the first time. You cannot see all that AirVenture has to offer in a day or even a week. Certainly you can wander, and spending some time doing this rewards you with satisfying surprises, but the best way to get the most out of your AirVenture adventure is to make a plan.

Thus, armed with a preliminary idea of the chaos and excitement ahead, let's see what we can make of this Classic Wisconsin Weekend.

WHEN AND WHERE TO GO

The fly-in takes place over one week, Tuesday through Monday, usually spanning the last weekend in July. The best time to go is a weekday, when crowds and traffic are the lightest. But be prepared for rush hours and traffic jams at any time, especially after the afternoon air show brings down the curtain.

AirVenture is held at Oshkosh's Wittman Field, conveniently located along Highway 41. If you've traveled 41 before, you've probably seen the big EAA sign and the mounted airplane along the highway across the road from the outlet mall. Ring a bell now? Exit at the junction of Highways 41 and 44. Just follow the signs. There are five parking areas, and parking is about $6 a vehicle. Gates open

The Experimental Aircraft Association's annual fly-in, held at Oshkosh's Wittman Field, is one of the premier aviation events in the world.

at 8 a.m. You may have to walk a ways to the main drag, but you're going to be hoofing it all day anyway, so enjoy the exercise. As you arrive, the number of people, size of the site, and the rows and rows of magnificent aircraft are simply overwhelming. (If you were to walk up and down each row of airplanes, you would cover 5.2 miles . . . but don't do this.)

Once parked, foot traffic is directed to the main gate. Admission is $29 a day for non-EAA members, $16 for youngsters ages 14 to 18, $11 for ages 8 to 13; children 7 and under are free. EAA AirVenture costs compare favorably to any other world-class event or similar family activity. The EAA has also responded to participants' feedback and lowered costs in a number of areas, including some food and drink prices. You'll get your money's worth and more.

For more information about the event, phone (920) 426-4800 or go to the Web site at www.airventure.org; this is one site that can help you drop your landing gear before hitting the pavement.

MAKING A PLAN

Once inside, you're faced with some choices about what to marvel at first.

Continuing with our city analogy, think of the major fly-in areas as districts composed of different types of aircraft, ranging from ultralight and vintage aircraft on the south side of the Main Street to homebuilt aircraft and Warbirds to the north. Other areas specialize in dining and shopping and even a university, where you can attend aviation forums, seminars, and workshops.

Within the designated districts are neighborhoods that are devoted to a particular group of aircraft. One neighborhood is devoted to Van's Aircraft, another to Rutan-designed planes, and so on.

According to Scott Spangler, editor of the EAA's Web site whom we thank for the analogy, "People with similar interests naturally gather so they can share knowledge and experiences and learn from each other. If you share their interests or want to learn more about their particular passion, visiting their neighborhood is a must. Naturally, what communities and neighborhoods you want to visit depends on your interests."

For internal transportation, shuttles run constantly from one end of the grounds to the other. Shuttle stops are well marked and routes are color-coded for simplicity. Save some time and energy by catching the nearest shuttle to travel between areas, otherwise you'll be on your feet a lot.

WHAT TO WEAR

Spending a day on a dusty flight line under a scorching July sun is no place to be caught unprepared. Wear loose-fitting, light-colored clothing and lots of sunscreen. You should wear a hat. Sunglasses help. Drink plenty of water—more than just enough to satisfy your thirst. Take several pairs of comfortable walking shoes if visiting more than one day. If you get new shoes, start breaking them in before the event. Even if you don't need new shoes, taking a walk every day, and increasing the distance you cover over time will benefit you all year, not just during AirVenture. If sitting on the grass during the air show isn't for you, bring a folding chair. Think about getting a lightweight backpack to carry all your essential items. It's also a good place to stash water bottles and all the literature and goodies you pick up during the day.

In other words, use your head—not your feet—to make your AirVenture experience as pleasant and worthwhile as possible.

THE AIR SHOW

Predicting each day's rush hour isn't difficult; it's after the afternoon **Air Show**. The daily shows are the featured attraction, the most-anticipated highlight of AirVenture. The afternoon show is a traditional part of AirVenture, dating back to the first fly-in in 1953. The lineups include some of the finest aerobatic competitors in the world, as well as heart-stopping team aerobatics, and Warbird formations and performances (with pyrotechnics). With daredevils, speed demons, dive-bombers, it's the finest air show you will see anywhere, a three-hour spectacular. The afternoon show starts at 3:15 and is best viewed from the grassy areas along the flight line. You're welcome to sit among the parked aircraft as you watch.

A BIT OF HISTORY WITH THE WARBIRDS

For most people, the Fly-in is synonymous with **Warbirds**. There's something about the old Corsairs, Spitfires, and P-51s that can stir the emotions like nothing else. Nearly 400 Warbirds make the fly-in. Heavy on World War II classics, the show also features Cold Warbirds, and modern fighting craft are well represented, too. A modern stealth fighter visited AirVenture in 2001 and hovered over the site like a giant bat.

There are only thirteen B-17s in the world today, but you'll find several B-17 Flying Fortresses at AirVenture. Tour the historic bombers for a few bucks, or for the ultimate experience, fly in a B-17. The price is steep: As much as $375 for non-EAA members to ride 30 minutes. Price is no deterrent, apparently, since the flight schedule is usually booked solid. Your mission includes a 30-minute preflight briefing. Once airborne, passengers have the opportunity to roam freely throughout the aircraft, imagining life as a waist gunner, bombardier, radio operator, or navigator while the four, 1,200-horsepower engines roar outside.

What is it about the Warbirds, arguably the most popular attraction at AirVenture? "It's the history involved," said John Booker, a volunteer tour coordinator for the *Aluminum Overcast,* the B-17 owned by EAA that offers regular flights. "It's like this airplane—the major factor of us winning the war in Europe. It's a piece of history that we have here to let people see and fly on it if they want to." Booker added, "It's something that simply will not be here very much longer. One of these days all of us (veterans) are going to be gone and the planes are going to be gone and you won't have the opportunity." The Aluminum Overcast

Warbirds, such as this vintage Corsair, are among the most popular exhibits on the EAA flight line.

has been lovingly restored in authentic detail, as have all the Warbirds at AirVenture; it tours regularly. Call (800) 359-6217 for more information.

The Warbird parking area is open to visitation much of the day, but it's closed every afternoon before the air show to permit safe taxiing operations.

For those looking to travel further into history, the EAA owns a **1929 Ford Tri-Motor**, affectionately known as the "Tin Goose," which offers passenger flights for $40. You have to sign up early in the day to reserve a spot. (Once a year, EAA holds the Ford Tri-Motor Ground School, a three-day program that lets lovers of the old bird revel in its history and intricacies.) Phone (920) 426-6815.

MAIN STREET

Plenty of food and beverage vendors line Main Street. And there are plenty of people patronizing those vendors, especially on weekends around lunchtime. To save time and aggravation, you should plan to get hungry at a convenient time. All the typical comfort foods can be found (pizza, pita sandwiches, brats, smoothies; prices range from $3.50 to $6). In addition, each neighborhood has a café where you can sit down in the shade and enjoy breakfast, lunch, or dinner. One place offers a Wisconsin fish fry.

In addition to the neighborhoods, the exhibit buildings, and Main Street, the area where aviation equipment is displayed and sold is a popular destination.

Just about every aviation widget is found here. Instruments, avionics, insurance, aircraft parts, and for those of us not in the market for that special propeller, there's no lack of memorabilia, books, videos, and clothing to look over.

SEE THE SEAPLANES

If you're looking for an out-of-the-way place with loads of character (and characters), try the **seaplane base** located on Lake Winnebago. The base is relatively unknown to the casual visitor and is a bit hard to find, located along a part of Winnebago that is more sleepy lagoon than Wisconsin lake, covered with moss and shaded by willow trees. Here, you can sit at a picnic table or on the grass, snack on roasted corn, and watch some rugged individualists come and go in their seaplanes. Fun is the name of the game here. You might see men dressed in grass skirts and coconut bikini tops as part of evening entertainment.

As much as the Warbirds exhibit evokes nostalgia, the seaplane base showcases the spirit of wanderlust. "Seaplane flying is by its nature recreational," said Michael Volk, president of the National Seaplane Association. "We're all here to have fun. You won't find people wearing ties for business trips. What you will find is people having a picnic on a remote lake somewhere, fishing, camping, hanging out with other seaplane pilots. It's very much oriented to having fun."

And it's an exclusive group if only by sheer numbers. The seaplane association has 7,500 members worldwide. It's hard to know where a seaplane pilot may be located most weeks of the year, except at the end of July. The EAA fly-in is a unique event at which pilots can experience the camaraderie of like-minded brethren, renew old friendships, and swap tales of exotic places they've visited.

For loads of character—and characters—the seaplane base on Lake Winnebago is the place to hang out.

They share a common notion that land-based pilots visit many interesting places, but seaplane pilots go where nobody else can. Seaplane pilots are "on their own," Volk said. "There are no control towers. There's not really an instrument flight system that they can use. They are primarily flying visually outside of the clouds. They don't have weather observing stations or air-traffic controllers to rely on. They rely on themselves."

Founded in 1949, the well-hidden base can be visited by catching a ride on a school bus from the ultralight neighborhood located on the south end of the AirVenture grounds.

IS THIS A KID-FRIENDLY EVENT?

Is there any doubt that youngsters would love this place? The spectacle of AirVenture alone will fascinate them. But there's more. KidVenture is located adjacent to the museum and a great place for fun and frolic. Here, children can build model airplanes and watch them fly, take a tethered hot air balloon ride, fly in a virtual F-18, or build and launch straw rockets. The NASA pavilions near the EAA control tower have displays suitable for all ages.

WHERE'S THE FISH FRY?

Get this—you don't have to leave AirVenture. A Wisconsin fish fry café is located on the grounds near the Warbirds. If you are visiting on a Friday, go to the seaplane base for a delicious walleye fry and a jumpin' polka band!

SLEEPING IN ISHPEMING?

Of all the events held in Wisconsin, AirVenture probably puts the greatest strain on local accommodations. The entire Fox Valley, Green Bay to Fond du Lac, is booked solid, including campgrounds, UW–Oshkosh's dorm rooms, and private residences. Even Milwaukee and Madison see overflow from the event. But before and after the weekend—Friday afternoon, Saturday, and Sunday morning that records the greatest influx of EAA visitors—finding a hotel room is less of a problem. Consider attending the first couple days or arrive on Sunday. Many of the hotels in Appleton and Green Bay run bus service for a nominal fee. In any case, if you're thinking about a hotel room, start looking now, and keep an open mind about making a day trip. Remember, weekdays are ideal for visitors: easy in and out and more available hotel rooms.

THE AIR ADVENTURE MUSEUM

If you don't make it to AirVenture—or even if you do—by all means visit the EAA's **Air Adventure Museum** at your convenience. Located right along Highway 41, this museum is a premier state attraction in its own right. The huge, gleaming 100,000-foot facility displays more than 90 full-size aircraft. The sport planes, gliders, and barnstormers are all here, as well as antique and military aircraft; multimedia exhibits and models, engines, propellers, components, and skeletons round out the display.

Located next to the museum as a result of its popularity at the 2001 fly-in, the **MaxFlight FS2000**, a full-motion simulator, duplicates an F-16 jet fighter experience, complete with loops and spirals and the roar of machine guns. For $5 you can get a taste of the wild blue yonder without leaving the ground. Pilots are belted into a module not unlike a roller coaster's seat. An overhead hatch closes to isolate riders from the outside world. Joysticks send commands to the simulator—just like the real deal—while the visuals are projected onto a 58-inch screen with state-of-the-art programming. It's a virtual video game and a roller coaster ride combined, with the passengers having control over the ride. What you don't have control over are the enemy fighters stalking you. It's harrowing and supremely entertaining.

The museum is open daily year-round except some holidays. Admission $7; those over 62, $6; ages 8–17, $5.50; family rate, $19. Phone (920) 426-4800. (Your paid admission to AirVenture includes free admission to the museum and an introductory EAA membership.) Take a virtual museum tour at museum. eaa.org.

For a few dollars you can explore the inner workings of a vintage B-17. For a few dollars more (quite a few more) you can ride in one of the handfull still flying.

READ ALL ABOUT IT

Most daily newspapers cover the fly-in, especially the hometown *Oshkosh Northwestern*. The *Milwaukee Journal Sentinel* has extensive coverage. A free fly-in newspaper is distributed daily at the gates.

HAVE YOU HEARD?

WOSH, 1490 AM, has live coverage of the fly-in.

HORICON MARSH
It's for the Birds

Although Horicon Marsh is the focal point of this Classic Wisconsin Weekend, there are other attractions nearby that are worth more than a casual glance. During a two- or three-day tour of this area, which lies southwest of Lake Winnebago in Dodge and Fond du Lac Counties, travelers can experience a wide variety of things to do and see.

HORICON MARSH WILDLIFE AREA

If you want to know about the wonders and secrets of Horicon Marsh, Rollie Zuelsdorf is your man. He can tell you all about the wetland and the birds that flock there. He can also tell you about the lost art of catching snapping turtles that were "as big as people" and the finer charms of the women of Mayville: "Oh, they loved to drink beer. Right out of the bottle."

Zuelsdorf has been guiding people through Horicon Marsh for four decades, which is slightly more than half the total number of years he has spent in and around the marsh. In this sprawling wetland of international importance, Zuelsdorf is the gentleman—patriarch, the man who single-handedly turned the marsh into an outdoor classroom for countless numbers of wide-eyed city kids, church groups on charter buses, and individuals from all walks of life.

Zeulsdorf founded **Blue Heron Landing Tours** in 1960, and it operates to this day near the bridge on Highway 33 in downtown Horicon. Up until that time, many of the marsh's visitors did not know the local roads, so he conducted tours in his station wagon for $1 per head. That vehicle was eventually replaced by a school bus, then a motor coach. A quarter of million people now come here annually.

Though known primarily for the annual migration of Canada geese, Horicon Marsh is increasingly drawing visitors throughout the spring, summer, and fall for bird watching, canoeing and kayaking, and duck hunting in-season. That's not counting the school groups and curious alike who only have to stray a few miles from Highway 151 in Dodge County for "the ultimate wildlife and birdlife experience," according to Zuelsdorf. "The ultimate. There's no question about it. In the world!"

The marsh was once the largest man-made lake in the world, replete with steamboats ferrying passengers and cargo from one end to the other. Not long afterwards it was drained and converted to farmland. Today, Horicon Marsh is much like the place favored by Native American cultures thousands of years ago, a 31,000-acre basin, 52 miles around, filled with silt, water, and cattails. The fauna—deer, fox, squirrel, raccoon, mink, skunk, opossum, muskrat, coyote—are year-round residents.

Then there are the birds, the marsh's claim to fame. Mallards, blue-winged teal, coots, ruddy ducks, cormorants, herons, terns are just a sampling of the water-loving migrants that visit Horicon. The marsh has been visited by 264 bird species, including some from South America—everything from the American bittern to the yellow-rumped warbler. Spring is the ideal time for bird watching.

The main attraction, of course, is the Canada geese. Fall is the best time of the year to see tens of thousands of these birds, as they start arriving in late September, with their numbers peaking in late October and early November. That's when they leave their breeding grounds near Hudson Bay, 850 miles north, and head for Horicon at speeds averaging 40 to 70 miles per hour, depending on tailwinds. The tourists flock to Horicon as well, many coming from other states, at speeds averaging 55 to 65 miles per hour along Highway 151, depending on traffic. The best times of day to see geese are sunrise and sunset, when feeding and roosting flights of thousands of birds create an aural and visual spectacle.

These geese winter in an area encompassing southern Illinois, western Kentucky, Tennessee, and Missouri. The tourists winter in an area encompassing the states of Florida and Arizona.

A good viewing spot, if you're not on the water, is **Conservation Hill**, accessible by the two-mile **Horicon Habitat Trail** at the north end of Palmatory Street in Horicon. Fall and spring dawns, you might hear sandhill cranes along with thousands of ducks and geese. However, geese spend the majority of the day away from the marsh. Weighing in at seven to ten pounds, they can be seen grazing in local crop fields.

Horicon's "Grand boubier" (big swamp), as it was called by pioneers and Native Americans, is recognized as a major wildlife refuge in North America.

Horicon Marsh is the largest freshwater cattail marsh in North America. And Zeulsdorf considers it one of the most important wildlife refuges in the world, putting it on the same level as the Everglades and the Okefenokee Swamp. The Wisconsin DNR manages the marsh's southern end, and the U.S. Fish and Wildlife Service takes care of the northern part. Camping is prohibited, as is hunting in the Federal area. Hunting is permitted in season with proper licenses and stamps in certain parts of the State area.

Canoeing and kayaking on the marsh is ideal, with flat water that is sheltered from the wind; it's really something to see and hear. You might want to drift up to a muskrat building a house or a heron on a log. Zuelsdorf's Blue Heron Landing offers guided and unguided canoe rentals April through September, $15 per day for two people.

Narrated tours are conducted aboard Zuelsdorf's pontoons, which depart every day May through September, 1 p.m. on weekdays, hourly on weekends; $9.50 per adult, less for youngsters. The Strictly Birding Tour is offered on weekends from May through September. These popular tours visit the heart of the marsh to view heron and egret rookeries; $17.50. Call ahead for schedule. The Blue Heron Landing Web site is www.horiconmarsh.com; phone (920) 485-4663.

The **Marsh Haven Nature Center**, located on Highway 49 at the northern edge of the marsh area, contains a wildlife art gallery, gift shop, and educational display. Self-guided nature trails and an observation tower are worth visiting. Open May to mid-November. Adults $1; children under 14, 50 cents; (920) 324-5818.

Horicon Ledge Park covers 83 acres along the Niagara Escarpment—a feature whose eastern edge is responsible for Niagara Falls—subsequently offering a beautiful vista of the marsh and some neat rock formations. The upper park is heavily wooded and offers picnic areas, group shelter, hiking trails, campsites and the Fort Ledge playground. Located between Horicon and Mayville, just off County TW. Camping allowed April–October, call (920) 387-5450 for reservations.

For general information about the entire area, contact the Horicon Chamber of Commerce at (920) 485-3200 or visit www.horiconchamber.com, the chamber's Web site. The DNR field office is located at the north end of Palmatory Street in Horicon. Phone (920) 387-7877 or (920) 387-7860.

No genuine attraction in Wisconsin is complete without an annual celebration. Horicon has two. The **Horicon Marsh Bird Festival** is a relatively new event held in mid-May (on International Migratory Bird Day) with wildlife shows, bird hikes, and seminars for beginning birders. The **Autumn Art on the Marsh** is a big hoo-ha held the fourth Sunday in September. For more than 25 years, about 5,000 people have attended this fine arts and crafts show at Horicon's Discher Park. Wildlife art and photography are featured. Phone (920) 485-3200.

If you're looking for even more marsh-related activity and want to get a better idea of the marsh's size, tour the 52-mile driving loop comprising the **Horicon Marsh Parkway**. Look for the brown and white signs leading in and around Horicon, Mayville, Waupun, Burnett, and Kekoskee. The DNR service center is located a couple miles north of Horicon on Highway 28; the U.S. Fish and Wildlife Service visitor center is found on the marsh's northeast corner on County S.

Finally, the **Wild Goose State Trail** skirts the marsh on a 34-mile route between Fond du Lac and Clyman Junction south of Horicon. Indian burial mounds can be found east of the trail on County E northwest of Horicon, an area that was known by early residents as the "grand boubier" (big swamp). You won't see much of the marsh along the route, but the birds and wildlife that make the marsh home are abundant.

Locals Know

Like many communities, the local high school team moniker reflects the region's most prominent feature. In Monroe, for example, the teams are called the Cheesemakers. In Horicon they cheer . . . the Marshmen.

MAYVILLE

Mayville hosts Audubon Days in October. Racing beds along the main drag is one of the featured events. The town is home to the **Audubon Inn**, a national historic lodging named one of the great inns in the U.S. by *National Geographic Traveler* magazine. Its restaurant is considered one of the state's best, too. Located on Main Street, the 1896 inn features four-poster beds, double whirlpools in every room, and a beautiful bar. Rates start at $109. Phone (920) 387-5858. The **Mayville Inn** is a family-owned lodging with 29 units on Highway 28, 701 S. Mountain Drive; (920) 387-1234. Rates start at $52. **J & R's Sherm Inn** is an 1870s Cream City brick bed and breakfast with rates starting at $55, 366 N. Main Street; (920) 387-4642.

A CHEESE STOP

Looking to make a cheese run? Six miles east of Mayville is **Widmer's Cheese Cellars** in the town of Theresa. The Widmer family has been handcrafting cheeses since 1922 in the cheese factory below their house. The cheese making techniques brought to America by John Widmer have been handed down through the family, including the traditional way of pressing brick cheese . . . with bricks. The cheese maker produces some of the finest brick, cheddar, and Colby cheeses in the world.

"Much like a limited edition book or lithograph, every piece of Widmer cheese is handcrafted in small batches to ensure quality," said Joe Widmer, grandson of John, who is one of only eight certified Wisconsin Master Cheesemakers in America, a program combining the art, education, and science necessary to run a cheese plant today. In-store sales are available at the factory, or visit www.widmerscheese.com to order a wedge. (You'll find some great recipes, too!)

Widmer's suggests that aged brick cheese is best served with pumpernickel bread, mustard, and onions. A pale ale is the perfect accompaniment. Draft beer, apple cider, or dark beers are also delicious. Who can argue with that?

The factory store and viewing area are open, Monday through Saturday between 5 a.m. and 5 p.m.; Sundays, June through October, 10 a.m. to 4 p.m. Guided factory tours for groups are available if scheduled in advance. Call (888) 878-1107.

WAUPUN

Located at the northwest corner of the Horicon Marsh, Waupun is synonymous with its imposing state prison. Saying you spent some time in Waupun might result in a raised eyebrow or two, but the town is certainly worthy of your (free) time. Here, you'll see the best collection of outdoor sculptures in the state, with eight sculptures located within the city limits and more nearby. Several works are breathtaking.

They are here because of the generosity of Clarence Addison Shaler, a self-made millionaire inventor who developed a love for sculpture late in his colorful life. Shaler commissioned some of the works and personally created more than a dozen others.

The most famous sculpture—and one of the most enduring images of the nation—stands in the city park; it's James Earl Fraser's **End of the Trail**, the unforgettable representation of a Native American on horseback, his head bowed and spear lowered. The bronze sculpture is 11 feet high and weighs three tons. Of the various forms and sizes of this sculpture that Fraser modeled from 1894 to 1929, this is the only monumental-size *End of the Trail* that the artist personally supervised. The sculpture was entered into the National Register of Historic Places in 1975. *End of the Trail* took two years to complete at a cost of $50,000 by the time it was unveiled in 1929. Its value today exceeds a million dollars. "This statue fills my race with weeping," said Roger Tallmadge, a Native American known as Chief Little Eagle, at the statue's rededication in 1979. You do not see us proud and standing on a hill facing our God, but at the lowest ebb of our history."

In Waupun's Forest Mounds Cemetery stands another stunning sculpture, **The Recording Angel**, dedicated to Shaler's wife, Blanche, and located at her gravesite. In 1921, Shaler commissioned Lorado Taft, who was responsible for such great works as *Spirit of the Great Lakes*, which can be seen outside Chicago's Art Institute, to create a masterpiece in her memory.

The Recording Angel depicts a seated angel contemplating the Book of Life. The work is made of bronze, is nine feet tall, and weighs nearly three tons. The back of it, made of polished Massachusetts Quincy gray granite, is ten feet tall and weighs 16 tons; the entire sculpture was chemically treated to give it an aged appearance. It is the only Lorado Taft work in Wisconsin. Nearly two years in the making, this work is considered to be one of Taft's finest. Set among the shade trees in the quiet cemetery, it imparts an overwhelming feeling of serenity. *The Recording Angel* was Waupun's first sculpture and is one of the highlights of Shaler's considerable reputation.

The dramatic *End of the Trail* is one of many sculptures in the Waupun area commissioned by local entrepreneur Clarence Addison Shaler.

He was born near Waupun and attended nearby Ripon College. While working on a farm after college, Shaler, always a tinkerer, invented replacement covers for umbrellas. He turned a vacant flax mill into a manufacturing plant and made his first fortune. In 1905, Shaler, reportedly the second person in Wisconsin to own an automobile, invented a patching method for flat tires called a vulcanizer. This second enterprise made him a millionaire.

Shaler also went on to invent custom-made golf clubs, the heating pad, and automobile headlights. There were so many other inventions he was responsible for that he never bothered to patent many of them. Within a few years of his retirement in 1928, at age 70, he began his sculpting career.

One of Shaler's most impressive works lies twelve miles to the northwest of Waupun in a small rural cemetery on the Mackford Prairie. *Morning of Life* depicts a life-size young girl seated on a large rock, eyes gazing heavenward. Shaler sculpted *Morning of Life* in 1936 in memory of his twin sister, Clara, who died at age 18. Another one of his impressive works is a bas-relief of geese in flight on display at the Waupun Public Library. (A renaissance man if ever one existed, Shaler also wrote short stories and published a few books.)

Shaler never sold any of his works. *Lincoln*, a bronze that took Shaler three years to complete, was given to his alma mater. *Lincoln* stands in front of an oak tree on the Ripon College campus. Another work, *Genesis*, a bronze work depicting a female face and arm emerging from a block of stone, was placed on the campus opposite the library.

RIPON

Twenty miles northwest from Horicon on Highway 23 is Ripon, best known as the "birthplace of the Republican Party," but perhaps the only place in the world founded by socialists *and* Republicans. The area was first settled in the early 19th century by a group called the Wisconsin Phalanx, whose guiding principle was community ownership. They named their settlement Ceresco after the Roman goddess of the harvest and located it in a valley nestled between two hills. Before long, it was the home of more than 200 idealists. The members constructed several communal dwellings called long houses, one of which still stands on its original site. The experiment folded in 1851 and the Phalanx returned its profits and holdings to members. Sounds like dividends.

Enter Alan Earl Bovay. One of the town's first lawyers, Bovay was a political reformer with the Whig Party on the East Coast. He called the famous March 20, 1854, meeting in the Little White Schoolhouse, where the Republican Party was formed. The group was outraged by the opening of the Kansas and Nebraska Territories to slavery. "We went into the little meeting held in a schoolhouse Whigs, Free-Soilers, and Democrats. We came out of it Republicans and we were the first Republicans in the Union," Bovay later wrote. It was his friend, newspaper publisher Horace Greeley, who boosted the name to national prominence. **The Little White Schoolhouse** is located at 303 Blackburn Street; (920) 748-6764.

Take a walk through Ripon's downtown, a square lined with turn-of-the-century brick architecture. In the last decade, the square has been brought back to life with facade restorations, the installation of ornamental streetlights, banners, and landscaping. While communities razed entire blocks of buildings for urban renewal in 1970's, the Watson Street Commercial Historic District remained relatively unchanged. The residential area south of the downtown has several fully restored Victorian homes.

The serene campus of **Ripon College**, a fine, private liberal arts school, is just west of the business district. The campus stands prominently on top of the hill with 22 buildings and nicely landscaped courtyards. The college was a major leader of the anti-slavery movement in Fond du Lac County. Its classrooms fueled sentiments that resulted in the founding of the Republican Party. Alan Bovay was a founding member of the college.

WHERE'S THE FISH FRY?

The Pub in Mayville, the **American Legion post** in Beaver Dam, and **Mother's Day** in Horicon are three reliable establishments in the area.

READ ALL ABOUT IT

The *Beaver Dam Daily Citizen* circulates to 14,620 locals; the *Horicon Reporter, Ripon Commonwealth Press, Waupun Neighbors*, and the *Mayville News* are the weeklies.

HAVE YOU HEARD?

WXRO, 95.3 FM, for country music and the "Old Barn Show" weeknights; WRPN, 90.1 FM, Ripon College's station; WBEV, 1430 AM, for news and talk.

CHAPTER SEVEN

KETTLE MORAINE AREA
History Coming Alive

Before embarking on this tour of Wisconsin's Kettle Moraine area, a couple of definitions are in order for those of us who were dozing in grade-school science. Kettles are bowl-shaped depressions in the landscape, and moraines are hilly belts of connected ridges and mounds. Kettles were formed by the melting of large ice blocks buried in glacial drift; moraines usually formed along the glacier's edge.

In the area between Fond du Lac and Sheboygan, running north–south between Greenbush and Kewauskum, lies the Kettle Moraine State Forest Northern Unit, a 30-square-mile band of hills, ridges, and pockmarks left at least 10,000 years ago by retreating glaciers. Running diagonally through southwestern Waukesha County and northwest Walworth County is the forest's Southern Unit. In between the two units, in Washington and Waukesha Counties, are more than enough rolling kettles and moraines, as well as some distinctive places to stop—Greenbush, Plymouth, Holy Hill,

Hartford—to constitute a Classic Wisconsin Weekend. And don't forget that Milwaukee is just a short drive away from all of this.

KETTLE MORAINE STATE FOREST: NORTHERN UNIT

Starting at the top, the forest's Northern Unit holds 367 year-round campsites and loads of trails on 29,000 acres of land. There's year-round recreation for campers, swimmers, hikers, bikers, cross-country skiers, horseback riders, and snowmobilers. Hunting and fishing is available. A fire tower offers nice views. Main forest entry is located in Campbellsport. Phone (262) 626-2116.

GREENBUSH

Located at the very northern tip of the Kettle Moraine is Greenbush, a town where history is preserved in the form of the **Wade House and Wesley Jung Carriage Museum**. In its day the Wade House was the only civilized stopover for travelers making the bone-rattling journey on a plank road between Sheboygan and Fond du Lac. The Wade House provided home-cooked meals and soft beds along the inhospitable road. It was the kind of place that mid-19th-century travelers might expect in civilized New England, but hardly in the Wisconsin wilds. "Here in the tiny pioneer hamlet of Greenbush, a stately and gracious inn contrasted sharply with its hard-bitten frontier setting," according to the Wisconsin Historical Society.

In the 19th century, Sylvanus Wade settled in the tiny hamlet of Greenbush. Today, the inn Wade built for weary travelers is a state historic site.

Founder Sylvanus Wade was convinced Greenbush would become the hub of commercial activities in the region. It didn't. Wade House faded into obscurity until the 1950s when preservationists came to the rescue. Greenbush is still very much a tiny hamlet.

The Wesley Jung Carriage Museum houses more than a hundred horse-drawn and hand-operated vehicles. The collection ranks as Wisconsin's largest—and one of the largest in the nation. Admission to the Jung Carriage Museum is included in the cost of admission to Wade House.

The newest addition to the grounds is the reconstructed **Herrling Sawmill**. The original mill stood at the same location from 1854 to 1910. The new mill is one of a few working water-powered sawmills in North America. The turbine-powered sawmill draws energy from a reconstructed millpond, fed by the Mullet River, to saw lumber daily as a historic demonstration for mill visitors.

Wade House is open May to October 31. Adults $10, seniors $9, children $5. It's located 18 miles east of Fond du Lac on Highway 23. W7747 Plank Road, Greenbush, (920) 526-3271.

Greenbush is a town that not only preserves history but also reenacts it. A good time to visit is September, when it hosts the annual **Civil War Weekend**, the Midwest's largest encampment and battle reenactment. Although Wisconsin does not hold ground as hallowed as Antietam, Gettysburg, or Ap-pomattox, it is fitting and proper to note that those Civil War battlegrounds were consecrated by the blood of many Wisconsin veterans.

The Badger State's Civil War story is the story of the 2nd, 6th, and 7th Volunteer Infantry Regiments. Augmented with regiments from Indiana and Michigan, this fighting force became known in history as the Iron Brigade of the West. In proportion to its numbers, it sustained the heaviest loss of any brigade in the Civil War.

Talk about "living history." At the Civil War Weekend, history lives, breathes, marches, attacks, and explodes before your eyes. The gathering is held on the grounds near the Wade House. For young and old alike, the encampments bring to life the Civil War right down to the last brass button. No details are left undone.

Each re-enactor carries items such as the distinctive black Hardee hat, worn with the left brim turned up and a black plume on the right side. In addition, each soldier shoulders 25 to 30 pounds of equipment: tent, blanket, haversack, canteen, clothing, shoes. Optional equipment includes a Springfield 1861 or Enfield 1853 rifle, musket sling, waist belt with bayonet and scabbard, infantry cartridge box. Accessories might include tin cups, candles, knife and fork, lantern, mess plate, and frying pan.

The grounds also have tents selling Civil War era clothing. You can listen in on period music being performed by reenactors with traditional instruments. Children can volunteer for service and might have their first (and last) experience standing at attention for a drill sergeant.

Depending on the battle, the Iron Brigade forces may amass in the woods before trying to push their way up the slope. Spectators watch from a half-mile, crescent-shaped observation line stretching from the valley, up the slope, along the top of the hillside, and back down. All places offer a good view.

First come the cannon volleys, deafening and spectacular. Heavy clouds of powder smoke rise from the valley. Confederate cavalry charge the Union flanks, horses pounding along the viewing line. Soon Union troops, marching shoulder to shoulder, begin to emerge from the woods. The infantry are joined in a see-saw battle that culminates in hand-to-hand fighting. On the far side of the battlefield, the two sides are attempting flanking maneuvers. A priest follows to administer last rites to the dead and dying as the smell of gunfire hangs heavy. The reenactment takes about an hour. It is an unforgettable experience.

Take a walk through time. Talk to the reenactors and ask questions. Taste some hardtack. Smell the gunpowder drifting from the battle. Guaranteed, you'll remember the Iron Brigade.

Double Take: The Iron Brigade

Years after the Civil War ended, General George McClellan was reminiscing with General John Callis of Lancaster, Wisconsin, about the legend of the Iron Brigade. The following story, as told by McClellan, was printed in the Iron Brigade's program during the reunion of 1900:

During the battle of South Mountain my headquarters were where I could see every move of the troops taking the gorge on the pike (National Road). With my glass I saw the men fighting against great odds, when General Hooker came in great haste for some orders. I asked him what troops were those fighting on the pike?

His answer was, "General Gibbon's Brigade of Western men."

I said, "They must be made of iron."

He replied, "By the Eternal they are iron. If you had seen them at Second Bull Run as I did, you would know them to be iron."

I replied, "Why, General Hooker, they fight equal to the best troops in the world."

This remark so elated Hooker that he mounted his horse and dashed away without his orders. After the battle, I saw Hooker at the Mountain House near where the Brigade fought.

He sang out, "Now General, what do you think of the Iron Brigade?"

PLYMOUTH

Just six miles east of Greenbush is a town that has made tremendous strides in preserving its downtown: Plymouth. Located at the intersection of two important roads (the Military Road of the 19th century and Highway 57, a major road between Green Bay and Milwaukee for much of the 20th century) Plymouth is a good walking town retro-fitted with coffee shops, cafes, and antiques stores. A self-guided tour features more than 50 historically significant homes, businesses and buildings; two are listed on the National Register of Historic Places. Brochures are available by calling (920) 893-0079 or (888) 693-8263.

Snap an obligatory photo of the giant dairy cow. All in all, Plymouth is a fine place to spend an afternoon in the Kettle Moraine area.

The town's charm is accentuated a number of exceptional B&B's, the most notable being **52 Stafford**, an Irish-style guesthouse. Owner Sean O'Dwanny has created a unique 19-room inn featuring custom-made carpeting and brass chandeliers. Guest rooms are plush, gourmet food is served in the dining room, and a beautiful pub is located on-site. Stop in for a pint o' Guinness. Located at 52 Stafford Street; phone (920) 893-0552.

At the annual Civil War Weekend, held on the grounds of the Old Wade House, history is living, breathing, marching, and firing cannons, leaving the air thick with smoke.

Other nice lodging establishments in or near Plymouth include the **B. L. Nutt Inn**, a historic home, (920) 892-8566; **Beverly's Log Guest House**, a modern lodging overlooking the **Kettle Moraine Forest**, (920) 892-6064; **Hillwind Farm Bed & Breakfast Inn**, (920) 892-2199; **Spring Tulip Cottage**, (920) 892-2101; and the **Yankee Hill Inn Bed & Breakfast**, (920) 892-2222.

ALLENTON

At the southern end of the forest is **Allenton's Addison House**, a historic building now serving as a B&B on Highway 175. Located on another historic crossroad, where the Fond du Lac and Decorah Indian Trails once met, the building was first a saloon in 1840. (A brewery and brothel also figure prominently in the building's history.) Big breakfasts and three acres of walking trails are part of the amenities. Caves built to cool beer are located on the grounds. Phone (262) 629-9993

SOUTH TO HARTFORD

Leaving the forest's Northern Unit and driving for 20 or so miles southwest, you'll come to the small town of Hartford in Washington County. Here, a former canning factory is home to the **Wisconsin Automotive Museum**, the largest collection of vintage vehicles in the state. Hartford?

Actually, automobile history runs deep in Hartford. The town was the manufacturing site of the Kissel, a luxury vehicle favored by movie stars and other well-healed personalities from 1906 to 1931. The most famous Kissel model was the Speedster, affectionately called the Gold Bug. The two-passenger model was owned by the likes of silent-film comedian Fatty Arbuckle and aviation pioneer Amelia Earhart. In its time, the Kissel was "every inch an automobile," according to advertising.

The Kissel plant is long gone, but the renovated canning factory provides the rare opportunity to see the largest assembled group of Kissel autos in the world. Of the 35,000 produced, only 150 are known to exist today. Many are here. And a fine collection it is, including four-passenger sedans, coupes, and touring cars; fire engines and trucks are also found in the huge building. Another featured car is the Kenosha-produced Nash, which first rolled off the assembly line in 1916. All told, more than 90 rare vehicles (including Reos, Pierce-Arrows, Pontiacs, Studebakers, Chevrolets, and Fords) are displayed on the two floors of the Art Deco-inspired interior.

Automotive artifacts on are hand as well—license plates, spark plugs, oil cans, signs—plus a collection of industrial engines and outboards built in Hartford from 1936 to 1992. The building is wheelchair-accessible. A park with picnic facilities adjoins the large parking lot. It's located one block from Hartford's Main Street at 147 N. Rural Street, (414) 673-7999. Admission $6 adults; children under 7 free. There is a gift shop on the premises.

The **Schauer Arts and Activity Center**, located next to the auto museum, regularly hosts nationally known performers; (262) 670-0560.

PIKE LAKE STATE PARK

A few miles east of Hartford lies **Pike Lake State Park**, which is becoming one of the most popular parks in southeastern Wisconsin. One of the reasons is that it offers about a dozen miles of wonderful hiking trails of various difficulty levels. Another draw is cone-shaped Powder Hill, one of the highest points in the region and a good place for a picnic. The National Ice Age Scenic Trail also makes an appearance here, as it briefly winds through the park, which is located at 3340 Kettle Moraine Drive, Hartford, (414) 670-3400.

HOLY HILL

One of the state's top photo opportunities is available at **Holy Hill, National Shrine of Mary**, five miles south of Pike Lake on Highway 167. At 1,350 feet above sea level, the shrine and cathedral, run by the Discalced Carmelite Friars, is renowned for its stunning silhouette above the rolling farmlands and for the view of southeast Wisconsin from the shrine itself. The site is one of the most visited and photographed places in the region.

The shrine holds fascinating stories as well, such as the hermit of Holy Hill: The hermit, Francois Soubrio, was discovered in the 1860s by local farmers who gave him food and built a small cabin. One account says Soubrio's mysterious presence at Holy Hill came as penance for the murder of someone he loved, or that the hermit was miraculously healed of a partial paralysis after spending the night in prayer on the hill's summit.

But there's more to the story. Before coming to Holy Hill, Soubrio worked for a professor in Quebec, Canada, when he found an old French diary and a parchment map dated 1676. The map showed the region and the route used to reach a very high hill in southeastern Wisconsin. Many believed the documents belonged to Father Jacques Marquette. Indian folklore supports the belief of a Jesuit missionary in the area. But records dispute that Marquette ever traveled to what is now Holy Hill.

We do know that modern-day pilgrims come to Holy Hill every day to worship. Others come as sightseers or hikers. Families frequently come to Sunday mass and remain to picnic on the wooded grounds. Weekday and Sunday masses are offered. Confessions are heard half-hour before mass on weekends and upon request. For more information, contact, Holy Hill National Shrine of Mary, Discalced Carmelite Friars, 1525 Carmel Road, Hubertus, WI 53033, (414) 628-1838.

The township of Erin surrounds Holy Hill, settled in 1841 by Irish immigrants who saw their homeland in the lush, rolling hills.

A RUSTIC ROAD

After taking in the grandeur and serenity of Holy Hill, you may want to cruise the open road for a wonderfully scenic tour of the surrounding area. Then head out to County K, just west of Holy Hill. This north–south route has been designated as **Rustic Road 33**. It's one of the best examples of Wisconsin's Rustic Roads System, which was created in 1973 in an effort to help citizens and local units of government preserve what remains of the state's scenic, lightly traveled country roads. This 12.1-mile stretch is a winding, hilly route offering terrific views of Holy Hill. In addition, there are other roads in the area that are part of the Kettle Moraine Scenic Drive; these are marked by acorn-shaped signs.

ASHIPPUN

One reason to visit Ashippun in Dodge County, about 10 miles west of Holy Hill is **Honey Acres Museum**. Located two miles north of Ashippun on Highway 67, the property has been owned by family beekeepers since 1852. You can take in a 20-minute multi-media presentation on pollination, then taste five varieties of honey and view active beehives; there is a nature trail on the grounds. Call (920) 474-4411.

Follow the acorn-shaped signs for scenic tours through the rolling Kettle Moraine region.

OCONOMOWOC

If you're new to Oconomowoc, you may think you ended up in Lake Geneva: Oconomowoc has a similar feel. Located west of Milwaukee in Waukesha County, the town became a popular 19th-century vacation place for wealthy families of the Midwest. Large and elaborate mansions grace the lakeshores of the area, as well as accessory buildings to service their owners. Victorian homes on shade-filled streets, gazebos and boardwalks, a lakeside band shell, and a picture-postcard downtown surrounded by sparkling water harken back to a bygone era. The only fieldstone train depot left in the Midwest is found here.

The most notable accommodation in the area is the majestic **Inn at Pine Terrace** in Oconomowoc, 351 Lisbon Road, recipient of many "best of" awards. The mansion has been restored to accurately reflect the prestigious lake estate of two brothers who built the showplace in 1879. Phone (888) 526-0588.

THE SOUTHERN UNIT

To get to the **Kettle Moraine State Forest's Southern Unit**, follow the acorn-shaped Scenic Drive signs through beautiful (and posh) areas such as Oconomowoc, Chenequa, and Hartland. Highways 67 and 83 both lead to the forest area.

Outstanding mountain bike trails are found in the Southern Unit, located in southwest Waukesha County and northwest Walworth County. Both the John Muir and Emma F. Carlin trail systems offer a great opportunity to test your riding skills. The Muir trails offer five different loops each varying in difficulty and lengths from 1.5 to 10 miles.

The Southern Unit encompasses 21,000 acres and has 332 camping sites, 50 of which have electrical hook-up. For more information, contact the Kettle Moraine State Forest Visitor Center at (262) 594-6200.

OLD WORLD WISCONSIN

Nearly 600 acres of prairie and woodland in the Southern Unit, just south of Eagle in Waukesha County, are the setting for **Old World Wisconsin**, a huge museum dedicated to America's rural heartland heritage. The complex, the largest exhibit of its kind in the world, opened in 1976 to commemorate 200 years of American history.

Old World Wisconsin includes numerous 1870s village buildings and an assortment of ethnic farmsteads. The state's history of immigration and resettlement in the late-19th and early-20th centuries are thoroughly recounted.

The visitor center includes the octagonal Clausing Barn and offers cafeteria-style restaurant. Ramsey Barn contains an orientation theater and museum gift shop. Caldwell Farmers' Club Hall once served as headquarters of an organization of progressive farmers. Hands-on activities are available for museum visitors. In addition, you can view a bit of living history on weekends every fall, when Old World's "Autumn on the Farm" performances show how Wisconsin

71

farmers used to prepare for Wisconsin winters, right down to butchering a live pig. Adults $11; children (5–12), $5.50; senior citizens (65 and over), $9.90. An all-day tram pass is $2 per person. Located 1.5 miles south of Eagle in Waukesha County, just off Highway 67. Phone (262) 594-6300.

WHERE'S THE FISH FRY?

In January 2001, fire destroyed one of Wisconsin's great fish fry palaces, the **Eagle Springs Pub**, a popular rural Waukesha County tavern in the town of Eagle. The only thing remaining after the fire were great memories of a country tavern built in 1930—and the secret fish fry recipe, committed to memory by the owners, John and Diane Oliver, a couple who would not go quietly into the dark night. The new Eagle Springs Pub has risen phoenix-like from the ashes and been rebuilt true to its heritage, with lots of knotty pine walls and fried fish served on paper plates.

Waukesha County, the link between the northern and southern Kettle Moraine, has any number of good restaurants catering to Milwaukee and local clientele. When passing through Oconomowoc, the **Main Street Depot**, 115 E. Collins Avenue, serves breakfast, lunch, and dinner in a restored building; (262) 569-7765. **The Red Circle Inn**, N41W33013 Watertown Plank Road, Nashotah, is one of the state's oldest restaurants and features fish, veal, beef, lamb, and poultry with a French flair; (262) 367-4883.

READ ALL ABOUT IT

The *Plymouth Review, Random Lake Sounder, Campbellsport News, Hartford Times-Press, Palmyra Enterprise,* and *Mukwonago Chief* are weekly papers throughout the Kettle Moraine region. The *West Bend Daily News* and *Waukesha Freeman* are daily publications.

HAVE YOU HEARD?

WTKM, 104.9 FM and 1540 AM, is the only radio in the world playing polka music all day, every day. A dinosaur? An anomaly wrapped in an enigma hidden in a tuba bell? Think again. Out of 400 stations that are being broadcast on the Internet through Warpradio.com, 50-year-old WTKM is in the top-ten. It's the only way Europeans can hear a polka station. For those of us taking it for granted, WTKM has 80,000 listeners in southeast Wisconsin and the Fox River Valley, and 25 percent of the audience is under age 50!

MILWAUKEE
Sampling the Melting Pot

Ve get so soon oldt und yet so late schmardt better ve take one.

Make mine Blatz.   —ad for Blatz Beer

This bit of homespun wisdom was seen on an old beer ad hanging on a tavern

wall nowhere near Milwaukee. It represents one of the most enduring

hallmarks of the city, one of the symbols by which the rest of the world has

come to recognize this melting pot by the lake. The ad also underscores that

Milwaukee's industrial charms are predicated on its ethnicity—from Germans

who left an indelible mark on the city (and the language) to recent waves

of Hispanic and Asians who are making a new life in old Brewtown.

Milwaukee, the country's 19th largest city, has been called the most foreign

city in the nation. Germans, Czechs, and Irish immigrated in the 1840s;

Poles arrived following the Civil War; Italians, Slovaks, Greeks, and

Hungarians came in the late nineteenth century while African-Americans

sought jobs here during the world wars.

Sometimes melting pots are a little too messy for chamber of commerce brochures, but melting pots are as American as the huddled masses slogging through the doors of Ellis Island. Milwaukee is our melting pot. Yes, its ethnicity sparked tension at times, but far more prevalent today are the distinctive neighborhoods, festivals, and foods that give Milwaukee its distinctive sense of place.

And we expect certain things from metropolises: museums, parks, concrete, concerts, sports, traffic, zoos, skylines, honking horns. For all her well-deserved blue-collar reputation, Milwaukee also delivers these modern trappings.

Milwaukee's Riverwalk cuts through the heart of the historic downtown.

CULINARY DIVERSITY

One of the best ways of experiencing Milwaukee's rich cultural mix—not to mention some terrific food—is to spend a few days sampling the city's ethnic restaurants. You'll not only taste some marvelous dishes but also have a chance to meet other customers, some of them locals who have may have been frequenting a place for years and swear by the food. You'll meet others, like yourself, who want to sample the culinary delights of a particular culture. Milwaukee has a list of restaurants longer than we could munch through in a lifetime. Fine, casual, ethnic, cheap eats—miss out on eating out and you'll miss the flavor of Milwaukee.

Among the city's most famous eateries are two German restaurants serving up schnitzel, sauerbraten, and spaetzle from Old World recipes: **Karl Ratzsch's** and **Mader's**, each owned and operated by their respective families since the early 1900s. Visiting dignitaries typically visit one or the other, but you don't need to be a head of state. Sadly, John Ernst's restaurant, one-third of the long-time Milwaukee trinity, closed its doors in May 2001 after more than a century in business. Karl Ratzsch's is located at 320 E. Mason, the junction of E. Mason and N. Milwaukee; (414) 276-2720. Mader's is found at 1037 N. Old World Third Street; (414) 271-3377.

If German food is a little too Milwaukee for your tastes, try the Mandingo Warrior Platter at the **African Hut Restaurant**. True to its name, the place dishes up authentic African cuisine and has been voted one of Milwaukee's best restaurants. There's a strong emphasis on vegetarian entrees, as well as seafood and poultry. African pudding pie is on the dessert menu. Owner Yinka Adedokun learned to cook in his mother's restaurant in western Nigeria. The restaurant is located near Mader's at 1107 N. Old World Third Street; (414) 765-1110. **Sanford Restaurant** has been mentioned in the same breath with some of the great fine dining establishments in America; it's certainly one of the best in Wisconsin—one of only two AAA-rated Four Diamond restaurants in the state (the American Club's Immigrant Room, Kohler, is the other). Located inside the modest building that was once a grocery owned by his father, Sanford D'Amato offers multiple courses from a French-influenced menu. It's located at 1547 N. Jackson, at the corner of Jackson and Pleasant; Phone (414) 276-9698. D'Amato also draws rave reviews at his more casual **Coquette Café**, 316 N. Milwaukee Street in the Historic Third Ward; (414) 291-2655.

Bill Clinton took a rain check on the usual German fare when he visited Milwaukee a few years back (and he was hosting German Chancellor Helmut Kohl!), stopping instead at **Miss Katie's**, a 1950s era diner serving meatloaf and ribs, 1900 W. Clybourn; (414) 344-0044.

The everyman's restaurant is **George Webb**, found at locations throughout the city and maintaining the great American tradition of all-night diners. Think Edward Hopper's painting *Nighthawks*. The **Third Street Pier**, 1113 N. Old World Third Street, has a scenic location on the Milwaukee River. Steak and seafood are the specialties with live jazz featured on weekends; (414) 272-0330. Two longtime favorites catering to the upper echelons downtown are **Watts Tea Room**, 761 N. Jefferson, (414) 290-5720, and **Celia** in the Pfister Hotel (formerly the English Room), 424 E. Wisconsin; (414) 390-3832.

For authentic ethnic cooking, Milwaukee has scores of restaurants representing all corners of the globe. **La Casita Mexican Café**, 2014 Farwell, offers south-of-the-border fare and a seasonal patio; (414) 277-1177. **Old Town Serbian Gourmet House**, 522 W. Lincoln, makes goulash and other Serbian cuisine from scratch; (414) 672-0206. The **Three Brothers Restaurant** is famous for its location in a former Schlitz brewing company building, 2414 S. Saint Clair Street, and for its Eastern European and Hungarian dishes; (414) 481-7530. The

West Bank Café is a highly regarded Vietnamese restaurant in a residential neighborhood at 732 E. Burleigh; (414) 562-5555. **Yen Ching**, 7630 W. Good Hope Road, has Mandarin cuisine; (414) 353-6677.

Albanese's, 701 E. Keefe, (414) 964-7270, dishes out Italian food from family recipes. **Taqueria Azteca** serves Hispanic food from scratch using the Sanchez family's secret ingredients, 2301 Howell; (414) 486-9447. **Izumi's** Japanese cuisine is popular at 2178 N. Prospect; (414) 271-5278.

Located in the University Square neighborhood at Locust and Oakland on Milwaukee's lower eastside is **Shahrazad**, a Middle Eastern restaurant serving lunch and dinner daily; the owners hail from Jerusalem, 2847 N. Oakland Avenue; (414) 964-5475.

West of the city, **Singha Thai**, 2237 S. 108th in West Allis; (414) 541-1234, is among the best of the many Thai restaurants serving trademark noodle dishes; it's causal and reasonable. For Creole, it's **Crawdaddy's**, 6414 W. Greenfield, West Allis; (414) 778-2228. For native Indian cooking, try **Tandoor**, 1117 S. 108th, West Allis; (414) 777-1600.

The north side of Milwaukee is home to Jack Pandl's **Whitefish Bay Inn**, a favorite for 80-plus years. It has a turn-of-the-century cottage atmosphere with homemade soups and roast duck. The house specialty is whitefish; Sunday brunch is popular, 1319 W. Henry Clay Street, Whitefish Bay; (414) 964-3800.

Bartolotta's Lake Park Bistro offers tremendous French dishes in an equally impressive setting on Lake Michigan. This is fine dining at its best, with Sunday brunch served in three courses. The restaurant itself is in a renovated pavilion in Lake Park, 3133 E. Newberry Road; (414) 962-6300. Joe Bartolotta also serves some of the most authentic Italian dishes in Wisconsin at **Bartolotta's Ristorante** in Wauwatosa, 7616 W. State; (414) 771-7910.

For dessert or an off-hours treat, try the custard at **Gilley's**, 7515 W. Blue Mound Road, Milwaukee's oldest custard stand; ditto for **Leon's**, 3131 S. 27th, the inspiration for the drive-in featured in Happy Days.

WHERE'S THE FISH FRY?

There are some good ones: Friday night at Pandl's is a tradition. Out in the suburbs, **Dick Manhardt's Inn**, 14000 W. North Avenue, Brookfield, packs 'em in with lake perch and potato pancakes. The **Silver Spring House** on Green Bay Avenue, a landmark tavern since 1856, serves walleye and lake perch with coleslaw and marble rye bread for standing room only crowds. **The Red Rock Café**, 4022 N. Oakland, received kudos from Juliet Child when she sampled the beer-battered perch! These are just four among dozens of places to consider. You'll get the definitive answer from every person you ask, and every definitive answer will be different.

Two venerable Milwaukee spots swim to the head of the school when it comes to Friday fish—American Serb Memorial Hall and Turner Hall. **Serb Hall** in South Milwaukee, 5101 W. Oklahoma Avenue, reportedly serves more than

4,000 people on Good Friday, maybe 1,500 or so on an average Friday night.

Hundreds of pounds of fish are served Wednesdays and Fridays with banquet hall seating for 600 and another 100 or so in the bar area. Drive-through window too! Serb Hall rests in the Saint Sava neighborhood, marked by South 51st and 60th Streets and West Oklahoma and Morgan Avenues, a compact community named after the Saint Sava Serbian Orthodox Cathedral. The impressive Byzantine-styled church is the heart of Milwaukee's considerable Serbian community. Nearby is the only Serbian parochial school in the United States.

The cathedral, built in 1957, is a landmark, and so is Serb Hall. Constructed as a memorial to American Serbs who served in the military, Serb Hall is a popular place for weddings, union meetings, and political rallies. The hall's bowling alley is open daily. Deep fried cod or haddock offered. Sample the Serbian style butter-baked fish served with tomato sauce. Reservations suggested; (414) 545-6030.

Turner Hall is a popular downtown gathering place across from the Bradley Center at 1034 North 4th Street. The interior of the 1883 building has been renovated to resemble the Schlitz Palm Garden. The original intimate dining room remains. You get a thick slice of Milwaukee culture with your dinner: murals are inscribed in German and original Turner photographs hang on the walls. (Turner halls, once the social clubs for German-Americans, emphasized physical fitness, art, literature, and music.) The dining room has Old World lampposts and stained-glass windows. Turner Hall makes for a memorable casual dining experience. The prices are $7.95 for cod or $9.95 for perch. Phone (414) 276-4844.

Paddleboats parked at a sleepy lagoon in Milwaukee's Lake Park; the city's lakefront contains a 10-mile ribbon of parkland.

WHERE TO START

Befitting a large city, there's a lot do in Milwaukee. Here are a few two- to three-day itineraries to help narrow your focus.

Quick tip: Don't overlook the obvious, such as spending a day in the park. Great cities are distinguished by great parks: New York, London, Paris. Sure, Milwaukee's **Lake Park** lacks the prestige of Central Park or Hyde Park, but the prejudice is undeserved. A day at the beautiful 140-acre lakefront park is a sure bet. Bike and kite rentals are available (lake breezes are ideal for kites); rent a paddleboat or aqua bike and float in the park's sleepy lagoon, watch a rugby game, envy the boaters in the marina, or people-watch. Milwaukee's lakefront is a 10-mile ribbon of parkland from Bender Park in Oak Creek, to Grant Park and Warnimont Park in Cudahy, to Bay View Park and South Shore Park in Saint Francis, to Veteran's Park and Lake Park in the central city. Lake Park is the crown jewel.

MILWAUKEE'S FIVE B'S

A good way to spend a Classic Wisconsin Weekend in Milwaukee and sample much of the stuff that made it famous is to take the "Five B's Tour:" beer, bratwurst, bowling, baseball, and bikes (and I'm not talking Schwinn). In particular, the itinerary would include visits to Miller Brewing and the Pabst Mansion, Usinger's sausage, Hollar House bowling, the Milwaukee Brewers, and Harley-Davidson motorcycles.

Frederick Edward John Miller, born in Germany in 1824, was sent to France for seven years to become a brewmaster at the ripe old age of 14. Miller came to Milwaukee in 1855 to flee his homeland's political strife, part of the first wave of German immigrants who were dodging military conscription, among other things. With $8,000 in gold, Miller set up shop in an abandoned brewery.

If he could see the place today. **Miller Brewing Company** is the second largest brewer in the United States. (Don't mention the other one in this part of the Upper Midwest.) Located at 4251 West State Street, the brewery offers free guided tours Monday through Saturday. Call (414) 931-BEER. The Girl in the Moon Gift Shop is open Monday through Saturday, 10 a.m. to 5:30 p.m. Closed selected holidays.

Another Milwaukee brewing giant was **Captain Frederick Pabst**. His mansion is located at 2000 West Wisconsin and open for tours. Listed on the National Register of Historic Places, the home is a wonder of the age of beer barons, a Flemish Renaissance-style giant built in 1892 and containing 37 rooms, 12 baths, and 14 fireplaces, (414) 931-0808.

What better Milwaukee souvenir than a box of bratwurst or blood sausage. Step into **Usinger's Sausage Shop** and savor the aroma of meat that is made from century-old recipes. Usinger's wurstmachers are still located on the site of the original store, where they adhere strictly to family recipes from the 1880s. Today, fourth generation Usingers lead the firm.

The sausage shop, 1030 N. Old World 3rd Street, contains tile floors, marble counters, and wood beams that have been in place since the early twentieth century. Best of all is the smell of all that sausage when you enter the store. Open 8:30 a.m.–5:00 p.m., Monday through Saturday. Tours not offered due to food sanitation requirements.

Old World Third Street's heritage is retained in this historic neighborhood downtown along the river walk. In addition to world-famous Mader's restaurant and Usinger's, you will find the African Hut Restaurant, Wisconsin Cheese Mart, the Milwaukee County Historical Center, and the Spice House, all located along cobblestone streets.

For a bit of sports nostalgia in a thoroughly Milwaukee setting, consider visiting **Holler House**, the oldest bowling alley in the nation. The nondescript building contains just two alleys, but they're tended by human pinsetters. Women's undergarments (autographed, of course) hang from the fixtures, old photos tell the history. The American Bowling Congress sanctioned Holler House in 1910. Located at 2042 W. Lincoln, (414) 647-9284, open at 4 p.m.

If you want a more contemporary twist to your sports viewing, new **Miller Park** is worth the short and convenient trip to Milwaukee's west side. It took some bruising political fights and untold millions of dollars to finally get here, but the home of Milwaukee Brewers baseball is an impressive venue that is marketed as a year-round destination. Tour information is available at (414) 902-4400.

The stadium's retractable roof eliminates those 30-degree home openers and summer rain delays that many fans endured at old County Stadium. Some things stayed the same, namely the secret stadium sauce for its bratwurst. Miller Park seats 42,500, and the playing surface is natural grass. The height of the outfield wall is eight feet in left and center field, six feet in right field; left field power alley—371 feet.

Tickets may be purchased at www.milwaukeebrewers.com 24 hours a day. A per-ticket convenience fee will be charged. Call (414) 902-4000 or (800) 933-7890. If you make a game-day decision, tickets will be held at will call. Ask about the three family sections if the kids are in tow. Ticket prices range from $5 for bleachers to $50 for field-side box seats.

The Brewers provide a number of automated information telephone lines to keep guests updated on promotions and special events, ticket and parking availability, even game recaps and player injuries. The information hotline, (414) 902-4300, is a 24-hour service.

If you like your recreation a bit more on the wild side (or least like to fantasize about roaring down the highway on a "Hog," head on over to the Harley-Davidson museum for the fifth stop on the "B Tour." The story of the company is one that "no one on earth could have made up," reads the **Harley-Davidson** Web site. "Four young men experiment with an internal combustion in a tiny wooden shed. Not only does the shed burn down, but the motorcycle they build goes on to serve over 100,000 miles under five owners. And that's just the beginning."

The legend of Harley-Davidson will be preserved for the ages in a $30 million museum complex occupying the former Schlitz ("the beer that made Milwaukee famous") Brewery. Talk about a marriage made in heaven. The 1894 brew house, a 75,000-square-foot fortress at 213 W. Galena Street had been standing idle for years.

The museum is a work-in-progress. It's scheduled to be open for Harley-Davidson's centennial celebration in March 2003.

BRIGHT LIGHTS, BIG CITY

There are many other reasons to like Milwaukee, and to spend some time there, besides the Five B's. The **Milwaukee Art Museum's** recent $100 million expansion includes a dramatic wing-like sculpture rising high above the lakefront, giving Milwaukee's skyline a unique signature piece. The museum itself contains about 20,000 artworks, including drawings, photography, decorative arts, and American and Haitian folk art collections. There's also a good collection of old masters. Located at 750 N. Lincoln Memorial Dr.; Phone (414) 224-3200.

Walk through the lakeside park at Lincoln Memorial Drive or have lunch at the trendy restaurants and cafes in the **Historic Third Ward**, a turn-of-the-century neighborhood that once served as a wholesale and manufacturing district. Not to be mistaken for the Old World Third Street not too far away, the Third Ward has a concentration of art galleries, antiques shops, restaurants, the Broadway Theater Center, the Milwaukee Institute of Art and Design, and the Eisner Museum of Advertising and Design.

Restaurants, galleries, and specialty shops have given new life to Milwaukee's Historic Third Ward.

In the area, **Edelweiss Cruises** offer narrated tours of the Milwaukee River; two-hour champagne brunch and moonlight tours depart 1110 Old World 3rd Street, (414) 272-3625.

Another old neighborhood that's becoming new again is **Brady Street**, located on the downtown's happening "eastside" between the Milwaukee River and Veteran's Park. This area once served as the hub for Irish, German, and Polish settlers during the 1840s, with the ethnic character of the area changing predominantly to Italian during the 1930s and 1940s. It's the city's trendiest

Milwaukee's Pabst Theater and City Hall typify the Old World flavor of Wisconsin's largest city.

neighborhood and within walking distance of the shores of Lake Michigan. It's highlighted by ethnic restaurants, nightclubs, coffee shops, cafes, and specialty food shops.

The downtown Theater District is composed of the **Marcus Center for the Performing Arts** (home of the Milwaukee Symphony Orchestra, Milwaukee Opera, Milwaukee Ballet). Also located in this district are the Milwaukee Repertory Theater, the gorgeous Pabst Theater, Renaissance Theaterworks, the Riverside Theater, and the African dance company Ko-Thi. Nearby, enjoy a walk or dinner at one of the riverside cafes along Milwaukee's RiverWalk, which winds its way through the heart of downtown.

Contributing to the eclectic character of the downtown area is the **Bradley Center**, home to the Bucks (NBA basketball), the Marquette University Golden Eagles (college basketball), the Milwaukee Wave (indoor soccer), the Admirals (hockey), and the Mustangs (indoor football). Major concerts are also held at the center, 1001 N. 4th Street, (414) 227-0400.

The opulent **Pfister Hotel**, 424 W. Wisconsin, is worthy of a visit even if you are not staying at the historic lodging-Old World luxury combined with a priceless art collection and modern amenities. Throughout the Pfister's public areas guests can gaze at the largest collection of Victorian artwork on permanent display in any hotel in the world. There are three outstanding restaurants. Or just hang in the Lobby Lounge, the place to be seen in Milwaukee, or Blu, the Pfister's new 23rd-floor cocktail lounge, which is often filled to capacity. Celia is the Pfister's new fine dining restaurant. The Café Rouge presents a Sunday champagne brunch, a Milwaukee tradition. The Pfister is one of the world's grand hotels. You don't have to go to New York, London, or Paris to savor the luxury; (414) 273-8222.

Finally, for a quick change of pace, fans of Schlitz should genuflect at the **Brown Bottle Pub**, 221 W. Galena, opened in August 1938 as a meeting place for brewery tours. The place was named in honor Schlitz's brown beer bottles, introduced in 1911 as protection against sunlight; (414) 271-4444.

FAMILY FUN

Milwaukee is also a kid-friendly town, with enough attractions to keep the little ones occupied for hours, maybe even days. One of the top attractions is the **Milwaukee Public Museum**, which contains the world's largest dinosaur skull, the last word on the argument that size matters. (Just ask any dinosaurs you see.) Kids will love the life-sized tyrannosaurus rex and stegosaurus. The collection has grown to more than 6.2 million artifacts. Then travel to a totally different era and walk the lamplighted streets of old Milwaukee in a life-size diorama of immigrant Milwaukee or learn more about rainforests or Native Americans in engaging exhibits that will interest children and adults. More than three floors of exhibit area. Located at 800 West Wells, (414) 278-2722. Open daily, 9 a.m. to 5 p.m.; admission $5.50; children $3.50.

Housed in the same complex is the **Humphrey IMAX Dome Theater**, a six-story extravaganza that shows movies throughout the day. You can select from several films and buy your tickets well in advance of the show time. **Discovery World/James Lovell Museum of Science, Economics, and Technology**, also located in the museum complex, features 150 interactive exhibits, live theatre performances, labs, and workshops. Called one of the top five interactive museums in the nation, the facility is named after the Wisconsin-born astronaut; phone (414) 765-9966.

A short distance away is **Betty Brinn Children's Museum**, designed specifically for youngsters ages 10 and under, with interactive programs such as a walk-through human digestive system. It was cited by *Parents* magazine as "one of the 10 best children's museums to visit nationwide." Located at 929 E. Wisconsin Avenue, (414) 390-5437.

The **Milwaukee County Zoo** should be considered for every Milwaukee itinerary, whether or not it involves children. One of the top zoos in the nation, the zoo is home to approximately 2,500 specimens representing more than 350 species of mammals, birds, reptiles, fish, and invertebrates.

The animals live in five continental groupings in natural settings; predator and prey inhabit the same habitats, just as in real ecosystems. The setting is truly impressive. Visitors will feel like part of the scenery. The newly renovated Aquatic and Reptile Center, a $25 million project, exhibits polar bears and seas lions through underwater windows. The Apes of Africa is popular as well.

Educational tours aboard zoomobiles give a good overview. Plan on spending at least half a day. Located at 10001 W. Blue Mound Road, just 10 minutes west of downtown; (414) 771-3040; admission $8, less for seniors and children. Zoomobile rides are $1.50. Free family days are offered.

Miller Park offers three family sections where the serving and drinking of alcohol is prohibited. For information on family section seating when ordering tickets, contact the Brewers ticket office at (414) 902-4000.

READ ALL ABOUT IT

The *Milwaukee Journal Sentinel* is the tale that wags the dog—Wisconsin's most widely read newspaper. The daily *Waukesha Freeman* caters to the metro area's western suburbs. Every community surrounding the Milwaukee area has a weekly paper, and the central city is home to newspapers catering to any number of specific audiences.

HAVE YOU HEARD?

There are 19-some radio stations in the Milwaukee area. All the usual formats can be found, and a number of others work to capture Milwaukee's diversity. You'll hear formats described as smooth jazz and ethnic (WYMS, 88.9 FM); urban contemporary (WMCS, 1290 AM); and rhythmic oldies (WJMR, 106.9 FM). Push the scan button and take it in.

MILWAUKEE'S SUMMERFEST
Party for the People

You've heard of "the Big Easy," the euphemism for New Orleans devil-may-care living and hospitality. Welcome to Milwaukee's version, Summerfest, best characterized as "the Big Sweaty."

Okay, that's not the official nickname. It's actually called "the Big Gig." The second official nickname is "the World's Biggest Music Festival." Come May and June, you'll hear both monikers used ad nauseam. The common denominator here is that Summerfest is a Big Something, an 11-day festival under the summer sun and stars that has grown so large it defies easy explanation. That's why this extravaganza, which runs from late June to early July, is a natural for a Classic Wisconsin Weekend.

One indication of Summerfest's magnitude comes when it draws to a close and the event proudly releases its "fun facts": 1,022,250 people in attendance;

grounds crew collected over 85,000 pounds of garbage; patrons used 7,800,000 feet of toilet paper (that's 1,477 miles); 37,129 shots were attempted at the Hole-In-One challenge; 120,000 mozzarella sticks were served; and on and on.

What's missing from these carefully compiled and potentially numbing factoids is the spirit that transcends the festival. A whopping 90 percent of Summerfest patrons are repeat attenders, with the average number of years in attendance currently resting at 12.

Summerfest is a subculture. As such, it deserves at least a brief anthropological investigation. Consider, for example, people who establish Web sites devoted solely to their Summerfest experiences and count the days to the next event. Consider the groups of people who meet at the same time and beer tent year after year like members of a Summerfest fraternal order. Or consider starry-eyed men and women who feel Summerfest is the ideal venue to meet . . . and marry. Yep, in 2000, ten couples were married on the Ticketmaster Legends stage as observers milled around eating enormous roasted drumsticks or cracking wise from the nearest beer stand. The matrimonies were discontinued in 2001, but there's nothing stopping fest-goers from a do-it-yourself ceremony.

FEST FEVER AND HOW IT GOT THAT WAY

Summerfest is the patriarch of what has become Milwaukee's niche: festivals. The calendar includes PrideFest, Asian Moon, Polish Fest, Festa Italiana, German Fest, African World Fest, Irish Fest, Mexican Fiesta, Indian Summer, and Arabian Fest. All are held on the Summerfest grounds along the lakeshore. All are good events, but each and every one is overshadowed by Summerfest. Remember, it's "the World's Biggest Music Festival!"

All this fest mania sprung from the well-intentioned proletariat brainstorm of the late Milwaukee Mayor Henry Maier following a visit to Munich's Oktoberfest in the 1960s. A festival for the people, Maier believed, would reenergize downtown Milwaukee, then suffering from urban blight, and provide a sense of local pride. In this respect Summerfest has exceeded Maier's wildest dreams. Economic impact is estimated at more than $126 million annually and supports 1,720 full-time jobs. Hotels in the city are booked solid during the fest. (Without an early bird registration you'll have to find a room out in Waukesha County.) And Milwaukee has become Festival City, U.S.A.

In 1970, the festival moved to Milwaukee's lakefront. At the time, the site was a former 15-acre Nike missile site, abandoned and post-apocalyptic. Plywood stages were built on concrete blocks. Festival-goers slogged through muddy pathways when rain fell. By the 80s, permanent stages had been built and the place was looking spiffy. Still does.

Recent additions include the Leinie Lodge at the Koss Pavilion and the Pepsi Comedy Pavilion. The lakewalk on the north end of the festival site has been completely relandscaped, a permanent first-aid treatment center was introduced, and a respite center was built. A new 20-year lease ensures that regular upgrades will be made by the city.

And a million people can't be wrong every year. Maier wanted those who were unable to afford summer getaways to have a vacation in their own backyard. Most attendees live in metro Milwaukee, 19 percent come from the rest of Wisconsin, 11 percent are from across the Illinois border. July 4th crowds are hard to fathom. Big, small, short, tall, young, old, beautiful, those with great personalities only—you'll see people if nothing else.

GETTING THERE AND PARKING

The earlier you arrive, the easier it will be to find parking. Simple enough. But please be aware that Summerfest has long held the opinion that it runs shows, not parking lots, so you must fend for yourself. If you read all the material that Summerfest churns out, parking information is conspicuous by its absence: "Milwaukee County Transit, the Department of Transportation and Summerfest encourage patrons to ride the bus for a convenient and easy ride to and from the festival."

Parking, however, is indeed available at the festival gates and in the nearby Third Ward neighborhood. However, the traffic can degenerate into gridlock when the gates close each night. With few exits, you may find that your car has moved very little after 45 minutes.

The answer, as suggested by the fest folks, is mass transit. The number of visitors arriving by bus has grown from a few thousand people a year in the mid-1980s to roughly half of the people attending Summerfest now. There are a number of options, courtesy of the Milwaukee County Transit System. For more information on MCTS routes and services, call the MCTS Bus line at (414) 344-6711 or visit www.rideMCTS.com to get info online.

The Freeway Flyer Service runs every half-hour (15 minutes on weekends) from park-and-ride-lots located throughout greater Milwaukee; the fare is $4. Downtown shuttle service runs every 6 to 10 minutes every day of Summerfest, 11 a.m. until 12:30 a.m. Stops are made at city bus stops marked with the Summerfest smile logo; $2.

There are nine Downtown Shuttle parking lots located throughout the central city area, all of which offer reduced parking rates. These lots are all located near the Summerfest shuttle bus routes.

Wisconsin Coach Lines offers service from Waukesha, Racine, and Kenosha; Waukesha Metro Transit has service, as does the Ozaukee Express Bus. Amtrak gets in on the act, too, running service from Chicago that includes free admission with a validated train ticket.

STAYING IN TOWN

The best acts finish their sets at midnight so driving home can mean a late night if you're headed back to the Fox Valley or Madison. Half the people staying overnight impose on local friends or relatives. For those who can't, there are roughly a dozen decent hotels in the city—including the Pfister, the finest hotel in the state—and many more in the metro area. Rooms are at a premium during Summerfest, as are the prices. You may have to do some looking. For information on lodging at hotels and motels, call the Greater Milwaukee Convention and Visitors Bureau at (800) 231-0903 or visit their Web site at www.officialmilwaukee.com.

Summerfest offers great opportunities for people watching. The music is good, too.

WHAT ABOUT THE WEATHER?

When it comes to weather, you have to pay your money and take your chances. Even the Summerfest gods cannot control the weather. You'll be outdoors and subject to whatever Mother Nature delivers.

Weather has always played a crucial role at Summerfest. The first Summerfest was held in 1968 at 35 locations throughout the downtown. Crowds were enthusiastic, festival planners were encouraged, and a small profit was made. Year two was an unmitigated disaster when the event expanded to 60 locations only to get pummeled by rain. The final day had to be cancelled altogether. A $164,000 debt was rung up. The private sector stepped up to the plate and saved Summerfest by sponsoring stages, a trait that makes Summerfest what it is today. (The Pabst stage went the way of the venerable brewer, but where else can you find venues called the Briggs & Stratton Big Backyard, the Harley-Davidson Roadhouse, and Miller Oasis?)

In 2001, Summerfest exceeded the million-person attendance milestone for the first time due to near-perfect weather throughout the entire run. The year before, one rainy day cost the festival an estimated 70,000 patrons.

HOW MUCH WILL IT COST?

Your visit to Summerfest will be affordable . . . if you stick to a budget. As of 2002, a single day advance ticket cost $8 ($2 savings) and a three-day pass $21

($9 savings). Gate prices for adults were $9 Sunday through Thursday, and $10 Friday and Saturday. The best way to go: Summerfest admission pins are available at participating Milwaukee locations for $3, or, even better, free admission is offered every day with promotions.

Not bad at all, but don't forget about incidentals: parking, food, drink, midway rides, and maybe a hotel. Parking lots near the fest grounds cost $10 to $15 a day. Beer is $3.50 a cup, a gyro plate $4.50, and soda $2.50. The midway rides are $4, the Sky Glider $2.50, and the Footsie Wootsie foot massage, 25 cents.

Performances—the big names—inside the Marcus Amphitheater require admission to the Summerfest grounds and a reserved seating ticket. A limited number of free general admission grass and/or bench seats will be available the day of the show on a first-come, first-served basis only with hand stamps available on the day of the show. Hand stamps go fast. Reserved seats for amphitheater shows cost whatever the going rate may be for a big-name act on tour, anywhere from $25 to $75 (rates subject to change). All other Summerfest stages are open to festival attendees.

Festival promotions run every day during designated hours and can get you inside at no cost, sometimes with as little effort as donating nonperishable food item.

If you are especially budget conscious, ride a bus to the grounds, take advantage of free gate promotions or buy a $3 pin. These tips can save $25 per person right off the top. Roughly 25 percent of all Summerfest attendees walk through the gates free or with a pin. On the other hand, that means roughly 75 percent are ready to spend, spend, spend. Of course, automated teller machines are located on the grounds, just in case.

With a little know-how, Summerfest can be an affordable event. Just take it easy on the indulgences.

ONCE YOU'RE INSIDE

If you're like most visitors, you come here for the three staples of Summerfest life: music, food, and drink. Music is the raison d'etre for the whole shebang, and you'd be hard pressed not to find one or two of your favorites performers; some artists that have performed here have gone on to superstardom. Others have performed long after their stars have descended. With such an extensive calendar (13 stages, 12 hours a day, 11 days) quantity sometimes supplants quality. Chumbawumba anyone?

You might want to pass on the come-back attempts (even if they evoke memories) and see top-notch regional and national acts of every musical genre on free stages—acts that kick butt under the lights and leave you hooting for more. The music is it. This is after all, "the World's Biggest Music Festival!"

The array of food nearly matches the variety of the music. To quote a bit of Summerfest publicity, "In addition to a diverse assortment of music and comedy, the festival provides a smorgasbord of appetizing cuisine to tempt anyone's palate." That means that you can find nearly anything on a stick. The food is actually better than other large-scale festivals. Fifty of Milwaukee's favorite restaurants run concessions. You can get Venice Club eggplant, John Hawk's fish fry, Gumbo Ya Ya gumbo, Mader's Viennese chicken breast, Zorba's gyros, Pitch's ribs, or Culver's custard, just to name a few. For those who prefer their food on a stick, well, you can find that, too.

As far as drinking, the third element of the fest equation, you have to remember (as if you could ever forgot) that this is Milwaukee, Wisconsin. The product that made both the state and city famous is served in oceanic quantities. At last count, there were 28 beer vendors dispensing the sudsy stuff, but the quantity sold is never, ever revealed, and bartenders are prohibited from talking to the media. The highly visible police and festival security people will tolerate a certain amount of goofy behavior. But they take a very dim view of fighting and anything else illegal. Those activities will get you booted—and fast—and will land you in jail.

Having said that, Summerfest scores points for cleanliness and security. Clean facilities and a sense of safety are big reasons that 90 percent of the people who attend Summerfest return. In addition to the omnipresent police and festival security, medical help is on-site.

The fest in the daytime is great for children. (But note that it can get hot and crowded, especially on weekends and July 4th.) There is plenty of kid-friendly activity, including a children's theater and play area, water shows, sports demonstrations, and amusement park rides. Strollers are not allowed inside, but rentals are available for a fee and with a deposit. Stroller and wheelchair rentals are located near the south gate in the south pavilion and near the north gate area. A lost children's/person area is located on the grounds as well.

So, there you have it: stage after stage of the best performing artists of our day juxtaposed with acts whose best days are behind them; a nice, clean lakeside venue offering an infinite variety of food and drink; and an atmosphere and clientele that shouts, "This could only happen in Milwaukee!"

Another Fest: Let's Hear it for the Irish

Milwaukeeans swear Irish Fest rivals Summerfest on the fun meter. (Note that these same Milwaukeeans trace their lineage to the Emerald Isle.)

Anyway, the Milwaukee Irish Fest has been considered the world's largest Irish culture festival since premiering in 1981, and you'll get a healthy dose of Celtic music, history, dance, drama, and sports. Held annually during the third weekend of August, the three-day event hosts 100,000 guests from around the globe. A couple of things stand out.

The arts comprise a main element of Irish Fest. Top Irish and Irish-American entertainers from around the world, as well as numerous regional groups perform on the festival stages. In addition, roaming performers dressed in traditional costumes entertain guests as they stroll the grounds.

Each year, the last day of Irish Fest is celebrated with a Sunday liturgy for peace and justice. Principle celebrants have included Milwaukee's archbishop, as well as other noted clergymen. Attended by more than 10,000 worshippers, the liturgy collects nonperishable food items to be donated to area food banks.

To help families trace their Irish heritage, genealogical resources and organizations are on-site, including the Wisconsin Irish Genealogical Society. For those with a competitive nature, Irish Fest offers plenty of contests: rugby, hurling, currach racing, and Gaelic football. Competitions, such as internationally sanctioned tug-of-war, children's red hair and freckle contests, bingo, treasure hunts, and a baking contest are also held. Additionally, The Top O' the Morning Run/Walk is held during the weekend of Irish Fest.

Summerfest favorite Pat McCurdy usually performs his wacky brand of music under a giant pig's head.

Double Take: Pat McCurdy

Pat McCurdy has been a Summerfest (and Wisconsin) favorite for more than a decade. His sardonic humor and original tunes—"I Don't Come From No Monkey," "Goofy Town," "Sex and Beer"—have earned the Milwaukee native a highly devoted and boisterous following throughout the Midwest.

McCurdy, with his faithful soundman known as Pipe Jim, performs at least twice daily at Summerfest. Listen for the huge crowd singing songs in the key of G with the artist known as Pat, usually on the Piggly Wiggly Stage, which is clearly marked by a giant pig head. One year, someone put a speaker in the pig's mouth and turned off the rest of the sound system so that McCurdy's voice became the voice of the pig. He said, "It had a huge reverb, like the voice of God."

Here's his take on his performances: "The afternoon show is a real mix of people—kids to senior citizens. It's a challenge because I want to entertain everyone. If they stay for one song, then they'll understand what's going on, that it's not going to be serious. I'm kind of making fun of everything, but gently. I don't want to be hateful. I want everyone to leave smiling. The nighttime shows are usually the wildest. I've been flashed, people have come up on stage in super hero outfits. One night for some reason women decided to take off their underwear and the stage was covered with bras."

Pat McCurdy is Summerfest's troubadour and is determined not to relinquish his role anytime soon: "If Summerfest wants to hire me, I'll play there till I'm dead."

CHAPTER TEN

LAKE GENEVA
Strolling past the Good Life

Lake Geneva is famous for several things: the beehive of tourist attractions (not nearly on par with Wisconsin Dells, though); the posh resorts, spas, and golf courses; that big, blue, spring-fed lake.

But Lake Geneva's most prominent characteristic is its opulence. Its table is set, if you will, with fine china and crystal, its lawns groomed like French toy poodles, for the air in this summer vacation town is perfumed with the scent of money rising from the incredible mansions ringing the lake, easily the greatest concentration of old money homes found in Wisconsin.

Eau Claire has its lumber baron's Victorian homes nestled in old neighborhoods along the Chippewa River, Neenah its string of paper-company-executive manors in the shadow of the mills on Wisconsin Avenue. Kenosha's industrialists built their villas downtown along Lake Michigan. All are worthy of seeing, but Lake Geneva's mansions play in another league altogether.

Look over there, it's Jay Gatsby and Daisy Buchanan frolicking carelessly on the rolling lawn, champagne glasses in hand. "What shall we do today, tomorrow, for the next 30 years?" Daisy asks. So this is what F. Scott Fitzgerald was talking about. As such, it's fitting and proper that Lake Geneva is often characterized as the "Newport of the West" (Newport, Rhode Island, being the summer getaway for the likes of Cornelius Vanderbilt and Claus von Bulow).

It wasn't always this way. Before the Civil War, Lake Geneva was part of the Underground Railroad used by slaves escaping from the oppressive conditions they endured on Southern plantations (see Milton later in this chapter). After the war, the town became a resort for wealthy Chicago families, many of them brought here by the city's great fire of 1871. Many had lost their homes and businesses and moved to Lake Geneva temporarily during reconstruction. Invariably they fell in love with the natural surroundings and commuted via rail to their businesses in Chicago or made Geneva a second home. The weekend trains became known as "Millionaire Specials."

A few of the grand estates have remained in their original families. Most, however, are owned by the nouveau riche, the era of the Wrigleys, Maytags, and Wackers, having faded away. Still, the difference between New Money and Old Money is irrelevant to those with Less Money. For visitors who want to see enormous and beautifully maintained mansions, along with sundry outbuildings and neatly trimmed lawns slopping down to the water, a walking tour is just the thing—a perfect centerpiece for a Classic Wisconsin Weekend (but ironic that it occurs at a place that Chicagoans consider their very own).

A GRAND WALKING TOUR

That's where *Walk, Talk, and Gawk* offers both an invaluable service and the inside track for the weekend. This written guide to seven separate lakeshore walks, ranging from two to three and a half miles, provides fascinating information and historical anecdotes about the mansions as you cross their lawns like a wayward Fuller Brush man.

Some of the gentry don't like this, but the 20.6-mile footpath that follows the shoreline is open to the public by law, and property owners are required to maintain sections that cross their yards. The result is a range of surfaces as different as the personalities of each property owner—grass, dirt, bricks, concrete, ceramics, spare change. No matter the surface, this is arguably the most unique walking trail in Wisconsin: beautiful Lake Geneva on one side, showpiece mansions, on the other, everything but the kitchen sink underfoot.

The entire Lake Geneva shore path could be walked in eight to nine hours. The smaller segments take anywhere from 40 to 75 minutes at a moderate pace. When walking the entire distance, and some people do go the distance, start at the Riviera Docks in downtown Lake Geneva and walk clockwise. This tackles the more challenging portions of the trail first and finishes with the easiest. But the path most traveled, as we shall see, starts from the same location but goes counter-clockwise around the lake.

No matter which way you choose, when walking a single segment, consider wind direction and time of day for temperature or shade preferences. You also need to arrange to get picked up when you're done with a segment, or plan on backtracking to get to your starting point. Some people use two cars.

Walk, talk, and gawk. A footpath circling Lake Geneva offers up-close and personal views of luxurious local mansions.

Walk, Talk, and Gawk is available at local stores or by mail order. It lists points of interest, distance, path conditions, public access, and parking information. With help from local historian Charlotte Peterson and the Milton High School desktop publishing class, the handy guide is the best (and most inexpensive) thing to do amidst the tourist detritus. Contact P.O. Box 413, Lake Geneva, WI 53147, for copies.

I don't know what Daisy will be doing today, tomorrow, or for the next 30 years (wait, Jay gets shot in his pool, and Daisy and Tom Buchanan carry on), but if you are visiting Lake Geneva and want to *do something*, then this handy guide is the ticket.

You may want to follow the lead of most people who walk along the lakeshore path and begin at the Riviera Docks in a counter-clockwise direction. This will put you on a seven-mile-long path to Williams Bay. There, you can board a boat to return (the return ticket should be purchased before leaving Riviera Docks, and make sure that you get the boat's departure time from Williams Bay). You can, of course, turn back on the path any time.

Among the highlights on this leg is **Maple Lawn**, the lake's oldest mansion, dating back to 1870. The Wrigley estates (Green Gables) once lined this mile of lakeshore. The surviving mansions in the area are homes formerly belonging to American business giants Montgomery Ward and Sears. Another site was owned by Levi Leiter, a business partner of Chicago department store baron Marshall Field, whose oldest daughter married the Viceroy of India under Queen Victoria.

The House in the Woods was built as a surprise birthday gift for Mrs. A. C. Bartlett in 1905 and was constructed under a Ringling Brothers Circus tent. In 1909, the *Ladies Home Journal* carried a two-page collection of pictures of the mansion and said it was one of the most beautiful country homes in America. The property remains intact as a private estate today. **Glen Annie**, the home with blue carpet steps and matching birdhouse, was the site of *Amos 'n Andy* radio show broadcasts.

The leg from Williams Bay to Fontana, approximately 3.5 miles, features **George Williams College Educational Center**, a 150-acre campus of brown cottages where the **YMCA** was founded. **The College Inn** offers snacks and ice cream.

At Fontana the **Geneva Yacht Club** stands as one of the oldest such clubs in the world. Built in 1874, the club still holds races here every summer. Another

Tours offered by the Lake Geneva Cruise Line are the most popular way to see the sights and enjoy Geneva's big, blue lake. One boat, the *Walworth II*, serves as an official U.S. mail boat.

one of the old mansions is **Black Point**, built in 1888 as a summer home for Conrad Seipp, a south side Chicago beer baron. (He became especially wealthy after the 1871 Chicago fire because so many of north side breweries burned down.) Black Point was reached initially only by boat. Guests were brought over by steamboat from the city of Lake Geneva and returned a week or more later. As many as 90 meals a day were served in the large dining room and surrounding veranda. It has been called "the best surviving example of the great summer houses in Wisconsin and Illinois."

The path near Linn Pier showcases **Aloha Lodge**, distinguished by six white pillars, built for Tracey Drake in 1901. Drake knew a few things about comfort. His hotel in Chicago, which carries his name, is one of the most luxurious in North America.

Walking toward Big Foot State Park, you'll see **Fair Lawn**, C. H. Wacker's estate—the man for whom Chicago's Wacker Drive is named. Fair Lawn was built in 1892 and contains a hand-operated elevator.

Once past the state park and near Geneva, you can't miss the most ostentatious estate on the lake. **Stone Manor**, also known as Younglands, the 18,000-square foot Italianate palace with a 250-foot veranda and sumptuous grounds, is visible from downtown Lake Geneva. It was built for over a million dollars in 1901. Gold-plated fixtures, a basement bowling alley, and a third-floor miniature golf course astonished even the wealthiest neighbors. A succession of proprietors (a school and restaurant included) came and went. By the 1980s the mansion and remaining property were purchased for back taxes, reportedly for $74,000. It has recently been restored and converted to six condominiums ranging in price up to $1.6 million.

CRUISING THE LAKE

For those who would rather relax a little and enjoy a somewhat more sedentary lake experience, the same sites can be enjoyed on one of the **Lake Geneva Cruise Line** tours. Tours operate late April through the last weekend in October; more frequent tours operate from June 15 through the last Sunday in August. The fleet includes the *Lady of the Lake*, the *Belle of the Lake*, and *Walworth II*. The Walworth II is an official U.S. mail boat, a longtime favorite because of the unique mail delivery system (a courier leaps onto the private docks) and the close-up views of the homes it provides. Lunch, champagne brunches, and sunset dinner cruises are offered in addition to the basic half-lake and full-lake routes. Phone (262) 248-6206.

The cruises depart from Lake Geneva's focal point and the logical starting point for a walk along the lake, **Riviera Docks**, which are connected to a beautiful WPA-constructed pavilion and beach. Many famous musicians performed here during the Big Band era; today the ballroom is available for receptions. The Lake Geneva Visitor's Bureau is located at 201 Wrigley Drive, just east of the docks, (262) 248-4416; www.lakegenevawi.com.

BIG FOOT STATE PARK

Located on the lake, Big Foot is one way for the budget-conscious to avoid the resort-levels prices and enjoy the area's ambiance. The park contains 100 campsites on 271 acres—by no means a large park. It's open mid-May through October; (262) 248-2528.

The classic WPA-constructed Riviera Docks pavilion is the place to begin a Lake Geneva tour.

YERKES OBSERVATORY

The imposing **Yerkes Observatory** occupies a small but beautiful campus in Williams Bay, 373 W. Geneva Street. The observatory is owned by the University of Chicago's department of astronomy and astrophysics, and holds public programs every Saturday throughout the year at 10 and 11 a.m., and noon. The free guided tour will entertain kids and adults alike. Visitors will explore the 90-foot dome, one of the largest of its kind ever built. Displays show spectacular images of outer space. For information about special tours and programs, phone (262) 245-5555.

WHERE TO STAY

As one would expect, the greater Lake Geneva area offers wide-ranging accommodations. Resorts and B&B's are numerous, in addition to the standard chain hotels and mom-and pop motels. Ranking above all is the **Grand Geneva Resort and Spa**. Spread across 1,300 acres of countryside, this is one place that surely contributes to Lake Geneva's reputation as the Newport of the West. The

AAA Four Diamond resort's focus is on recreation and pampering, from several fine golf courses and horseback riding to steam rooms and salons. Of course, it features excellent restaurants as well. Downhill skiing, snowboarding, and cross-country skiing make the Grand Geneva an attractive winter destination. Phone (262) 248-8811.

Among the best-known B&Bs is **General Boyd's**, a vintage 1843 Colonial Revival farmstead located at the junction of County BB and Highway 120. Phone (262) 248-3543. The **T. C. Smith Historic Inn** is another excellent example of pre-Civil War homes, complete with Tiffany chandeliers and Persian rugs. The building combines Greek Revival and Italianate styles. Phone (262) 248-1097. The **Budget Host Diplomat Motel** is the best of the no-frills places to stay; phone (262) 248-1809. In Fontana, on the west side of the lake, the **Abbey** is another large resort offering spas, villas, and restaurants; (262) 248-8811.

LEAVING LAKE GENEVA

In contrast to the bumper-to-bumper traffic and parking hassles of downtown Lake Geneva, the surrounding area offers some nice drives: north to the Southern Unit of the Kettle Moraine State Forest; northeast to East Troy and Burlington; east to Bong Recreation Area; northwest to Delavan, Milton, and Fort Atkinson. You'll see sprawling horse farms, clean little towns with cafes and antiques stores, a pastoral countryside characterized by steep hills, hidden valleys, and oak savannas.

EAST TROY AND BURLINGTON

About 14 miles north of Lake Geneva is the small community of East Troy, probably best known as the western terminus of the **East Troy Electric Railroad**, which runs from Mukwonago. This is not a round-the-Christmas-tree kind of electric train. Built in 1907 by the Milwaukee Electric Railway & Light Company, it continues as both a living short line and mobile museum. The basic ride (dinner trains and charters are scheduled regularly) is the 10-mile round trip from the East Troy Depot at 2002 Church Street to the Elegant Farmer Farm Store located at the intersection of County ES and County J south of Mukwonago. The actual running time is 20 minutes in each direction, with a 20- or 25-minute layover at each end.

You can begin your ride at either depot. If there is no agent at the Elegant Farmer Station, you can still board there and ride to East Troy where the agent works. At the East Troy end, in addition to the gift shop and museum displays in the depot building, most trips include a two-block walk to the East Troy Shop, where the restoration of the cars takes place. This is chance to see (and roam through) cars that aren't in use.

Popular dinner train and tea train excursions make leisurely trips to Phantom Lake and return to East Troy after a pause on the shoreline. Chartered trains are available as well. Reservations are required, (262) 548-3837.

There are two B&Bs of note in East Troy: **Pine Ridge Bed & Breakfast and Cottage**, an outdoor getaway at W3895 Timber Lake Road, and the **Pickwick Inn**, 2966 Union Street. Pine Ridge, once owned by beer baron Rudolph Pabst, is situated on 18 secluded acres of wooded lakefront property. There is a separate cottage, pier, rowboats, in-ground pool, and hiking trails through the wooded grounds. Phone (262) 594-3269. The Pickwick Inn offers a small-town America experience on East Troy's old-fashioned square. Phone (262) 642-5529.

Burlington, about 13 miles southeast of East Troy, is best known as home of the Burlington Liar's Club, which gathers on New Year's Day every year to swap tall tales. It is also home to **Chocolate Fest**, held every May. Burlington maintains its small-town charm, mainly because the historic significance of the city's buildings has led to efforts to preserve the quaint downtown, including attempts to have the area designated a historic district.

If you're in the mood for more walking (sans mansions and enormous lake), head southeast from Burlington to the **Bong Recreation Area** in Kenosha County. With more than 4,500 state-owned acres, Bong offers 217 campsites, 16 trails, fishing, and beach areas.

NORTHWEST TO DELAVAN AND MILTON

The town of Delavan has always been a bit of a little sister to Lake Geneva (from an economic point of view, most towns in the country could also play that role). But Delavan, 10 miles west of its big sister, has its own charms, including some circus history. In the 19th century, the town was the headquarters of several traveling circuses. There are hints of this association scattered around town, including the graves of circus performers in the local cemetery. Stroll the town's brick main street and read the historical marker to get the scoop. After browsing Delavan's antiques shops, most people head to **Millie's** on County Road O for a taste of Pennsylvania Dutch cooking.

One of the most notable B&Bs in the state is located a couple blocks down from Delavan's main drag at 511 E. Walworth Avenue. It's impossible to miss the 9,500-square-foot **Allyn Mansion**. The lodging is restored so immaculately that it won the National Trust's Grand Prize for Historic Preservation (as well as some of the state's most prestigious preservation awards). Guests have three large parlors to relax. The owners encourage visitors to hang out in the kitchen while they make homemade breads and jellies. Phone (262) 728-9090.

Finally, if you venture 20 miles northwest to Milton, be sure to visit the **Milton House**, built by Joseph Goodrich, a fervent abolitionist, in 1844. Goodrich allegedly dug the 50-foot tunnel from his cabin to the inn as part of the Underground Railroad for fugitive slaves. The tunnel connected Goodrich's cabin to a hidden basement room at the inn. The history has never been verified, but there are many oral accounts of local people in Albion, Milton, Rock River, and Walworth aiding fugitive slaves. While the tunnel has been enlarged, it was large enough in its day to allow a person to crawl through, making it plausible that the tunnel could have been used in aiding fugitive slaves. The inn itself is an attraction, a hexagon-shaped building designed so that every room could accommodate a stove; the chimney ran through the middle of the building. The Milton House is located at the junction of Highways 26 and 59. Open for tours daily, 10 a.m.–5 p.m., Memorial Day through Labor Day, (608) 868-7772.

WHERE'S THE FISH FRY?

There are two reasons to visit **Scuttlebuts** in Lake Geneva: The fish fry and the view of the lake. Better yet, you don't have to live the life of Gatsby to pay the check at this family restaurant with a nice selection of sandwiches and salads. Specialties are of the Swedish variety. It's located at 831 Wrigley Drive. **Hanny's Restaurant**—look for the beautiful, vintage neon sign at Dodge and Broad Streets—has been a fixture since 1938 and still uses original recipes; a comfortable, family-friendly restaurant; (262) 248-4850.

Ten minutes southeast of Lake Geneva is Fitzgerald's **Genoa Junction Restaurant**, 727 Main St., Genoa, a historic octagon house featuring outdoor fish boils a la Door County; (262)279-5200.

READ ALL ABOUT IT

Weekly newspapers in the area include the *Burlington Standard Press, Delavan Enterprise, East Troy News, Elkhorn Independent, Lake Geneva Regional News, Sharon Reporter, Walworth Times, Whitewater Register*, and the *Twin Lakes Wetosha Report*.

HAVE YOU HEARD?

WBSD in Burlington, 89.1 FM, plays a unique mix; WLKG in Lake Geneva, 96.1 FM, plays adult contemporary for summer vacationers; hear just about everything considered alternative from UW–Whitewater's station, WSUW, 91.7 FM.

Double Take: National Dairy Shrine

Located in the bucolic community of Fort Atkinson in Jefferson County, the **National Dairy Shrine and Hoard Historical Museum** should be a required stop for every Badger State traveler. You'll be served—proudly—a tall glass of Dairy State pride: "From the earliest recorded history, nearly 8,000 years ago, man has depended on the dairy cow as one of the chief sustaining forces of human life. Only in the past 100 years has science discovered why milk is man's most nearly perfect food." No wonder they call this a shrine.

Visitors see a 20-minute, self-guided multimedia tour of the past, present, and future of dairy farming in the United States. The Hoard Museum tells the pioneer history of Jefferson County and the unique archeology of the Lake Koshkonong area. The museum and shrine are open Tuesday–Saturday, 407 Merchant's Ave. Call (920) 563-7769.

MONROE AND NEW GLARUS
Cheese Daze

What would a Classic Wisconsin Weekend be without one of the state's gifts to the world: cheese? And there's no better place to celebrate this ubiquitous symbol of Wisconsin than Monroe—especially during its **Cheese Days** festival—and New Glarus.

But first, we need some background about how cheese came to celebrated in this part of the country. In one respect we can thank soggy cabbage.

By the second half of the 19th century, Green County's farmers had been through the wringer. Wheat crops had failed, and they turned to dairy farming, cheese making in particular. When they succeeded in perfecting cheese, misguided local officials outlawed its production. (Ok, their cheese may have been good, but it was Limburger, the cheese with the aggressive aroma, and the powers that be couldn't take it anymore.) The transportation of Limburger in and out of Monroe, the county seat, was banned.

Legend has it that in 1873, entrepreneur Arabut Ludlow staged a revolt on the courthouse square, or maybe it was just revolting, but wagons stacked high with bricks of Limburger left their mark hanging heavy in the air that day. Free trade resumed.

By 1889, Green County's farmers—proud, hardworking Swiss immigrants—had established 200 cheese factories and creameries manufacturing 10 million pounds of cheese annually. The county would eventually produce nearly all of the Limburger made in the U.S., more than 11 million pounds a year by the 1920s. Things were looking up.

Then came the cabbage.

Monroe was being upstaged by Forreston, Illinois, of all places, for something called Sauerkraut Day, of all things. Sauerkraut—a limp, pickled concoction made from cabbage. Sauerkraut was nice, but how much artistry does it take to chop cabbage compared to lovingly, painstakingly, handcrafting and aging Swiss, cheddar, or Limburger cheese?

Monroe's citizens thought that cheese making was a loftier skill and certainly more worthy of a festival. After a trip to Sauerkraut Day, the townsfolk, in just 19 days, organized the first Cheese Days celebration. People came in droves, four thousand strong, from far and wide, on a cold and rainy September day in 1914. A year later the governor, the state food commissioner, and teams of Swiss tumblers made Cheese Days an event for the ages. So much for sauerkraut.

MODERN CHEESE DAYS

Here in the 21st century, dairy princesses are crowned and honored and there's dancing in the streets. Parade units numbering 225 slowly make their way past who-knows-how-many tens of thousands of cheering people. The sounds of alphorns ring through the hillsides. A celebratory 200-pound wheel of Swiss is made on the courthouse lawn. The New Glarus Yodel Club is called back on stage by the kind of applause that rock stars can only dream of. A world-famous tumbling team warms up in the wings. In the surrounding countryside, busloads of tourists are taking cheese factory and farm tours, transported on buses that leave the town square hourly. At night, the Cheesemaker's Ball packs historic Turner Hall and a street dance erupts in a giant swirling mass of sound and color.

Cheese Days is held on even-numbered years to celebrate and promote the area's rich heritage. And why not? All they do is make the best cheese in the world. Not to mention that cheese making is damn hard work. Cheese makers continue to endure relentless challenges, from undependable milk prices (it takes 10 pounds of milk to produce 1 pound of cheese), to labor shortages and consumer idiosyncrasies. The quaint problems of yesteryear pale in comparison to those of today. Wisconsin, however, will always have what other states desperately want: the finest specialty cheeses and a deserved reputation for quality, ensuring that Wisconsin remains America's Dairyland despite the fact that another state has surpassed it in the amount of dairy products produced. Green

County is our ace in the hole.

Cheese Days encompasses equal parts pride and fun. A volunteer working in the souvenir tent summed it up best without ever saying a word. Her festive red sweatshirt contained two words: Swiss Power. Whether or not you attend Cheese Days, spend a weekend in Green County. You'll gain a deeper appreciation of one of Wisconsin's national treasures.

The shirts say it all. Monroe's heritage, celebrated at its annual Cheese Days festival, is built on the hard work of Swiss immigrants who mastered the art of cheese making.

GETTING AROUND ON CHEESE DAYS

All Cheese Days activities are open to the public and conveniently located around Monroe's charming courthouse square. A midway with the usual rides is located one block south. Food vendors dominate the square: local beef and pork producers grilling their products; dairy princesses serving heaping helpings of ice cream and cream puffs; community groups providing standard brat-and-soda fare.

Two stations draw the heaviest pedestrian traffic. One is the cheese tent, where local producers offer free samples and sales of packaged cheese. About 15 tons of cheese will be bought during this weekend.

The other place to be is the **Monroe Optimists**' booth, where you can stand in line for some deep-fried cheese curds, but it's well worth the wait. Two bucks will get you a snow cone cup stacked high with fresh fried curds. Busy workers (it's a good thing they're optimists) churn out curds assembly line-style—the serving counter is lined with holes that have been cut into the wood to rest curd cups—but the lines do get long. Nobody minds. One and a half tons of cheese curds will be consumed during the weekend. The Optimists' stand is located next to the stage, ground zero for the weekend.

The hills are alive with sounds of alphorns at the Cheese Days festival.

Cheese Days is kicked off on a Friday afternoon in mid-September (again, on even numbered years only), with opening ceremonies featuring alphorns, the parade of canton flags, Monroe's Swiss Singers, and a memorial to volunteers who have passed away since the previous festival. Expect some down-home speechmaking and personal greetings from the Swiss Consulate. An impressive children's costume parade follows.

Among the weekend events are cow milking contests, 5K and 10K runs, a golf tournament, arts and crafts fair, antique car and tractor show, cheese factory/ farm tours, and Swiss folk fare.

A full slate of live music is featured from roughly noon to 1 a.m. all weekend: oldies and polkas keep the crowd dancing in the streets, but don't miss the Monroe Swiss Singers or New Glarus Yodel Club. World famous tumblers are likely to be flying around, too. Beer gardens with live music can be found just off the square.

Locals Know

Keep your eyes peeled for the hilarious Huber Bock Run, an unofficial Cheese Days event. Starting at Turner Hall with a blast from an alphorn, the event is a race along three city blocks with a halfway stop at a Bullet's Tavern for a pint of Huber Bock—characterized by one participant as "motor oil"—and ending at the Huber Brewery's hospitality room. The Royalty Ball and the Cheesemaker Ball take place at Turner Hall on Friday and Saturday nights respectively. Both are open to the public for a $6 cover charge.

The weekend reaches its crescendo during Sunday's spectacular parade. For more than two hours, hundreds of units wind around the courthouse square. As many as 175,000 people attend the weekend festival—it seems most of them are at the parade. (Locals put down lawn chairs a day early and sometimes camp along the route.)

Needless to say, sleepy Monroe (population 10,200) gets crowded. It's the only time the number of people surpasses the number of cows in Green County— really! Book accommodations early. If making a day trip, arrive early to avoid traffic jams. Shuttles are available at the shopping mall on Highway 11, buses departing every half-hour for $1. For more festival information, phone (608) 325-7771 or (800) 307-7208, or write Cheese Days, P.O. Box 606, Monroe, WI 53566.

MONROE AT OTHER TIMES

It's said that a fence could be placed around Monroe and admission charged to enter. And it would be worth admission. Better yet, Monroe can be savored for no charge at all and done easily by foot. The yards are tidy and deep green under shade trees, the houses stately yet humble in a Midwestern way. In other words, you don't need Cheese Days to enjoy a classic weekend in Monroe.

The first thing visitors notice is that the streets are numbered—all the streets are numbered. If you attend the Saturday morning farmer's market, for example, you may find yourself standing at the corner of 16th and 16th. Avenues run north–south, streets run east–west.

The second thing visitors notice is the predominance of Swiss culture, right down to the architecture of the nursing home and the city parking ramp. This authentic Swiss influence, however, never reaches the kitschy level found in some communities. These are proud people, not tacky people. One building to definitely check out is the **Green County Courthouse**, a beautiful Romanesque

Baumgartner's Cheese Store and Tavern has been serving faithful patrons on Monroe's town square since 1931.

structure built in 1891 by local masons for $52,390, showcases the town square. If the numbered streets get you turned around, just point yourself toward the red brick courthouse with the white trim.

Standing shoulder-to-shoulder around the town square are storefronts dating from the 1880s. Justifiably, the most famous local establishment is **Baumgartner's Cheese Store and Tavern**, located on the west side of the square at 1023 16th Avenue. Baumgartner's claims to be Wisconsin's oldest cheese store. No argument here—step through the door and back to 1931. The store carries 35 domestic and imported cheeses and the three other necessities: mustard, sausage, and rye bread.

Cheese connoisseurs will marvel at Baumgartner's selection: six types of Swiss, four cheddars, three kinds of brick, Gruyere for fondues, Muenster, Jacko (Colby and Monterey Jack), champion domestic Crème Havarti, Gouda, Edam, onion cheese, salami cheese, farmer cheese, pesto cheese, mozzarella, Brie, imported Danish Blue, English Stilton, and the cheese that will live in infamy, Limburger, famous for it's self-assertive aroma. Order forms for shipping are available at the counter along with tips on how to preserve your cheese (one of them is to put it in a fruit jar and add 3 to 5 drops of water).

Walk through the archway separating the cheese store from the tavern and Baumgartner's becomes something of a community headquarters, with beers on tap and dollar bills stuck to the 18-foot-high ceiling. Proudly featuring locally brewed Huber and Berghoff, the tavern purportedly serves more Huber and Huber Bock than any tavern worldwide. Opposite the bar, a mural details the counties of Switzerland. Photos of proud Limburger queens are scattered about.

Don't think about leaving Baumgartner's without trying a cheese sandwich and a local brew—a marriage made in heaven, sort of like vanilla ice cream and chocolate sauce. Some seating is available in the storefront, more in back. Two bucks will buy you a cheese on rye, another 50 cents for sausage with that. Add your own helping of brown mustard. The mother of all Baumgartner's sandwiches is Limburger and braunschweiger (liverwurst) with raw onions and horseradish on rye bread. Yee-hah! They'll know you've been to Monroe.

Also lining the square are the Kourt House (offering "Bowling, Tanning, Laundromat, Spirits, Cheese, Sandwiches"), Schultz Pharmacy, the old Goetz Theater, and many other storefronts. At 1217 17th Avenue, the **Turner Hall Club** contains the obligatory exercise room, a bowling alley, and restaurant. The present building was constructed in 1937 after fire destroyed the original. The hall was once the thriving social center for area Swiss. Still is.

Local history is told at the **Green County Historical Society Museum**, housed in a former Universalist Church, 1617 9th Street. Outside is the oldest schoolhouse in Green County. Both are open summer weekends 2–5 p.m., admission $1 adults, 50 cents children.

The **Joseph Huber Brewing Co.** still turns out bottles of exquisite malt beverages just as it has since 1845 (not counting Prohibition, of course). The present plant, at 1208 14th Avenue, was built in 1875. The brewery recently started offering tours. Contact www.berghoffbeer.com for more information or phone (608) 325-3191. Huber has won numerous awards for its products.

An 1880s depot houses the **Historic Cheesemaking Center** on Highway 69 just south of town, (888) 222-9111. The depot was meticulously restored in 1993 by volunteers and showcases artifacts about the famous local industry. And for those who have been sampling a bit too much of Monroe's famous products, the depot also marks the start of the **Cheese Country Recreational Trail**, a 47-mile multi-use path running to Mineral Point through the heart of rugged southwestern Wisconsin. You'll find 57 trestles and overpasses are along the way. Unlike some state-owned trials, multiuse activities are permitted, meaning that ATVs, mini-bikes, and horses can (and will) share the path.

On the north edge of town is the **Ludlow Mansion Bed and Breakfast**, 1421 Mansion Drive, a 17-room villa built in 1857 by Arabut Ludlow, of Limburger revolt fame, who desired a stopover on his frequent travels between Madison and Chicago. The mansion is listed on Wisconsin's Register of Historic

Places; (608) 325-1219.

At the corner of 20th Avenue and 10th Street is the **Frank Chenowith House**, (608) 325-5064, a four-room bed and breakfast with rates ranging from $84 to $139 per night. The im-pressive house, built in a San Francisco Renaissance style of Victorian architecture, dominates its corner lot with a grand covered porch and three-story turreted tower.

NEW GLARUS

In one respect, New Glarus and Monroe are like twin sisters. Both are fresh-faced little Swiss kids, all smiles and braids. If you see one, the other is nearby. Expect to be charmed in equal measure. New Glarus (population 1,582), however, has the edge when it comes to dining. Full on heavy Swiss foods? Walking the downtown hillsides can help work up an appetite or work off dinner.

Swiss pioneers, who saw their homeland in southern Wisconsin's hills and valleys, had perfected dairy farming and cheese making in the homeland. They had the know-how to change for the times when wheat crops went under. The Swiss had already been making cheese in Wisconsin and knew it could be a ticket to prosperity. Soon, the University of Wisconsin was preaching the gospel of dairying to farmers throughout the state. Perhaps the state slogan should be amended to "America's Dairyland—Thanks to the Swiss."

New Glarus is smaller than Monroe, its Swiss pedigree perhaps a bit more pronounced. Swiss music rings along streets. Swiss flags and flower boxes hang from windows all over town. The Wilhelm Tell Pageant (Labor Day) and the Heidi Festival (late June) are big to-dos every year.

New Glarus is nestled into a hillside behind the historical marker on Highway 69. Turning onto Sixth Street puts you squarely at the foot of New Glarus. Park the car and get ready to walk some modest inclines. An information kiosk is located at the corner of Sixth and Railroad streets; a depot serving as trailhead for the Sugar River State Trail is located across the street.

The **New Glarus Hotel** is the heart of the village. Constructed before the Civil War, the hotel was one of the first buildings in New Glarus. The main dining room was once the hotel's old opera house. Traveling stock shows and vaudeville revues were billed often at the old theater, and it later featured silent movies, complete with pianists.

More of a great restaurant and polka palace than a hotel, the place is famous for authentic Swiss cuisine (amiable owner and chef Hans Lenzlinger visits the homeland often). Breakfast is served daily, a popular breakfast buffet on Sunday, and Tuesday through Saturday the dinners draw visitors from near and far. Specialties include Swiss onion soup ($4.25 a bowl) and *geschnetzlets*, thin slices of tender veal, a European favorite ($15.50). The hotel most famous specialty is beef fondue Bourguignonne ($19.50)—cubes of raw, aged prime beef tenderloin brought to your table, along with copper fondue pans. You spear the steak cubes, plunge them in bubbling hot oil, and dip into the homemade sauces. Most dinners are served with *spatzli* (Swiss-style noodles) or roesti (Swiss-style potatoes browned with Swiss cheese and onion).

Polka music is performed every Friday and Saturday night. Under the hotel balcony is Ticino Pizzeria, named after the Italian-speaking canton in Switzerland. Dine in or carry out. The hotel is located at 100 6th Avenue, (608) 527-5244 or (800) 727-9477. The hotel offers six rooms starting at $59. Check out the Web site (half in Swiss, half in English), with links to the Swiss embassy, at www.swisstown.com; e-mail address is hotel@newglarushotel.com.

On top of the hill on Seventh Street, next to the town cemetery (containing some of the most picturesque views in New Glarus) is the **Swiss Historical Village Museum**. The village is an impressive assemblage of 14 buildings, some authentic. Included are a *kaserei* (cheese factory), *schmiede* (blacksmith shop), *wehr haus* (firehouse), *kramerei* (general store), and *druckerei* (print shop), as well as a log cabin, smokehouse, and bee house. Parking is provided in front of the welcome center.

The **Chalet of the Golden Fleece**, located at the corner of Second Street and Seventh Avenue, was built in 1838 as the home of Edwin Barlow, the force behind the town's Wilhelm Tell festival. Today it's a museum chock-full of European artifacts.

Looking to treat yourself after traipsing around town or biking in the area? There are numerous places in town that will satisfy your sweet tooth and show you what Swiss food is all about. The **New Glarus Bakery**, 534 1st Street, is the place to do it. From-scratch baking and ethnic specialties have been made here since 1916. The little bakery ships its famous New Glarus stollen and cookies across the country. Climb the steps to the bakery into the sunny tearoom. Pastries to die for. Mail order at www.newglarusbakery.com. The **Maple Leaf Cheese and Chocolate Haus**, 554 1st Street, (608) 527-2000, sells, in addition to sweets, fondue accessories and local sausage.

Fondly known as the Stube, the **Garner Stube**, 518 1st Street, (608) 527-2216, serves up bowls of fondue big enough to float a boat. Decor is dark wood with hand-carved Swiss objects. Reservations not accepted Friday or Saturday evenings, so arrive early (and often). Drawing rave reviews for its fine dining is **Deininger's Restaurant**, located in a turn-of-the-century Victorian home atop Stonewall Hill. Some of the dinner specialties: *Königsberger klöpse*, meatballs and veal in a white wine and caper sauce ($13.50); frog legs Provençale with fresh garlic and white wine ($16.50). Reservations recommended. Look for Victorian frame house at 119 5th Avenue, (608) 527-2012.

Ruef's Meat Market ("The Wurst Store in Town," a sign on the door proclaims) makes its sausage from Old World recipes. Their *landjaegers, kalberwurst* (smoked brats), and *mettwurst* are outstanding, 538 1st Street; phone (608) 527-2554, or order online at www.ruefsmeatmarket.com.

Puempel's is the oldest tavern in town, dating to 1893 and in the Puempel family for over a hundred years. Current owner Chuck Bigler faithfully maintains it's warm traditions. On the patio seating in front you'll likely find bikers cooling off after a day on the Sugar River Trail. Inside, old-timers still play the Swiss card game known as jass on the antique tables. The original cherrywood bar is here, as well as the hardwood floors that served as a dance floor years ago and might host an occasional dance now and then. The hallmarks are four giant folk murals, painted on the tavern walls by a traveling artist in 1913. One depicts the arrest of Andreas Hofer, an Austrian patriot, by Napoleon's army. There are other beautiful, rare works of folk art. Puempel's serves daily soup and sandwich specials featuring local cheese. New Glarus Brewery products are on tap. Phone (608) 527-2045.

Outside of town, walk-in camping on wooded, secluded sites is available at small **New Glarus Woods State Park**. It's situated next to busy Highway 69, however, so automobile traffic can be heard all night. There are 18 drive-in sites, 15 walk-in, and 5 group sites in the 400-acre park, located a mile south of New Glarus; (608) 527-2335. A bike path leads from the park to the town and the trailhead of the Sugar River State Trail. The Sugar River State Trail runs 22 miles one-way between New Glarus and Brodhead, with Monticello and Albany located along the former rail bed. Open farmland, marsh, and oak trees characterize the scenery.

Puempel's tavern in New Glarus, dating back to 1893, contains rare folk art murals painted by a traveling artist.

Double Take:
Cheese, Wine, and Beer

Few cheese makers can offer tours of their facilities due to health codes (some accept reservations for group tours, others have observation windows to watch part of the cheese-making process). That's OK, because you can always enjoy Wisconsin's very best food and beverages in settings that match the quality of the products. *A Taster's Guide to Wisconsin Cheese, Beer and Wine*, produced by the Wisconsin Department of Agriculture, offers detailed descriptions of the state's 62 cheese factories, 29 breweries, and 11 wineries. The guide (and accompanying map) makes it easy to plan a day encompassing the world's best cheese, a glass of award-winning wine in the incomparable setting of a Wisconsin vineyard, or mug of premium beer in a local brewing company's garden. For free copy, write to the Wisconsin Department of Agriculture, Trade and Consumer Protection, P.O. Box 9811, Madison, 53708-8911.

READ ALL ABOUT IT

The *Monroe Evening Times* circulates to 6,000 area residents, making it one of the smallest daily newspapers in the state. The *Belleville Recorder*, the *Brodhead Independent Register*, and the *New Glarus Post Messenger* are smaller weekly newspapers circulating in the area.

HAVE YOU HEARD?

The programming at WEKZ radio, 1260 AM, is music to the ears of locals. The station has been playing Swiss music for more than 50 years. "The Swiss Program" features German- and English-speaking guests, plus yodeling and alphorns, 1:05 p.m. to 1:35 p.m., Sunday through Friday.

MADISON
Still Mad after All These Years

Weekends in Madison are transcendent, larger than life. There are at least a half-dozen occasions when this city, distinguished by two 800-pound gorillas, the state government and the University of Wisconsin, becomes the paragon of leisure-time activities and thus a great weekend location. If you can't find fun to your liking around here, you might want to check your pulse.

One such Classic Wisconsin Weekend occurs in late April when the ice has finally melted from the city's four lakes and spring fever sweeps epidemic-like through the 40,000-plus UW students. Loosely falling under the rubric of "Badger Weekend," Madison hosts the Crazy Legs Classic, a five-mile walk/run for 10,000 participants; the spring football scrimmage at Camp Randall Stadium; the first farmers' market of the season, the largest such event in the state, that rings Capitol Square. Throw in a concert at the Alliant Center (formerly the Dane County Coliseum), as well as live entertainment in smaller clubs throughout the city, and you'll have yourself quite a time.

Yet it's only the first in a series of weekends that brings legions of folks, young and old and in-between, to downtown Madison. If a capital city is supposed to be a state's crown jewel—some are, most aren't—then Madison may be the best example of the 50 choices. Some events during the warmer months include Art Fair on the Square, Badger State Games, Taste of Madison, Madison Blues Fest, and a string of autumn weekends when the Big Ten sports calendar is in full swing. At times, it seems like everything is going on here.

EXPLAINING MADISON

Former Governor Lee Dreyfus cemented Madison's reputation when he called the place "36 square miles surrounded by reality." And Dreyfus was only half-right. It's closer to 70 square miles. Madison's eclectic reputation lives on, thanks to the city's overt political correctness, the students' youthful exuberance, and the long-running comedic performances of the state legislature. The old joke says that when people living in the boondocks want to take an exotic vacation, they visit Madison.

Despite its reputation, Madison's reality today is a city on the move. Construction cranes share the skyline with the capitol dome. One of the benchmarks of the city's transformation came in 1996 when *Money* magazine named Madison the best place to live in America. Madison has been dealing uneasily with the good news/bad news ever since. A building boom invigorated the city, while housing values were sent into the stratosphere. Downtown has been rejuvenated. Some new restaurants and bars are decidedly upscale and, in a few cases, downright pretentious.

This is not your father's Madison. Latte anyone?

Look past the places trying too hard to be upscale and chic and you find that the true character of Madison is alive and well, a place best described as Gopher Prairie meets Madtown. Tear gas may not waft through the streets like it did in the turbulent 1960s, but you can count on the annual marijuana harvest rally producing its own unique aroma. And for every new fancy-pants cocktail bar serving nine-dollar martinis there are beloved mom-and-pop standbys, packed to the rafters on weekends, where everybody wears Badger red and drinks two-dollar Bloody Marys from bucket-sized cocktail glasses.

AN INTRIGUING PAST

It's a city marked by contradictions, but what do you expect—early pioneers described it as "beautiful but uninhabitable." Native Americans loved the four lakes region and lived here for 12,000 years. Fascinating remainders of the early Native American cultures can found all over Madison: burial mounds in the shape of animals that were built for the dead or for other ceremonial purposes. Most of the more than 1,500 mounds built in the area were destroyed through the years, but fine examples remain at the Mendota State Hospital grounds, Observatory Hill on the UW–Madison campus, and at the UW Arboretum near Lake Wingra.

Precariously packed on an isthmus between four lakes—Mendota, Monona, Wingra, and Waubesa—the swampy, mosquito-ridden land held little promise for settlement until the enterprising (criminal?) James Doty persuaded (bribed?) territorial legislators to move the government seat from Belmont, Wisconsin (where the first state capitol building was shared with pigs).

The years 1848 and 1849 were seminal for Madison. Statehood was granted, cementing Madison as the seat of government. Equally important, the state university was established—resulting in a fortuitous double play that has defined Madison ever since.

The university, as well as the town, has always enjoyed a reputation as places where divergent, oftentimes unpopular viewpoints are given full expression. And Madison's history of civil unrest during the Vietnam era can't be ignored. The UW–Madison campus was a hotbed of antiwar sentiment, the site of some of the nation's earliest and biggest campus war protests, some of which degenerated into tear gas and chaos and subsequently beamed into living rooms on the nightly news. The turbulence reached an awful climax when Sterling Hall was bombed in 1970, taking the life of a researcher and causing millions of dollars in damage. At the time it was the worst act of domestic violence in U.S. history. Madison, the bellwether of the 1960s, was the place where the era saw its denouement as well.

LET'S GET ON WITH IT

Whatever your particular brand of fun may be, there are multiple choices. University alums have their routine down pat when visiting (it usually involves a sports event followed by painful attempts to resuscitate lost youth at the bars), ditto for the white-collar locals at the Saturday morning farmers market.

For those who are truly tourists, Madison can be frustrating: downtown traffic patterns are a challenge, parking can be nonexistent at times, and hotel rooms, except for a few at the edge of town, fill up fast. It's best to narrow your focus, get a feel for the city, and keep going back for more. Let's look at some obvious options.

For tourist information, contact the Greater Madison Convention and Visitors Bureau, 615 E. Washington Avenue, (800) 373-6376, www.visitmadison.com.

STATE STREET AND A LITTLE BEYOND

Less than a mile walk down State Street will take you from Capitol Square to Bascom Hill, yet the entire weekend could be spent lingering here, the hub for the city, the county, the state. Hotels, restaurants, stores, galleries, theaters, bars, an arts district, museums—never a dull moment. It's quite possibly the most happening place in Wisconsin.

Just south of the square is the **Monona Terrace and Convention Center**, based on an original Frank Lloyd Wright design and one of the newer additions to Madison's architectural landscape, unveiled in 1998. Extending over Lake Monona, the rooftop terrace offers nice views while a pathway below is popular for walkers, bikers, and in-line skaters. Call (608) 261-4000 for tour information.

You can't miss the next site, nor should you. The **State Capitol Building** anchors downtown and dominates the city's skyline. Ordinances prevent new construction from obscuring the sight of the white granite beauty, the third such building standing on the present site. Topping the 2,500-ton dome is Daniel Chester French's Wisconsin, a gilded bronze statue also known as Miss Forward, a figure with a badger on her helmet. Take in the beautiful grounds around the building, then stroll through the rotunda. It's your building, citizens of Wisconsin.

Constructed in 1917 in Roman Renaissance style, the capitol is easily one of the best-looking statehouses in the nation. Walk around, look at the murals, stare into the dome, pity the lobbyists sweating profusely in their dark blue suits.

Guided tours of the rotunda, governor's conference room, state supreme court chambers, and senate and assembly chambers are offered; phone (608) 266-0382. It's worth planning a trip during the holiday season when a two-story-tall tree is erected in the rotunda.

Wisconsin's largest farmer's market is held in the shadow of the State Capitol.

Capitol Square, a social focal point of Madison, hosts many of the afore-mentioned weekend events, including the Art Fair on the Square, Taste of Madison, and Concerts on the Square. The showcase event is the **Dane County Farmers Market**, which completely surrounds the capitol grounds. Held every Saturday morning, spring through fall, it hosts thousands of people who prowl the various stands looking for fresh produce, fresh coffee, and baked goods. They are also there to see or be seen. It's the state's largest and most impressive market.

Locals Know

Neither the farmers market nor the art fair are suited for the claustrophobic or those hoping to take a brisk walk; the parade of humanity is plodding at best, with children and wagons slowing foot traffic. Pamplona, Spain, has the running of the bulls, Madison has the shuffling of the Birkenstocks. The major events held on the Capitol Square are all designed for foot traffic, but if you're looking to take a brisk hike, stick to the trails.

State Street is anchored at both ends by an impressive collection of museums and other cultural attractions. At the east end, on or near Capitol Square, lie the Wisconsin Historical Museum, (608) 264-6555, 30 N. Carroll; the Madison Art Center, (608) 257-0158, 211 State Street; Madison Children's Museum, (608) 256-6445, 100 State Street; and the Wisconsin Veterans Museum, (608) 267-1799, 30 W. Mifflin Street. Near the west end (neither are located on State Street) are the Wisconsin Historical Society and the Elvehjem Museum of Art.

The **Wisconsin Veterans Museum** on the square at the corner of State and Mifflin, is a real gem. Dedicated to the men and women of Wisconsin who served in America's conflicts, the museum features life-sized dioramas that portray historical events ranging from steamy jungles to snow covered-forests. The Nineteenth-Century Gallery houses exhibits recounting events of the Civil War and Spanish American War. Other full-scale dioramas depict the Battle of the Bugle and jungle warfare in New Guinea. Three aircraft are suspended from the ceiling: a Sopwith Camel, circa 1917; a P-51 Mustang circa 1944, and a Vietnam War era "Huey" helicopter. Also displayed are scale models of military ships and 17 bronze figures that personify Wisconsin veterans.

In between the more cerebral attractions offered by museums, State Street becomes a sensory extravaganza. You'll see bald-headed women and supreme court justices; you'll smell fresh coffee and stale beer; you hear Chilean folk music and American jazz; you'll taste Mediterranean entrees and grilled brats. You can find pretty much anything you're looking for here.

Some longtime eating establishments include **Nick's**, the "Home of Good Food," a family-owned bar and restaurant with a great jukebox; **Radical Rye**, a build-your-own-sandwich shop; **Zorba's** for "gyrofriesandcoke"; **the Pub**, a college bar since 1949; **Husnu's** for Turkish and Middle Eastern cuisine; **State Street Brats**, featuring, you guessed it, grilled brats; **The Plaza**, just off State, home of the famous Plaza Burger; or **Gino's** Italian restaurant, where stuffed pizza is the best call on the street

At the west end of State, you'll be treading on UW turf. **Bascom Hill** offers a good workout and the obligatory Madison photo opportunity looking down from Lincoln's statue at State Street and the capitol building.

The **Elvehjem Museum of Art**, 800 University Avenue, (608) 263-2246, houses a permanent collection of more than 15,000 artworks dating from 2300 B.C. Noteworthy holdings include American and European paintings, sculpture, prints, and drawings as well as ancient and Asian art.

And located across from the Wisconsin Historical Society building (the "Gray Lady") is the **Memorial Union**, the heart and soul of the UW–Madison, a true Wisconsin place with Teutonic murals in the Rathskeller and a breezy terrace overlooking Lake Mendota. Some people who visit Madison go straight to the terrace and spend the weekend there. Not a bad idea. A walking path follows the lakeshore from the terrace to Picnic Point, a peninsula offering more good views of the city skyline.

The UW consistently rates among the best universities in the United States. The student population will claim, rightly so, that the school is among the best for having a good time. The Memorial Union and State Street is where much of the fun occurs.

RIDE A BIKE

Madison may be the best urban biking city in the United States. Here's one route: a perfect—in every way—10K circle around Lake Wingra, starting from the front of Vilas Zoo, winding behind Edgewood College, and looping through the UW Arboretum under a canopy of trees before returning to the zoo. Visitors need not travel any farther to get a taste of the very best of Madison: the zoo, a lake, beaches, picnic areas, nature preserve, frozen custard. Grab your bike or walking shoes. Paddleboat and canoe rentals are available. Popular Monroe Street eateries include the Laurel Tavern, Pasqual's, Bluephies, and Michael's Frozen Custard.

While you're in the area, hop off that two-wheeler and stop at the **Henry Vilas Zoo** on Lake Wingra, one of the few free zoos in the country. It contains 175 species of animals, including 12 that are endangered, and a children's zoo. It's open year-round. Vilas Beach is located across the street, (608) 266-4732.

The **UW Arboretum** consists of 1,260 acres of land bordering the southern half of Lake Wingra. There are two main vehicular entries: the northernmost is where McCaffery Drive, North Wingra Drive, and South Mills Street intersect near the zoo and St. Marys Hospital; the southernmost entry is north of the Beltline near the intersection of McCaffery Drive and Seminole Highway. There are parking lots and bike racks within the Arboretum. It's open year-round from 7 a.m. to 7 p.m. daily.

Madison, supposedly, has three bikes for every two cars. The entire city is interconnected with paths. Noteworthy routes include one that circumnavigates

Lake Monona (13 miles) and another on the university's lakeshore path leading to Picnic Point. Your best bet is to begin and end your Lake Monona tour at the Monona Terrace Convention Center. If you want the definitive glimpse of Madison's spectacular skyline, check out the view from Olin Park on the way, located across the road from the Alliant Energy Center. From this vantage, you'll see Monona Terrace hanging out over the lake, with the city skyline serving as a backdrop. It's particularly breathtaking at night.

Follow the Badger tracks into one of the great Wisconsin traditions: Big Ten football at Camp Randall Stadium.

Finally, the Capital City Trail skirts the southern edge of the city and links to the Military Ridge Trail in Verona. Madison is the hub for bike trails that stretch from Milwaukee to western Wisconsin.

WATCH THE BADGERS

Athletics is where the UW–Madison flexes its muscle, drawing students, alumni, and sports fans from near and far for Big Ten action. Football Saturdays on sparkling autumn days, with tailgaters and beer gardens and red sweaters and busy stores and restaurants, is one of the all-time great Wisconsin experiences. The UW marching band, which performs and generally carries on after games as part of the famous "fifth quarter," alone is worth seeing. Of course, the UW puts on a full slate of competition in other sports: men's and women's hockey and basketball, volleyball, softball, crew, wrestling, and more—you name it. And tickets for many events are much easier to snare than those for the football Badgers. And the best thing about any of them is that you don't have to like sports to have fun.

Not only is **Camp Randall Stadium** the home of Badger football but also it has a bit of nonsports history: it is built on the old training ground for Wisconsin's Civil War soldiers. More than 70,000 men trained for service within the boundaries of this camp. As a memorial, an arch was completed in 1912; this is where the UW band makes its grand entrance into the stadium after leaving pregame pep rallies at Union South.

With the downtown located on a narrow isthmus, the parking problem becomes acute during events at Camp Randall or the **Kohl Center**, the UW's facility for men's and women's basketball and hockey. Get to both places early if you are attending an event. Parking will be backed up through the neighborhoods near the venues. Regent and Monroe Streets and University Avenue are the main thoroughfares on game day. Best bet: park in a city ramp and take a bus, or walk a mile or two. Actually, walking to Camp Randall or the Kohl Center is the best way to take in the game-day electricity.

EAT, DRINK, BE MERRY

In recent years, Madison has seen a proliferation of restaurants, especially downtown, though there never was a shortage. The local phone book contains 19 pages of restaurants. Carnivores will need to consider the **Tornado Room**, **Smoky's**, and **Delaney's** for tremendous steaks, with **Johnny Delmonico's** being the newcomer. Seafood is the specialty at the **Blue Marlin**, **La Paella**, and the **Mariner's Inn**. **L'Etoile** has 25-plus years serving the some of the finest dinners in Madison. **Pasta Per Tutti** and **Porta Bella** do Italian just right.

Casual places are too numerous to mention, with one exception: for the best ribs in the country (that's country, not county, and the proprietor has the ribbons to prove it), head straight to **Smoky Jon's**, a casual little North Woods-type joint on 2310 Packers Avenue.

A local tradition continues in **Mickies Dairy Bar**, where the breakfasts are huge and it's always 1947. Mickies is a true-blue dairy bar/diner located just a Hail Mary pass from Camp Randall Stadium on Monroe Street. Booths, a long, horseshoe-shaped counter, and the original soda fountain contribute to the authentic atmosphere as much as the generous portions of yanks (pan-fried potatoes). Sunday is usually standing room only, 1511 Monroe Street, (608) 256-9476.

Being a Wisconsin college town, Madison has bars everywhere, some serving very good comfort food. The best hamburgers in town can be found at the **Blue Moon** on Old University Avenue, and they have good soups, too. The **Nitty Gritty** does justice to hamburgers as well, and it has an infamous past—it was the planning spot for the four radicals who bombed Sterling Hall in 1970.

If you thought there were copious places to eat, you'll be amazed by the number of places in town to quench your thirst. A decent number of clubs offers more than just four walls, ten stools, and four beers on tap. Live music can be found at **Luther's Blues**, a modern venue featuring top-notch musical performers (and two separate eateries); the **Crystal Corner Bar**, **Regent Street Retreat**, **Memorial Union**, and the **Club Tavern** in Middleton have live music on a regular basis, as do smaller venues scattered throughout the city.

WHERE'S THE FISH FRY?

Skip Zach's down-home **Avenue Bar** has the best-known Friday night fish in Madison. What started out as a small bar in 1970 has expanded over the years to serve lunch and dinner seven days a week. The Avenue's house specialty is boiled cod with all the fixings (potatoes, carrots, onions). Tasty fried lake perch is served as well. Get the hash browns with cheese and onions. Country-style breakfasts are served on weekends. Enough farm implements hang on the walls to cultivate a third world nation. Reservations are strongly recommended Friday nights. Located at 1128 E. Washington Avenue, (608) 257-6877.

ENJOY A LITTLE NATURE

Olbrich Botanical Gardens, 3330 Atwood Avenue, (608) 246-4718, across from Lake Monona, features 14 acres of outdoor specialty gardens, the Bolz Tropical Conservatory, and a botanical center. The rose garden has more than 600 individual rose bushes. A 50-foot high glass conservatory simulates a rainforest atmosphere and contains free-flying birds.

Madison has exceptionally scenic parks, though the maintenance is sometimes spotty. **Tenney Park**, by the locks on Lake Mendota, was created so the "laboring portion" of the city would have "a place of rest and recreation," according to the long-gone Madison Park and Pleasure Drive Association. (Even as far back as 1899 people needed a refuge from the government and university.) Several bridges were erected and a lock was built for passage between Lakes Mendota and Monona, which form the eight-block-wide downtown isthmus. In the winter, ice-skaters on the Tenny Park lagoon create a scene worthy of Currier &

Ives. Olin Park, Picnic Point, and Olbrich Park are other notable places to un-wind. A large park is being discussed for the central city, which means, in Madison terms, that it might be established in 60 years or so.

Art Fair on the Square is just one event that draws throngs to Madison's Capitol Square on weekends.

READ ALL ABOUT IT

Another only-in-Madison amenity: many cities nationwide have a free, alternative weekly newspaper, but few are as widely read as the provocative *Isthmus*. (And it provides the definitive weekly entertainment listings.) The *Wisconsin State Journal* and *Capital Times* are the two daily papers, the *Capital Times* is one of the few afternoon papers still around. The *Daily Cardinal* and *Badger Herald* are the UW student daily newspapers. The now-famous weekly publication of satire and humor, *The Onion*, had its humble beginning in Madison; free copies can be found at most newsstands.

HAVE YOU HEARD?

Madison's broad range of citizenry is reflected in radio stations of every stripe. The usual formats are found in addition to college-oriented music at WMAD, 92.1 FM, and the progressive-music radio station WMMM, 105.5 FM. Community-supported WORT, 89.9 FM, is quintessential Madison, running the gamut from classical music to surf punk, with doses of political activism in between. WHA, 970 AM, is Wisconsin Public Radio, which broadcasts on high power during daylight hours.

Double Take: The Argus

You'll find no lack of watering holes around here, but **The Argus**, 123 E. Main, (608) 256-4141, might be the best representative of the cultural intersection known as Madison. It's located in the shadow of the capitol building to begin, and this is the place where local folk, politicians, students, bureaucrats, reporters, bleeding-hearts, and stuffed-shirts mix easily within the confines of an original downtown building.

In fact, the Argus is located in Madison's oldest commercial structure, dating to 1847 when the community was a swampy village of 1,166 people. The building's first tenant was the Wisconsin Argus newspaper, which became Madison's first daily newspaper in 1852 when it merged with the *Wisconsin Democrat*, now the *Wisconsin State Journal*.

Over the years the upstairs was occupied by fraternal lodges, the main floor held a bakery and succession of bars, and the basement was a Turkish bath and steam room.

In 1988, after years of neglect, developer and renovator Cliff Fisher restored much of the 19th-century workmanship. Todd Dukes is the Argus's amiable owner and roaster of pigs for catered parties.

Lunch specials are served on weekdays, burgers on evenings and weekends. Great pictures of historic Madison hang on the walls, some include the Argus building itself. Take a gander at the ancient brickwork in the basement, or say howdy to your legislator, who can probably be found underneath the bar. Look for the old-time clock outside by the patio.

Other venerable joints include **Mickey's** on Williamson Street, the **Silver Dollar** just off the Square, and the **Harmony Bar** on Atwood Avenue. If you are looking for some good local hand-crafted beer, head out to the **Capital Brewery**, Middleton, home of award-winning brews, not to mention a beer garden with live music on summer weekends.

CHAPTER THIRTEEN

BARABOO AND THE DELLS
A Tradition of Fun

The pedigree of Wisconsin's two most popular destinations comes down

to six people who dreamt big dreams and tasted the fruits of success

after years of toil—but on their best days probably never imagined the

magnitude of what now exists in Baraboo and the Dells. These six people—

one guy with a camera living in Kilbourn City (as Wisconsin Dells was then

called) and five brothers living in Baraboo—honed their arts in the late 1800s.

Today Sauk County, home of Baraboo and the Dells, sees more than

$683 million in tourist greenbacks annually. One location has evolved into

an indescribable mass of American kitsch. The other place is a stupendous

collection of American showmanship. There's much to do and see in the area,

so don't be disappointed if you miss something. Just come back another day.

First, the showmanship.

BARABOO'S CIRCUS WORLD

Brothers Al, Otto, Charles, John, and Alf moved to Baraboo in 1875. Al, the oldest at 23, was a carriage finisher, a skill that would come in handy later. His true passion was performing, however, and he spent his free time cajoling the brothers to assist him in his "shows" and organizing local children into a small performing troupe. After seven years the family performed their first professional gig, a vaudeville act in which two brothers danced, two played instruments, and one sang. Al was a juggler, John a clown. With their first profit of $300, the brothers bought evening suits and top hats.

In 1884 the brothers began traveling by wagon with a rented horse. After two years of hard work, all they could afford to add to their performances was a donkey and a Shetland pony. Another four years passed before they bought an elephant and began traveling by rail.

Slowly but surely the act grew. The brothers began acquiring small circus troupes. By 1900, after 16 years on the road, they had accumulated one of the largest traveling shows around. When they bought James A. Bailey's circus in 1907, the five brothers—the Ringlings from Baraboo, Wisconsin—were proprietors of one of the most beloved spectacles on earth: The Ringling Brothers and Barnum & Bailey Combined Shows.

And every winter for 34 years, from that first horse-drawn wagon to the Greatest Show on Earth, the brothers brought their circus home to Ringlingville on the banks of the Baraboo River.

Last used by the circus in 1918, Ringlingville was rescued from disrepair decades later by John M. Kelley, who had been the Ringlings' personal attorney and general counsel. Kelley, a Wisconsin native, spearheaded efforts to establish a historical and educational facility. Following fundraising efforts, the museum was deeded debt-free to the state and opened to the public in 1959.

A top-notch museum with live performances under the big tent, Circus World Museum in Baraboo captures the spirit of the "Greatest Show on Earth."

Ringlingville today is home of the **Circus World Museum**. Not only a top-notch museum, the 50-acre site is a world of its own indeed—a living chapter of American entertainment with real, live Big Top performances and all the bally-hoo and spectacle one would expect from the Greatest Show on Earth.

This is, unquestionably, a must-see Wisconsin attraction. The museum preserves more than 200 circus wagons—masterpieces all—the largest collection in the world. Its library of posters, photos, films, heralds, and other rare pieces of circus memorabilia is the best in the world. Those are just static displays found in nine original Ringlingville buildings. The kids will be hoping for more, and they won't be disappointed.

The real deal is presented every day from early May to mid-September. Highlights include circus performances under a traditional canvas tent twice daily: high-wire acts from around the globe, elephant rides, trolley rides, clown skits, unique musical instrument concerts, parades, and train-loading demonstrations. All this is presented on the scenic banks of the Baraboo River without some of the rough edges that are normally associated with circuses and fairs.

The museum's shining moment occurs each July when it stages the annual Great Circus Parade on the streets of downtown Milwaukee. The event is attended by untold thousands of delighted spectators of all ages and seen by millions more via telecasts. If you can't make it to the Great Circus Parade, no problem, you'll see virtually the same things—and more—at the Baraboo museum.

The Circus World Museum is located in Baraboo via Highway 12 or Interstate 90/94. (Get off the Interstate at exit 92, Highway 12 at Lake Delton, or exit 106, Highway 33 at Portage.) Directional signs to Baraboo and Circus World Museum are located on all major highways. Within the city of Baraboo, signs will direct you to Circus World Museum, just blocks from the scenic Baraboo town square.

Admission ranges from $7.95 per child to $14.95 per adult during high season, less during off-season. Admission includes all shows, exhibits, and demonstrations. Food service, gift shops, carousel, and animal rides and trolley tours not included. Annual tickets available for $20 per adult, $10 children 5–11. Group rates available.

A picnic area is available in Ringlingville Park across the street from the main entrance. Bringing food and drink onto the grounds is prohibited. Contact Circus World Museum, 550 Water Street Baraboo, WI 53913-2597, (608) 356-8341. Twenty-four hour info available at (608) 356-0800; the Web address is www.circusworldmuseum.com.

THE REST OF BARABOO

When in Baraboo (population 9,200), take a stroll around the quaint town square and visit the **Al Ringling Theater**, one of America's finest entertainment palaces. The "Al" was gifted to the community by the oldest Ringling sibling, who, by 1915, was Baraboo's leading citizen and one of the best-known names in Wisconsin. Ringling had traveled the world in his day and became enamored of the beauty and majesty of European opera houses. The Al is the earliest structure that can be accurately called a "movie palace," according to the Theatre Historical Society of America. Al Ringling died seven weeks after the grand opening.

When's the last time you rode an elephant? Elephant rides and other Circus World amusements will keep the family entertained for hours.

Tours of the Al offer a mix of entertainment and education. A private concert on the mighty Barton organ completes the visit. The 45-minute tours are offered at noon, Thursday through Sunday, mid-June through Labor Day. Group tours are also available by reservation. Tours cost $2 per person. To schedule a tour, or for more information, please call the theater at (608) 356-8864, 136 Fourth Avenue; movie line (recording) (608) 356-8080; the e-mail address is ringling@baraboo.com.

Located next to the Al is the **Little Village Café**, a charming restaurant in the historic corner building that once housed the local newspaper.

A collection of captive cranes is maintained at the **International Crane Foundation**, headquartered a little more than five miles north of Baraboo on Shady Lane Road. The foundation demonstrates endangered-species management for the public. That includes watching people dressed in crane costumes nurture the birds. (This is true. Cranes will "adopt" a human in a crane outfit.) The ICF differs from most nature centers and conservation facilities in that its activities focus on a very specific subject—cranes—rather than treating the natural history and general ecology of a region. Phone (608) 356-9462.

DEVIL'S LAKE STATE PARK

Just four miles south of Baraboo on Highway 123 is Devil's Lake State Park, one of Wisconsin's crown jewels. Its 9,000 acres of quartzite bluffs tower above the placid lake surface and draw visitors from near and far throughout the year, especially during summer when the park's 406 campsites are booked solid. Hiking along the 22 trails that wind up and down the bluffs is the park's most popular activity. Aside from the trails, the park offers the best rock-climbing opportunities in the Midwest. The lake is ideal for canoeing and kayaking. A full-time naturalist, present during park hours, rounds out the amenities.

The bluffs consist of huge, red-brown and purple quartzite, fractured cleanly to leave sharp angles and smooth, almost shiny, surfaces—offering great vistas. Sunrise and sunsets from ground level, when light hits the rock, are picture-perfect; compares favorably to mountain and canyon settings of the West.

The best ways to take in the sights is through **Devil's Lake Nature Safaris**. The tours are led by geologists who discuss regional wonders probably not found on your own. Fans of the Discovery Channel or National Geographic will love it. The safaris are conducted by van.

Sites include 1,000-year-old Indian mounds, rare plants and animals, scars from the last ice age, ancient sand dunes, and historic iron mines. Tours of Parfrey's Glen, Ableman's Gorge, and the Wisconsin Dells are offered as well. Suitable for both families or adults, the tours are generally two and a half hours and cost $23 for adults and $17 for children ages 8–12; children ages 7 and under free. Ask about discounts. Kids get a cool trilobite fossil as a gift. Safaris are conducted on weekends in May and daily starting June 1, departing at 10 a.m. and 1:30 p.m. (Weekend tours among the fall colors offered in September and October). Group tours available year-round. Call (800) 328-0995.

WISCONSIN DELLS

Sports Illustrated features a weekly column called "Catching Up," in which athletes who have appeared on the magazine's cover decades ago are revisited. Recently the magazine caught up with an Olympic swimmer who revolutionized the breaststroke in the early 1960s. The swimmer went on to become a surgeon, a family practice doctor, and a kinesiology professor and swimming coach at Indiana University. He doesn't swim anymore, but every summer he drives his nine grandchildren north.

"We go the water parks in Wisconsin Dells," said the man who set 12 world swimming records. "When I go in the water there, I just bob like a cork."

Ah, the Dells . . . Wisconsin Dells . . . Goliath of the tourism industry in the upper Midwest . . . living proof to some folks that the downfall of civilization is beginning in Wisconsin . . . to others the greatest playground in the world.

Whatever your take may be, the Dells as we know it, the place of atomic monkey bars, swimming pools on steroids, and cash-fueled hotels, has little to do with the dells, those strange and mystical formations sculpted by the Wis-

Devil's Lake is a hugely popular destination for rock climbers, hikers, and canoeists.

consin River. That's too bad, because somewhere behind all that plastic is one of the state's foremost natural attractions. So while your kids will love the sensory overload and run to the nearest faux lagoon at the mere mention of sightseeing, there are some traditional activities, such as scenic boat tours, that balance fun and history.

But how did all this come to be? Henry Hamilton Bennett is the man who put the Dells on the map. Bennett returned from the Civil War with an injured hand, his life as a carpenter virtually over before it began. (Like Al Ringling, his initial trade would come in handy later on.) Bennett instead opened a photography studio and took a liking to outdoor settings because, as he said, "It is easier to pose nature and less trouble to please."

At the time Bennett opened his studio, common household devices called stereoscopes were used to view photographs, especially in well-to-do Victorian homes. In a stroke of pioneer marketing, he produced thousands of stereograph pictures mounted on cards—the name of his studio featured prominently—and sold them through agents who traveled the Midwest.

It can be said that the advent of modern tourism started with Bennett when his pictures started reaching comfortable Victorian living rooms. Visitors who could afford to travel were lured from across the country by the trainload. Wisconsin Dells became one of the most popular tourism destinations in the 19th-century Midwest.

127

Bennett lived in Kilbourn City all his life, painstakingly photographing the river's dells with cameras he crafted himself: nature scenes, pictures of everyday life, native Ho-Chunk people, frilly Victorian tourists among the Wisconsin wilds. Bennett's stop-action photo of his son Ashley leaping to Stand Rock in 1888 has turned up in desk drawers the world over.

While one has to wonder if Bennett was a better promoter than camera-man, a look at Bennett's works demonstrates that he deserves a place in the pantheon of great photographers. And you can judge for yourself at the studio Bennett founded in 1865.

The **H. H. Bennett Studio and History Center** lends much-needed perspective to amidst the tourism that distinguishes the Dells today. The center is the only preserved 19th-century photography studio in the country. More importantly, the studio contains a priceless collection of Bennett's prints, negatives, and antique equipment within 6,000 square feet of exhibit space. The center uses both traditional stereoscopes and the latest in stereo-imaging technology to create the three-dimensional effect. In the latter instance, viewed through liquid crystal 3-D glasses, subjects appear to leap out of 21-inch computer monitors. Kids have great fun here at half the cost of other places in town.

Continuously owned by successive generations of his family—making it the oldest family-owned photographic studio in the United States—the studio was acquired by the Wisconsin Historical Society in 1999.

The center is open May 15-Sept. 15. Open to school tours year-round. Adults $6; children 5–12, $3; senior citizens (65 and over) $5.40; family (two adults and two or more dependent children 5–17) $16; 215 Broad-way, (608) 253-3523; e-mail: hhbennett@mail.shsw.wisc.edu.

THE REST OF THE DELLS

The city is a tourist town like no other, with far too many attractions to describe here. A sample: American UFO & Sci-Fi Museum, Bay of Dreams Indoor Water Park, Big Chief Karts & Coasters, Crystal Grand Music Theater, Dungeon of Horrors, Family Land, Ho-Chunk Casino, Lost Canyon, Noah's Ark, Original Wisconsin Ducks, Ripley's Believe It or Not, Riverview Park and Waterworld, Storybook Gardens, Tommy Bartlett's Robot World and Exploratory, Tommy Bartlett Thrill Show, Wax World of the Stars, Wisconsin Deer Park . . . not to mention the restaurants, souvenir stores, and hotels, many of which contain indoor/outdoor water parks (and restaurants and souvenir stores).

At the very least try to pay homage to what started all of this: the river. **Dells Boat Tours** offer guided sightseeing trips through the Upper and Lower Dells of the Wisconsin River. Boats leave the Upper Dells Landing, juncture Highway 12 and Highway 13/16/23, daily every 30 minutes 8:45–6:00, June–August; every 1 to 2 hours, April–May and September–October. The 2.5-hour Upper Dells tour includes sandstone cliffs, rock formations and stops at Witches Gulch and Stand Rock for a walk along nature trails. Fare $17.75; ages 6–11, $9. The 1-hour nonstop Lower Dells cruise offers unusual rock formations, caverns, and the Rocky Islands. Fare $14.75; ages 6–11, $7.50. Phone (608) 254-8555.

The **Dells Ducks** are a longstanding tradition as well. Tours are made in amphibious Army surplus vehicles brought into the area after World War II. One-hour tours on land and water take in the famous natural sites. Daily April– October; adults $16; children 6–11, $8.75; 5 and under, free; (608) 254-8751.

A couple other monster attractions have become synonymous with the Dells as well, namely the Tommy Bartlett attractions and Noah's Ark water park. Bartlett changed Dells tourism by introducing a tourist attraction unrelated to the scenery—and by slapping bumper stickers on every car parked in his lot. **Tommy Bartlett's Robot World and Exploratory** contains Russia's original Mir space station and more than a hundred interactive displays. Open daily 10–4, longer Memorial Day weekend through Labor Day weekend. Admission $9, under 5 free. Phone (608) 254-2525. Bartlett's **Thrill Show** is an outdoor Las Vegas-style act performed on a single stage *and* water. The Dancing Gauchos, "direct from Argentina and performing dance, drumming and bollo mastery," were recent headliners. Jet skis, boats, water skiers, and human pyramids conduct stunts, comedy, and magic. The Thrill Show entertains more than 300,000 people each summer. Shows daily at 1, 4:30, and 8:30 p.m.; $11 general admission, deluxe seating $14, reserved $17, under 5 free on lap; (608) 254-2525.

The sensory extravaganza known as the Wisconsin Dells is the state's biggest tourist draw.

Noah's Ark bills itself as the world's largest water park. Who's checking, anyway? Thirty-three water slides, 4,000 lounge chairs, 20 picnic pavilions, 600 picnic tables, a couple of million-gallon wave pools. The park offers a variety of packages and ticket programs, including an All-Day Unlimited Use Pass good for 60 family activities: water rides, mini-golf, bumper boats, kiddie play areas, and a kiddie roller coaster for, $25.99. Call (608) 254-6351 for more information.

On a warm summer day, you'll want to arrive early (before the park opens at 9 a.m.) for parking spaces and lounge chairs. Head for water slides early and late in the day. When the slides are busiest, mid-day, go to the two massive wave pools. Crowds start to thin after 4 p.m., but the park stays open until 8 p.m. (Hint: late afternoon is a good time to go.)

Locals Know

June is the best time to hit Noah's Ark and other major attractions. Most families are planning vacations for July or August. Lines are typically shorter on Sunday, Wednesday, and Thursday. For more information, contact the Wisconsin Dells Visitor and Convention Bureau, 701 Superior Street, Wisconsin Dells, WI 53965; phone (608) 254-8088 or (800) 223-3557.

THE DELLS INDOORS

Your Dells weekend experience would not be complete without seeing what lurks inside the walls of some of the area's mammoth structures. Not long ago the Dells began to make yet another metamorphosis, from summer destination to year-round attraction, thanks to the emergence of indoor water parks. Like everything else here, the change was made in eye-popping proportions. There is no "season" anymore. People book hotel rooms at the mammoth hotels-cum-indoor-parks all year long. Most Dells lodging establishments, advertise an indoor water park or aqua center—keep in mind that one person's swimming pool is someone else's water park.

Among the new generation of hotels and resorts with indoor water facilities are: The Alakai, Antiqua Bay, Camelot, Carousel, Chula Vista, Copa Cabana, Grand Marquis, Flamingo, 4-Seasons, Great Wolf Lodge, Kalahari, Meadowbrook, Polynesian, Skyline, Tamarack, Treasure Island, the Wilderness, and Wintergreen. Some are significantly larger than others. For the easier-to-please families, most motels and budget hotels have hopped-up swimming pools.

DELLS DINING

Dining in the Dells is weighted heavily toward buffets and family eateries, as you can imagine. There are a handful of noteworthy restaurants.

The **Del-Bar** has been owned by the same family since 1943 and is best known for steaks and seafood in a fine dining setting. **Ishnala** offers great views of Mirror Lake with forty years of dining tradition. The **Cheese Factory** is a casual, strictly vegetarian restaurant that's popular for breakfast and lunches. **Monk's** is longtime bar and grill serving hamburgers. **Field's at the Wilderness** has raised the bar on fine dining since opening in 2000. **Thunder Valley Inn** offers a taste of the Old Country in both its farm setting and food; *the* spot for breakfast.

TWO STATE PARKS

Just a few miles from the Dells, two beautiful state parks, **Mirror Lake** and **Rocky Arbor**, have been combined by the DNR into a single working unit. The 2,100-acre Mirror Lake, just southwest of town, contains 147 campsites. To the northwest, Rocky Arbor holds another 89 sites on 225 acres. The parks' scenery and proximity to the Dells make it tough to find an open campsite in high season, but Mirror Lake has increasingly become a year-round park with sites available off-season. Mirror Lake contains a 200-foot beach with changing facilities, easy bike trails, and year-round fishing. Seventeen miles of cross-country trails have been developed recently. Canoe, boat, and bike rentals available. No powerboats are allowed on the small lake.

READ ALL ABOUT IT

The *Baraboo News Republic* is the smallest daily newspaper in the state. The Dells does not have a daily newspaper—who reads a newspaper while bobbing like a cork at a water park? *Dells Events* keeps locals apprised of news every week.

HAVE YOU HEARD?

WNNO, 106.9 FM, will provide the soundtrack to your Dells vacation with Top 40 and hit songs.

Double Take:
A one … and a Two … and a Three …

As a type of music or as a dance, the polka is precious to Wisconsinites. It comes naturally in a state that welcomed large clusters of immigrants from eastern and central Europe during its formative years. Polka in these parts has transcended the novelty of folk dance to become standard play on AM radio stations, sporting events, and every Saturday night wedding in Wisconsin.

Bohemians, Polish, Czechs, Dutch, Finnish, Germans—each culture had a hand in the evolution of this dance distinguished by the half-step, or hop. Wisconsinites are genetically programmed to polka. Lest there remain any doubt, the State Legislature ordained the polka as the official state dance in 1993.

Polka palaces are still the places to be in towns across Wisconsin. The New Glarus Hotel, the Dorf House in Roxbury, the Essen Haus in Madison are just three venues in Dane County alone where you can find a polka band playing virtually every weekend. WTKM in Hartford is the last radio station in the nation to have a polka-only format, and its broadcasts are wildly popular on the Internet. WPDR in Portage beams polka music to south-central Wisconsin. Many Wisconsin stations feature polka music for a couple hours every week.

Wisconsin Dells hosts two large polka gatherings every year. Polish Fest, which features traditional and modern folk music and foods as well as polka, schedules as many as a dozen bands for the weekend. The state polka contest is held at Polish Fest. Some of the biggest names in polka music perform, such as Eddie Blazonczyk's Versatones and Stas Bulandas, both from Chicago; Roger Majeski and the Harmony Kings from Mosinee; and Chad Przybylski from Pulaski. The event is hosted by Chicago radio personality and part-time sausage maker Patrick Henry Cukierka, aka "the Polka Party Animal," who regales audiences with his greeting, "So, how do you like my kielbasa!" Polish Fest is held in early September. **Polka Fest,** held in November, celebrates the music itself with . . . well, lots of you know what.

Polka. It's the law.

CHAPTER FOURTEEN

THE LOWER WISCONSIN
A River Runs Through Us

From it headwaters in northern Wisconsin, our state's namesake river runs through 430 miles of forest, sand country, and valleys before joining the Mississippi at Prairie du Chien. This waterway is a natural treasure. In 1989, the Wisconsin Legislature designated more than 92 miles along its southwest leg as the **Lower Wisconsin State Riverway** to protect the river valley's character. So it seems fitting that a Classic Wisconsin Weekend be devoted to getting more familiar with this natural wonder.

You can explore the Wisconsin by canoe or drive along Highway 60, which parallels it from Sauk City and Prairie du Sac to Prairie du Chien. Along the way, the longest stretch of the Wisconsin River that's been left undammed, there are a total of 62 species of endangered, threatened, or special-concern-status wildlife, as well as 34 unique plant species. All told, 350 species of flora and fauna are found along the Lower Riverway.

Driving Highway 60 is great for landlubbers, especially in autumn, and on-road biking routes are popular on the river's southern side. But for a truly remarkable experience, there's nothing like getting out on the river and paddling. If you're the indecisive type, you can do both: drive the highway, then find a spot where you can rent a canoe and take to the water. You can rent canoes from the many outfitters located along the river, then put in at one of its small towns. Better yet, pitch a tent on a sandbar in the river and see the majestic Wisconsin the only true way: from its slow rolling waters.

There is no whitewater along the lower Wisconsin, one reason that this stretch of river is a favorite for quiet canoeing, not to mention its beauty, wildlife (especially eagles), and small towns. And because of tricky currents and submerged trees and rocks, speedboats and jet skis are rare downriver from Lake Wisconsin.

STARTING OUT

Once you've decided to paddle, a good place to begin is at the **Sauk Prairie Canoe Center**, one of the longtime outfitters along the river, (608) 643-6589. Located at 932 Water Street, just a couple of doors west from the Highway 12 bridge, the business stocks 120 canoes and offers options ranging from an easy two-mile paddle to a 90-mile, six-day-trip to Wyalusing State Park. Return shuttle rides are offered on all routes. Paddlers bringing their own canoes can use the shuttle service for a fee. On a nice summer weekend, the outfitter will send a hundred or more canoes a day downriver.

One of the best ways to experience Wisconsin's namesake river is through the many canoe outfitters found along the river's southern region.

A popular short trip is a seven-mile route downriver to Ferry Bluff. Paddle time is 2 to 3 hours, punctuated by a hike to the bluff top for a great view. The most popular trip is to Spring Green, a 25-mile paddle, where wilderness camping on sandbars and islands maximizes the quality times (sunset and sunrise) on the river. Costs are graduated depending on the trip length, starting at $10 for a half-day excursion Monday through Friday, to $140 for the long haul to Wyalusing. The Ferry Bluff paddle will run you $30 on a weekend, $15 for shuttle service only; Spring Green will cost $60 on a weekend, $35 for shuttle only.

If you're traveling along the river's southern roads, keep your eyes peeled for Ole & Lena's Tavern. I don't know if Ole and Lena can be found at Ole & Lena's, but I bet you can hear some good anecdotes about the couple's ongoing marital challenges.

SAUK PRAIRIE

Your introduction to the Lower Riverway, whether traveling by canoe or car, begins in Sauk Prairie—the abbreviated name for the twin cities of **Sauk City** and **Prairie du Sac**. The towns rest above the river and they share Water Street. They also have a heritage that includes a colorful character by the name of Aguston Haraszthy. Arriving in 1841 with loud clothes and big ideas, the Hungarian championed free thought in the Wisconsin wilderness. Those free thoughts were likely prompted by the wine making Haraszthy established in the area before moving on to California, where he started vineyards in a then-little-known valley called Napa.

What's important to remember from this fractured history lesson is that really good wine is found at **Wollersheim Winery**, located opposite Prairie du Sac on Highway 188. Try the Prairie Fumé. Free thoughts will follow. Wollersheim is open daily 10 a.m.–5 p.m., closed New Year's Day, Easter, Thanksgiving, and Christmas Day. Phone (608) 643-6515 or (800) VIP-WINE. Wine tours and tasting are offered daily. Over the past 10 years, annual production at the winery has increased by 68,000 gallons. In 2001, Wollersheim unveiled the newly restored Great Room, which had served as a dance hall on the winery's third floor. Take a virtual tour at www.wollersheim.com.

SOARING WITH EAGLES, MUCKING WITH COWS

In Sauk Prairie, two annual rituals make it clear that you're not in Madison anymore: bald eagle watching and cow chip tossing. Viewing both activities is well worth the extra time. Eagles roost in abundance in the Wisconsin River valley. There are 775 active nesting pairs of bald eagles in the state, making them one of the great success stories among endangered species. Wisconsin's eagle pairs dropped to a low of 82 in 1970. The national symbol was placed on the state endangered list two years later. With justifiable fanfare, eagles were removed from the list in 1997, although they are still protected by federal and state laws.

Eagles hunt in exclusive areas during the summer, which means you are less likely to see more than one at a time in warm weather. Come winter, when ice has covered the lakes, eagles have to go where the getting is good—open water. Since the Wisconsin River rarely freezes over below the dam in Sauk Prairie, eagles can fish at their convenience. The two communities schedule **Bald Eagle Watching Days** in January with Department of Natural Resources presentations, bus tours, storytelling for kids, and lots of food. Rehabilitated eagles are occasionally released during the celebration. An observation platform is located on Water Street in Prairie du Sac; Veterans Park, a few blocks north of the Highway 60 bridge is another good viewing place. Look for the big, beautiful birds sitting in trees in and around the river.

What was that about cow chips? Well, those would be meadow muffins to the folks around here. And since you asked, the **Wisconsin State Cow Chip Throw** determines nothing less than who represents America's Dairyland at the national competition in Beaver, Oklahoma. Fun and frolic is part of the contest, held every year on Labor Day weekend. A parade called the **Tournament of Chips** and 5K and 10K runs take place, along with food, music, and—can you believe it?—beer. One event, Bovine Bingo, involves a cow roaming a giant grid. Participants guess where Bessy leaves her mark.

Chip tossers come from near and far come to flaunt their skill. Regulation chips (must be six inches in diameter) are selected by the Meadow Muffin Committee and placed on the official event wagon. Each tosser selects two chips. Winning distances have exceeded 137 feet, so wipe that smile off your face, or you might find yourself in a shoot-out with the quickest draw in these parts. One other thing—no gloves allowed.

OTHER SAUK COUNTY DELIGHTS

The intrigue of Sauk County doesn't end there. One of the most unique exhibits in the state is scattered across several acres at **Delaney's Surplus**, the home of Dr. Evermor's outdoor sculpture garden. A couple of strange, scrap metal sculptures mark the site across from the defunct Badger Army Ammunition plant on Highway 12 about seven miles south of Baraboo. Park the car and take a walk into Dr. Evermor's fantastical world of scrap metal thingamajigs. The centerpiece is the Forevertron, a 250-ton, out-of-this-world contraption that Guinness lists as the world's largest piece of scrap metal. Hundreds of pieces of artwork are scattered around the grounds: lots of insects and flamingo type-birds, but the subject matter is as limitless as your imagination. From the chaos of scrap—tools, musical instruments, motors, pipes, chains, and so on—Dr. Evermor crafts complex and beautiful folk art. The exhibit is free. Some of Dr. Evermor's animals are for sale. Now that's lawn ornament your neighbors will love.

History buffs will want to visit the historical marker on Highway 78 south of Sauk City, site of the 1832 Battle of Wisconsin Heights. Here, Chief Black

Hawk organized a holding action against the U.S. Army that is studied by military strategists to this day. Black Hawk's maneuvers enabled his people to safely cross the Wisconsin River. (The tribe, women and children included, would eventually be killed in the shameful Battle of Bad Axe on the Mississippi River.) Hiking trails are located at the site.

Dr. Evermor's fantastical world of thingamajigs includes these metal creatures, which appear to be scurrying across the snow.

MAZOMANIE

As you paddle down the Wisconsin or cruise along Highway 60, the next stop should be Mazomanie, in particular the **Old Feed Mill**. This excellent restaurant is not on the river, but it's close; it's housed in a restored 1857 stone flourmill just off Highway 14 at 114 Cramer Street (608) 795-4909. This is a great place to go for chicken potpie or bread pudding. Opened in October 1995 following a four-year restoration process, the site is listed on the National Register of Historic Places. It contains an antique marble soda fountain, bakery, and old-fashioned general store. It's open for lunch and dinner, Tuesday through Saturday, and for brunch and family-style dinner on Sunday. Reservations are recommended on weekends.

SPRING GREEN

Farther downriver is Spring Green. Its most famous attraction is Taliesin, Frank Lloyd Wright's home and studio. The area also offers the American Players

Theatre, an outdoor in-the-round venue offering Shakespeare on summer evenings. There's also the House on the Rock, a bizarre, gaudy tourist trap in the great American tradition of bizarre, gaudy tourist traps.

Spring Green is also home of **Tower Hill State Park**, located on County Highway C; (608) 588-2116. The restored Civil War shot tower is the last vestige of the Helena, a busy river port and railhead that aspired to be the territorial capital. The park has a mere 15 campsites, but the view from the shot tower makes the stop worthwhile. A bit of exploration (the trails are poorly marked) can find the tunnel at the base of the shot tower among the sandstone cliffs and swampy backwaters of the Wisconsin River. The Spring Green Area Visitors Council is located at P.O. Box 142, Spring Green, WI 53588-0003; phone (608) 588-2042 or (800) 588-2042.

TALIESIN

Frank Lloyd Wright may or may not have been born in Richland Center (the debate still rages), but there is no doubt that he chose Spring Green as the site for his home, **Taliesin**, and for his architectural school. As a result, Spring Green and south-central Wisconsin, with a concentration of Wright-designed buildings, is a mecca for Wright aficionados.

Take Highway 23 south from Spring Green to get to the Visitor Center, which is located along the highway three miles out of town. All tours of the Taliesin property begin at the Visitor Center, a Wright-designed building housing the Taliesin Bookstore.

Taliesin tours depart from this Frank Lloyd Wright building, the only restaurant designed by the famous architect, now serving as the Taliesin visitor center and bookstore.

Tours are May through October, and some require advance reservations. Off-season and group tours are sometimes available. Call (608) 588-7900 for reservations or log onto www.TaliesinPreservation.org for detailed information. In general, visitors have four options.

The one-hour Hillside Studio and Theatre Tour runs every day 10 a.m. to 4 p.m., May through October; $10. Visitors see the Hillside Home School, which Wright built for his aunts in 1902 and later revised to accommodate his community of architects and designers. It includes three of his most magnificent rooms: the living room, the theatre, and the 5,000-square-foot drafting studio.

The Country Walking Tour is a two-hour visit offered daily at 10:45 a.m. and 1:45 p.m., May through October, at a cost of $15. Visitors can take a guided tour through the bucolic grounds to see all of the Wright-designed structures.

The Taliesin House Tour is sold by advance reservation and operates from May through October. Only recently has the public been able to tour the interior of the house that was the architect's residence for nearly 50 years.

The Estate Tour is a four-hour, all-inclusive experience featuring the interiors of Hillside and Taliesin, an opportunity to see the exteriors of all the buildings on the estate as well as Unity Chapel, and a break for refreshments on Wright's private terrace. The tour operates Tuesday, Thursday, and Sunday at 8:30 a.m., May through October only; $65; no children under age 12. Reservations are required.

TWO CLASSIC ATTRACTIONS

In contrast to Wright's iconoclastic architecture, Spring Green's **American Players Theatre** is all about tradition—Shakespeare in the round. An amphitheater resting in the rolling hillside provides a natural venue to perform some of the world's greatest theatrical works. Shakespeare is the foundation for the APT's repertoire, although other masters (Moliere, Shaw, Wilder, etc.) are also incorporated into the schedule. The atmosphere is informal. Wear clothing suitable for outdoors (and insect repellent!). Matinee and evening shows are performed Saturdays. Picnicking is popular on the grounds. Gourmet boxed suppers can be ordered in advance through the box office. Concessions are available inside the amphitheater. The season runs early June through October. To receive a schedule or purchase tickets, call the box office at (608) 588-2361, or write APT, Box 819, Spring Green, WI 53588.

In the heyday of "motoring," roadside attractions beckoned tourists to drop their dimes on all sorts of dubious attractions. The tradition lives on today in the form of the **House on the Rock**, although the admission fee to this hodgepodge of . . . stuff is considerably more than 10 cents. Located nine miles south of Spring Green on Highway 23, the house was designed and built by Alex Jordan beginning in the 1940s. That's the easy part of the description for something beyond description. An off-the-charts house of gaudy trinkets accumulated by a preeminent huckster might be one person's definition of the House on the

Rock—but, hey, that's part of the appeal. The shear schizophrenia of the collection begs your attention. So, why not? Go ahead, indulge.

The multilevel house stands atop the chimneylike Deer Shelter Rock, 450 feet above the Wyoming Valley. Granted, the house *is* an architectural wonder, with pools of running water, waterfalls, massive fireplaces, and a whole lot more. The view from the observation deck encompasses 30 miles. The Infinity Room, extending hundreds of feet out over the valley below, also offers views through some 3,264 panes of glass. A 350-foot-long overhead walkway connects the gatehouse to the house. Other exhibits, including large display gardens, are on the 200-acre grounds. Self-guided tours take two to four hours.

Jordan built the house as a weekend retreat. When people kept asking to see the place, the proverbial light bulb went on in Jordan's head, along with the sound of a cash register. He started charging admission and the collection of "artifacts" was underway. Added were the Mill House, the Organ Building, the Doll House, the Circus Building, the Oriental Room, the Weapons Exhibit, the Armor Collection, and the Crown Jewel Collection.

And that's not all, folks. Now you can step right up to the newest and most spectacular attraction this side of Atlantis, the Heritage of the Sea exhibit, showcasing a 200-foot sea monster engaged in a titanic battle with a squid. During the holidays, the house features more than 6,000 Santas, because, apparently, if you've seen one Santa, you have not seen them all.

The complex is open daily 9 a.m. to dusk, mid-March through the last full weekend in October. Holiday tours are conducted daily 10 a.m.–6 p.m., early November to early January. Closed Thanksgiving and December 24–25. Admission to the complex is $19.50; ages 7–12, $11.50; ages 4–6, $5.50. Admission for holiday tour $12.50; ages 7–12, $7.50; ages 4–6, $3.50. Phone (608) 935-3639, ext.123.

LONE ROCK

Hiking and biking enthusiasts can try the **Pine River Trail** in Lone Rock. The 14-mile rail-to-trail project crosses 15 bridges between Lone Rock and Richland Center.

Bikers are treated to views of green-forested bluffs lining the broad valleys of the Pine and Wisconsin Rivers. Town Parks in Gotham and Lone Rock offer pleasant rest stops. On the south side of Lone Rock at Fireman's Park you can swim in a backwater slough of the Wisconsin River.

RICHLAND CENTER

Antique shops and bakeries can be found in Richland Center, hometown of Frank Lloyd Wright; it's also the location of one of his architectural masterpieces. In 1915 he built a warehouse like none other for local merchant A. D. German. Guided tours of the building are available by appointment; (608) 647-2808.

BOSCOBEL

Moving farther down the river, we next arrive at Boscobel, located in an area that was called the "beautiful woods" when Father Jacques Marquette and Louis Joliet paddled by in 1673. Its claim to fame, however, resulted from being a God-forsaken river city two centuries later.

In 1898, two traveling salesmen met in Boscobel's **Central Hotel** and pondered the creation of an organization to fortify fellow travelers with the Word of God. It had something to do with the hotel lobby, which, according to one of the salesmen, was occupied that night by "hang-abouts playing cards, shaking dice, smoking, laughing, cursing, yelling and singing with clinking glasses and men drunk and asleep in chairs." The two salesmen met twice more and created the Christian Commercial Travelers Association, which later became known as the Gideons, a name the gentlemen appropriated from the Book of Judges. The Gideons have distributed tens of millions of Bibles bearing their name to all manner of lodging establishments since then, not the least of which was the Boscobel. In 1960, Senator John F. Kennedy and wife Jacqueline rested in room 19—the same room used by the Gideon's founders—during a presidential campaign swing through the state. Legend—stress legend—has it that John Jr. was conceived here. Room 19 has been restored and the old hotel, built in 1863, contains a restaurant and bar. Located on Wisconsin Avenue. Call (608) 375-4714 for a tour.

RIVER'S END

Ask state park users about their favorite spots and **Wyalusing**, located seven miles south of Prairie du Chien, will be found near the top of the list. On Sentinel Ridge, high above the Mississippi River, elaborate, prehistoric mounds said to be the most valuable group in existence can be seen. Interesting rock formations,

Sauk Prairie's riverbanks are prime spots for bald eagle watching. An observation deck can be found on Water Street in Prairie du Sac.

canyons, and lookouts are found throughout the park. The park also contains a monument to the extinct passenger pigeon. No offense to the long-forgotten passenger pigeon, but it's the stunning view 520-feet above the Mississippi that sets Wyalusing State Park apart from the others. There are 110 campsites and 22 trails at Wyalusing. Book early if you want to camp. It's one of Wisconsin's first state parks due to its scenic grandeur. Phone (608) 996-2261.

PRAIRIE DU CHIEN

Located on the Mississippi just north of Wyalusing, Prairie du Chien has a long and colorful past. Predated only by Green Bay, the town has a recorded history dating to 1673 when Marquette and Joliet reached the confluence of the Wisconsin and Mississippi Rivers. Prairie du Chien is French for "prairie of the dog," a reference to Native American Chief Alim, whose name meant dog.

From 1685 to 1831 four forts were built and occupied at various time by French, British, and American forces as the fur market flourished. During the War of 1812, an American flag was raised here for the first time over an American fort. When some pro-British locals alerted the British, a force of 150 militia and 400 Indians besieged and captured the garrison. American Fort Crawford was built when the war ended, and it later housed Jefferson Davis and Zachary Taylor for a time.

Today, the community's attractions include several historic sites, including Villa Louis and the Fort Crawford Medical Museum. **Villa Louis** on Saint Feriole Island, was the estate of Colonel H. L. Dousman, fur trader and agent of John Jacob Astor's American Fur Company. You can imagine, in the days when this was a wilderness occupied by rugged fur traders and Native Americans, what a glorious site Villa Louis must have been—and still is. The present mansion, named for Dousman's son, was built in 1870 on an ancient Native American mound. It's a Victorian-style mansion containing one of the finest collections of Victorian decorative arts in the country. An icehouse and smokehouse are located on the grounds. The carriage house has been converted into a museum. A 12-minute slide program is given in the visitor center. Tours conducted by costumed guides begin in the visitor center next to the parking lot. Open daily, May–October. Admission. Phone (608) 326-2721.

The **Fort Crawford Medical Museum**, part of the Fort Crawford restoration 717 South Beaumont, exhibits medical procedures before the days of anesthesia, especially Dr. William Beaumont's groundbreaking studies of the human digestive system. His patient was a fur trader with a gaping belly wound; open May-October, (608) 326-6900.

A creepy old jail, rivaled only by the dungeon in the basement of the Kewaunee County courthouse, is located in the bowels of the **Crawford County Courthouse** in Prairie du Chien, 220 N. Beaumont Street. Call the county clerk for a tour, (608) 326-0200. The jail was built in 1843 and the largest cells measure five by seven feet-for two prisoners. Two cells are three feet wide. For solitary confinement, leg irons and arm chains were fitted in two windowless cells that barely provided enough room to stand up. Pretty grim stuff.

For the true diner experience, stop at **Pete's** downtown for a burger served in a retired caboose.

READ ALL ABOUT IT

From west to east along the Wisconsin River: the *Praire du Chien Courier Press, Boscobel Dial, Muscoda Progressive, Spring Green Home News, Sauk Prairie Star,* and the *Eagle* (Sauk City) provide plenty of river city happenings every week.

HAVE YOU HEARD?

Madison stations dominate the airwaves along the Lower Riverway until the country sounds of WPRE, 980 AM, and WQPC, 94.3 FM, Prairie du Chien, come into range.

Double Take: GRABAAWR

You can get to know the Wisconsin River as few other people have, from its headwaters near Michigan's Upper Peninsula to its confluence with the Mississippi River, 500 miles all in all . . . every mile on a bicycle.

The Great Annual Bike Adventure Along the Wisconsin River (GRABAAWR) is a popular six-day tour leading more than a thousand riders through the state using our namesake river as a guide. Most participants believe that Wisconsin's scenery and the kindness of fellow riders are the best parts of the tour.

GRABAAWR, like similar state tours, typically include transportation for riders to the starting point as well as support services along the way. Your camping gear will be hauled to each overnight location, usually a local high school where riders can refuel on generous dinners and breakfasts.

GRABAAWR's route starts in Eagle River, proceeds through the flat Central Sands area and the scenic Baraboo Bluffs, before finishing along the lower river valley where riders dip their tires in the Mississippi at Prairie du Chien. Overnight stays are made in Rhinelander, Wausau, Wisconsin Rapids, Adams-Friendship, Portage, and Spring Green.

The tours are designed for amateur riders. There is no prize for finishing first. The reward comes from enjoying the ride. That's not hard. The sights, sounds, scents, and tastes of Wisconsin will accompany you every step, or pedal, of the way. Call Bike Wisconsin at (888) 575-3640 for more information on GRABAAWR and other state tours, or visit www.bikewisconsin.com.

THE SOUTHWEST CORNER

If You Want To Be a Badger

Any fourth graders who paid attention to their local history lessons

can recite the story of how Wisconsin became the Badger State.

Before Barry Alvarez, way back in the early 19th century, miners poured

into the territory when word of lead deposits in the southwest corner of the

Wisconsin territory reached the East Coast and jumped the Atlantic Ocean.

Dull, gray, dirty lead is hardly as glamorous as gold, so our "rush"

will be overshadowed forever by the events in California circa 1849.

Make no mistake about it though, some 20 years before California,

the influx of more than 10,000 miners looking for lead in "them thar hills"

put Wisconsin on the map. Lead, as the cliche goes, was good as gold.

By 1836, Mineral Point had become the seat of territorial government and

the regional center for land sales. By the 1840, local mining was producing

half of the nation's lead. By 1848, Wisconsin was the 30th state.

Then there was Ron Dayne? No, some of the early miners who came to the area in search of lead were so resourceful that they lived in the holes that they had dug. People such as Jesse Shull, the father of Shullsburg, got the idea by watching badgers (the animals, not the miners) burrow into hillsides.

The area around what is now the town of New Diggings became the first Euro-American mining site in the Wisconsin lead region, named by miners who left "old diggings" at Galena, Illinois. The badgers (the miners, not the animals) created villages that reflected their rough-and-tumble lifestyles: Hardscrabble, Patch, New Diggings, Hoof Noggle, Tail Hole, Nip and Tuck. Most villages didn't last longer than the local lead veins, but others survived and their descendents persevere today through farming and small businesses.

So if you want to be a badger, just come along on this Classic Wisconsin Weekend to Shullsburg, Mineral Point, Platteville, and other locales where it was once fashionable to say your home was a hole in the ground.

Underrated as a tourist destination, the old lead-mining zone of southwestern Wisconsin offers the whole kit and caboodle: beautiful scenery among undulating terrain; intriguing small towns perfect for poking around; recreation ranging from bike trails to horseback riding to trout fishing; state parks, wineries, cheese factories; and, best of all, traditions that are (almost) as alive and palpable today as they were in 1836. One weekend, however, probably doesn't provide enough time to enjoy everything the rugged hill country has to offer.

SHULLSBURG

To get a taste of what badger life was life, our first stop is Badger Park on West Estey Street in Shullsburg, site of a humble-from-the-outside museum that belies its featured attraction. In the building along with the museum is the entrance to the **Badger Mine**, one of the most compelling and primitive of southwest Wisconsin's tourist attractions. A reconstructed general store, kitchen, and doctor's office are featured in the museum along with the requisite antique furnishings. Ask about the legend of the bullet-ridden hotel sign hanging overhead.

Touring the mine is worth the price of admission. You're following the footprints left by Jesse Shull some 175 years ago. Not much has changed down there. Visitors descend a narrow wooden staircase into the earth below the park. The ground beneath Shullsburg is honeycombed with tunnels, more than five miles all told (one of the reasons the town was not selected for a state prison). Many channels have never been mapped.

A half-mile section of the Badger Mine is open for touring. The damp passageways narrow to a height of five feet in some places. Along the walls are initials of early miners who burned their names into the rock with candles. Blasting holes are still evident. A dog skull is perched on one wall, the remains of a mine mascot who died in a blast. (The skull is said to be cursed, by the way.) Abandoned ore car tracks still lay on the rock floors. Any number of tunnels lead into darkness from the main passage. Your guide will shut down the lighting system

The Bevans Mining Museum in Platteville digs deep into the state's mining history.

and spark a candle to simulate working conditions that seem impossible by today's standards.

It's a gritty, and slightly claustrophobic, look at life in the mines. Badger Mine is as authentic as any attraction you will find in Wisconsin. It's open 10 a.m.–4 p.m. daily, Memorial Day weekend through Labor Day weekend; (608) 965-4860.

The grim livelihood of the early miner explains why Shullsburg's streets were named Charity, Faith, Friendship, Peace, and Truth. When Catholic missionary Father Samuel Mazzuchelli saw men living in hellish conditions underground, surfacing only to raise hell in town, he suggested the virtuous street names as inspiration. Judgement must have been added should the local folk have lost their way on Faith.

Shullsburg is an irresistible walking town, mainly due to its main drag, Water Street, which looks much like it did a century ago (but with antiques shops). Most of the buildings were constructed during the boom years. A town tour might start at the top of Water Street at its intersection with Judgement. (After weddings, it is a tradition to drive backward down Water Street.) Among the 45 featured structures are the **James Hatch Building**, 112 W. Water Street, built in 1833; the **Charles J. Meloy Hardware Store**, 127 W. Water Street, built in 1886; and **C. G. Miller Dry Goods Store**, 133 W. Water Street, built in 1855, today the site of **Jackson's Confectionery Store**. A Web site provides a detailed walking tour at http://wicip.uwplatt.edu/lafayette/ci/shullsburg/. After exploring Shullsburg above ground and below, stop by the **Brewster Café**, 208 W. Water Street, for the best eats in town.

NEW DIGGINGS

Not much has changed in New Diggings since it was built, which is reason enough to visit. See for yourself by stopping to admire the town, especially the **New Diggings General Store and Inn**. This is one of state's oldest taverns. Rooms are for rent upstairs, and there's live entertainment every weekend. The proverbial two-taverns-and-a-church-town, New Diggings is the site of Father Samuel Mazzuchelli's Saint Augustine's Church, built by the missionary in 1844 and still standing. (See sidebar.)

As venerable as any business in the state, the New Diggings General Store and Inn is still going strong as a popular gathering place for live music on weekends.

PLATTEVILLE

Along Highway 151, about 20 miles northwest of Shullsburg, lies another town nestled into the hillsides. Platteville is ripe for exploring and is the place that provides the area's most comprehensive look at its lead mining days. Platteville (population 9,700) is another early digging site, settled in 1827 by John Rountree, who had the town patterned after his native Yorkshire village. Although some lead and zinc are still mined, cheese production is a more common industry today. Platteville also is home to the University of Wisconsin–Platteville.

The **Bevens Mine and Mining Museum**, 385 E. Main Street, (608) 348-3301, traces the development of lead and zinc mining in the area through dioramas, equipment, relics, photographs, and the mine itself. It is the most complete presentation on the early mining days that you will find in Wisconsin. A guided tour includes a walk 50 feet underground into the 1845 lead mine, where the temperature remains a constant 52 degrees year-round. A visit to the hoist house and a train ride around the museum grounds in ore cars pulled by a 1931 mine locomotive are included in the tour. It's all great family fun. The museum is open daily 9 a.m.–5 p.m., May–October; self guided tours Monday–Friday, 9 a.m.–4 p.m., the rest of year. Admission is $4; over 64, $3.50; ages 5–15, $2.

The cost includes admission to the **Rollo Jamison Museum**, located next door. Rollo Jamison apparently never saw a trinket he didn't like. He started collecting arrowheads in his childhood. The arrowheads, along with 20,000 other diverse items, are part of the collection. Phone (608) 348-3301.

The **Mitchell-Rountree Stone Cottage** is the oldest homestead in Platteville and one of the oldest in Wisconsin, built in 1837 by a veteran of the Revolutionary War. Free tours are offered Memorial Day through Labor Day. Located at the corner of Lancaster and Ann Streets; (608) 348-8687.

Hard to miss is the huge letter M set into a hillside four miles northeast of Platteville, built by students of the Wisconsin Mining School in 1930. It is lighted twice a year, during UW–Platteville's homecoming and the school's springtime M Ball. Steps lead up the M for a nice vista.

For more information about the town, contact the Platteville Chamber of Commerce, 275 Highway 151, Platteville, WI 53818, or phone (608) 348-8888.

POTOSI

Another early mining community, Potosi was settled in 1829 after lead was found near the Saint John Mine. Named for the silver mining city in Bolivia, the village began as three separate settlements resting between steep valley walls and the Grant and Mississippi Rivers. In its mining hey-day, Potosi was a leading shipping port for lead ore and supplies and was one of the largest communities in the territory. By 1840 the harbor filled with silt and large vessels could no longer dock. The Gold Rush of 1849 took care of the miners. The **Potosi Brewery**, built in 1855, remained an important local business for more than 100 years, but today it provides the best brewery ruins in the state. Above the town are the remnants of miners' dwellings known as "badger huts." This self-proclaimed "catfish capitol of Wisconsin" supposedly also has the longest Main Street in the world without a single traffic stop (three miles), but who's counting?

Tours of **Saint John Mine** run six days a week from 9 a.m. to 5 p.m., starting in May; closed Wednesdays. The mine, which extends over 200 feet into the hillside, was left virtually untouched for the 99 years it lay closed. The guided tour takes an hour and is geared to all ages. Admission: $4.50, adults; $2.25, children 6–12; free to children 5 and under. Call (608) 763-2121.

CASSVILLE

For a nice change of pace, head over to **Stonefield Village** just north of Cassville, a spanking turn-of-the-century reconstructed community. It takes its name from the 2,000-acre farm of the state of Wisconsin's first governor, Nelson Dewey. Across the road is **Nelson Dewey State Park**, which offers a nice vista above the Mississippi and 44 camping sites; (608) 725-5374. Stonefield is a living history park, meaning costumed guides stay in character as they demonstrate how to make brooms, barrels, horseshoes, and other nineteenth-century necessities. It's open daily from Memorial Day weekend to early October. Phone (608) 725-5210. The village also features the **Nelson Dewey Home Site**, located near the park entrance.

LANCASTER AND BELMONT

There are two small towns in the area worthy of note—and a visit. In Lancaster, the **Grant County Courthouse** was influenced by classical designs. Think Saint Peter's Basilica in Rome, only on a small-town scale. It stands on a town square that is home to one of the country's first Civil War monuments. The courthouse's octagonal copper and glass dome is one of the most unique you'll ever see. Open during business hours. Murals line the rotunda inside. Two blocks from the courthouse is the resting place of Governor Nelson Dewey.

Blink and you'll miss Belmont, a pleasant little town with a significant history. Remnants of this history can be seen at **First Capitol State Park**, seven miles east of Platteville on County Road G. It contains two restored buildings that stood on the site where the first territorial legislature met. The site is likely the smallest state park in Wisconsin. Picnicking is permitted. The site is open daily 10 a.m.–4 p.m., Memorial Day through Labor Day, and is free to the public. Call (608) 987-2122 for more information.

MINERAL POINT

Some 13 miles farther northeast along Highway 151 lies Mineral Point, once the nerve center of the territory and still the main destination for many of the region's visitors. The roots of Mineral Point can be can be traced back to Cornwall, England. For centuries, the mining of tin, copper, and lead mining in Cornwall was done vertically into the rock hills, rather than horizontally. The Cornish subsequently became expert hard-rock miners and stone masons. When word of New World lead deposits reached England, the folks in Cornwall began packing their bags.

Tourism is Mineral Point's draw today. Visitors descend down narrow lanes past shops and homes and gardens; the town's rock-solid buildings were hand crafted by local masons. The structures are old, very old, but they look no worse

Pendarvis's unique stone masonry along Shake Rag Street is just one highlight for visitors to Mineral Point—the entire town is on the National Register of Historic Places.

for wear than they did in 1840. In December, when wreaths and Christmas trees decorate the town and a dusting of snow covers the ground, the scene recalls the pages of a Dickens novel.

The on-going restoration of the town is the result of preservation efforts that began in the 1930s. With more than 500 structures standing on plats drawn in 1837, Mineral Point was listed as Wisconsin's first district to be named to the National Register of Historic Places.

Restoration has preserved Cornish architecture and culture, including **Pendarvis**, a series of Cornish houses furnished with antiques and lead-mining tools. **Shake Rag Street** contains a concentration of stone cottages built by Cornish miners. The street was named, by the way, for the way in which the Cornish housewives summoned their miner husbands to lunch. The Pendarvis site also offers information about a self-guided tour of nearby **Merry Christmas Mine** hill to view abandoned shafts and badger holes, although no mines are open for touring. The hillside has been restored as native prairie. Guided tours of the Pendarvis complex are conducted daily from 9 a.m.–5 p.m., May–October. Admission is $8; over 65, $7.20; ages 5–12, $4. Phone (608) 987-2122 for information.

Mineral Point has evolved into a center for arts and crafts. Antique shows are held in June, July, and October. Each August the town celebrates its annual art fair.

Walking the street of Mineral Point is mandatory for those who hope to gain an appreciation for this historic town and the entire region.

The beautiful **Mineral Point Theater** has been a community focal point since 1915 when it was opened as a theater and opera house. Still active, it's the only performing arts venue between Platteville and Madison. Located at 139 High Street, (608) 987-2642.

SOME LOCAL FARE AND FUN

The **Red Rooster Café** is probably Mineral Point's best-known and most traditional eatery. For the real-deal Cornish experience, try a pasty, which holds a special place in Cornish culture and in the hearts of the Cornish people. The pasty is among the most traditional of Wisconsin foods and one that is most closely identified with the Badger State.

The pasty (it rhymes with nasty but can hardly be described as such) is a semi-circle-shaped pastry filled with meat, potato, carrots, and onions. For centuries the Cornish filled their pasties with almost any edible ingredient that could be scrounged up. Legend has it that the devil would never cross the River Tamar into Cornwall for fear of becoming filling in a Cornish pasty. When the Cornish rugby team plays an important match, a giant pasty is symbolically hoisted over the goalpost before the start of the game, a tradition that dates to 1908. (The original giant pasty is still used.)

The most traditional filling is beef and potato with sliced onion. Popular fillings through the ages have included egg and bacon, rabbit, apples, figs, and jam. In Cornwall, they sometimes add parsnip. The original pasties contained meat and vegetables in one end and jam or fruit in the other to provide two "courses" for miners, and Cornish housewives marked their husband's initials on the left-hand side of the casing should the miner save a portion for later. Traditionally, a piece of the crust was left for the *knockers*, mythical troll-like people who could cause all sorts of problems unless placated with food. Lucky trolls. The crust is the best part.

Visit the Red Rooster to sample what we're been talking about. The restaurant is located at 158 High Street; (608) 987-9936.

Another popular restaurant, with lodging accommodations, is the **Brewery Creek Inn**, located at the head of the Cheese Country Recreational Trail. Housed in an 1854 building, the inn has been drawing rave reviews for its brewpub (terrific food) and five upscale rooms (four contain fireplaces and double whirlpools). Call (608) 987-3298 or visit www.brewerycreek.com.

For a bit of outdoor fun after the pasties and other culinary treats, head out on the **Cheese Country Recreation Trail**, a three-county, 47-mile, rail-to-trail route between Mineral Point and Monroe that cuts through the cheese-making country of Iowa and Green Counties. Bikers note: this is a popular ATV trail. Features include an iron truss bridge west of Browntown. At Calamine, the trail connects with the Pecatonica State Park Trail, putting the biker and hiker in a link with some 200 miles of pathways located in nine southwestern Wisconsin counties.

DODGEVILLE

Along with Mineral Point and Platteville, Dodgeville (population 3,900) was a bustling lead-mining town during the 1820s and 1830s. The town bears the name of Henry Dodge, a colorful frontiersman who pioneered the mining industry, figured prominently in the defeat of Black Hawk, and served as the first territorial governor and later as U.S. Senator. Dodgeville is home to the **Iowa County Courthouse**, the oldest courthouse in Wisconsin, having been dedicated in 1861 and expanded in 1894 and 1927. The Doric columns and cupola have been restored to their 1861 appearance. The facility is open during business hours.

Nearby, **Governor Dodge State Park** is one of the state's larger parks at 5,000 acres, but it's the steep hills, valleys, two lakes, and waterfall that make this a popular attraction. Located just north of Dodgeville off Highway 23, the park has 270 campsites. And remember to book early. For more information, write Governor Dodge State Park, Route 1, Box 42, Dodgeville, WI 53533, or phone (608) 935-2315.

Dodgeville is also the western terminus of the **Military Ridge Trail**, a popular bike route that winds through the rolling terrain of Dane and Iowa Counties, tracing the path of the original military road built in 1835. The trail roughly follows Highway 151 from Dodgeville to just east of Verona, but wanders away from the highway through farmlands, prairie remnants, and woods. The ridge offers sweeping vistas of southwest Wisconsin's Driftless Region.

Looking for that 315-pound Brazilian agate? This is the place. The **Museum of Minerals and Crystals**, four miles north of Dodgeville on Highway 23, contains more than 3,000 rock, mineral, and crystal specimens from around the world. Fluorescent material is displayed in a black-lit room. The museum is open daily 9 a.m.–5 p.m., April 1–November 15. Admission is $3.50; individuals over 65, $3; ages 6–18, $2.50. One-hour horseback rides, available from an on-sire stable, cost $12; two-hour rides, $24. Phone (608) 935-5205 for information.

BLUE MOUNDS

The area east of Dodgeville boasts another exceptional state park, marked by two blue hills, the highest in south-central Wisconsin. **Blue Mounds State Park**, off Highway 18/151 west of the town of Blue Mounds, features two observation towers and picnic areas. Enjoy the 50-mile-plus views of the Wisconsin River valley and the Baraboo Hills to the north, Platteville and Sinsinawa to the south. Legend has it that Winnebago treasure is buried in the mound. The park offers 78 camping sites on 1,500 acres. Phone (608) 437-5711.

Cave of the Mounds, also off Highway 18/151 west of town, is a super underground attraction. This national natural landmark has theatrical lighting enhancing a variety of brilliantly colored stalactites, stalagmites, and underground pools. The grounds offer rock gardens and picnic areas. The attraction is considered the most significant cave in the Upper Midwest. Food is available in the summer. Open daily 9 a.m.–7 p.m., Memorial Day weekend through Labor Day; daily 9 a.m.–5 p.m., the day after Labor Day through November 15, and March 15 to the day before Memorial Day weekend; Open Saturday and Sunday the rest of the year. Guided one-hour tours along concrete walkways leave every 15 minutes in summer. Admission $12, adults; ages 5–12, $6. Phone (608) 437-3038.

WHERE'S THE FISH FRY?

Potosi likes its catfish, so you'll see plenty of the whiskered bottom feeders on menus. The **Potosi Yacht Club**, 6659 Highway 133, is an area favorite, (608) 763-2238.

READ ALL ABOUT IT

You'll find a slew of weekly papers in southwestern Wisconsin: *Grant County Herald Independent* in Lancaster; *Platteville Journal*; *Dodgeville Chronicle*; *Democrat Tribune* in Mineral Point, and the *Fennimore Times*.

HAVE YOU HEARD?

WGLR in Lancaster, 1280 AM and 97.7 FM, is the station for old standards, country music and local news; WDMP in Dodgeville, 99.3 FM, is all country music; Platteville has easy listening and oldies on WPVL, 1590 AM and 107.1 FM; UW–Platteville's WSUP, 90.5 FM, plays whatever it wants.

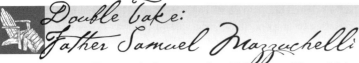

Double Take:
Father Samuel Mazzuchelli

No person had a more profound influence on Wisconsin's lead mining region than Dominican missionary Samuel Mazzuchelli. Born in Milan, Italy, the young priest made his way through the Northwest Territory, alone, by way of Mackinac Island, arriving in the lead zone in 1835.

Living among the miners, Father Mazzuchelli had his work cut out for him. Although shocked by the early settlers' lack of faith (see Shullsburg), he immediately sought to bring Catholicism to the area. In all, he built 17 churches from Mackinac to Muscatine, Iowa, and founded 40 parishes. He also developed the Chippewa Almanac, a work that that is kept in the Library of Congress rare book collection.

In 1844 Father Mazzuchelli established the College of Saint Thomas for men and the Congregation of Dominican Sisters of Sinsinawa, a community of teaching nuns at Sinsinawa Mound. He himself taught science, philosophy, history, and religion.

Annually over 32,000 guests find their way to Sinsinawa Mound, located on County Road Z off Highway 11, just a mile or so from the Illinois border. Pilgrims are struck by the beauty of the peaceful setting: 450 acres of lush woodlands, orchards, vineyards, prairie, and gardens. There is also a sustainable farm in operation seven days a week. The site is a popular location for retreats, and the Sinsinawa kitchens produce delicious cinnamon and zucchini breads and caramel rolls. Phone (608) 748-9700 for more information or log onto www.sinsinawa.org.

In New Diggings, mass is celebrated annually the last weekend in September in Father Mazzuchelli's weather-beaten church, Saint Augustine's. This pioneering priest died of pneumonia on February 23, 1864, after visiting the sick on a bitterly cold morning. He is buried behind one of the churches he designed and built, Saint Patrick's, in Benton. His tiny rectory stands next door.

CENTRAL WISCONSIN

The Heart of the Heart of the State

Location, location, location.

Central Wisconsin is both blessed and cursed by it.

Because of location, the advantages to travelers in this area are obvious. Motoring to Stevens Point, Wisconsin Rapids, Wausau, and all points in between will only take a few hours from most parts of the state. Business people have known this for years and have made the area, especially the Steven Point Holiday Inn Holidome, a convenient venue for statewide business meetings. Because of location, the University of Wisconsin–Stevens Point has drawn tens of thousands of students from all over the state to its campus.

The downside to all this is that most people driving I-39 (Highway 51 to natives) probably have the vehicle set on cruise control and are hell-bent on getting somewhere else, probably Minocqua and points beyond. The region also appears to be a yawner, aesthetically and culturally speaking, from the car window. It seems the most intriguing attraction for miles around is the Stevens Point Holidome's bar, called Mortimer's Show Palace, home of "Las Vegas Style Entertainment"—sans casinos, showgirls, and buffets.

But the recommendation from this intrepid traveler is to pull off Highway 51 sometime and take a closer look. You might be surprised by the region's unique features: sandstone buttes worthy of John Wayne; cranberry bogs that produce some of the state's finest autumn colors; flowages and wildlife refuges. There's plenty of underrated camping, and central Wisconsin is home of impressive state memorials dedicated to native sons and daughters who served in our nation's conflicts. Towns like Wausau, Wisconsin Rapids, and Stevens Point are convenient jumping-off points for exploring the area. In a word, central Wisconsin has all the ingredients for a Classic Wisconsin Weekend.

SOME GREAT STATE PARKS

A good place to take in many of the region's distinctly natural attributes is in the area southwest of Wisconsin Rapids. Here you'll be treated to the Petenwell and Castle Rock Flowages, the Necedah National Wildlife Refuge, the Black River State Forest, and Buckhorn and Roche-A-Cri State Parks.

Rock outcrops are especially prominent at **Mill Bluff State Park** near Camp Douglas and **Roche-A-Cri State Park**, Friendship. Mill Bluff offers spectacular views of the rock formations and 24 campsites; (608) 427-6692. Roche-A-Cri features a 300-foot high outcropping with a stairway to the top; 41 campsites in this quiet, diminutive park; (608) 339-6881.

Along with Mill Bluff and Roche-A-Cri, **Buckhorn State Park** forms a neat and accessible triad of state parks within a 25-mile radius. Buckhorn contains a long causeway across the Castle Rock-Petenwell Flowages on the Wisconsin River, leading to the 2,500-acre park. A guided boardwalk detours through desert-like terrain. There are only 24 campsites, but the sites are located near the water, (608) 565-2789.

Just north of the three state parks lies the **Necedah National Wildlife Refuge**, located in what was once glacial Lake Wisconsin, later dubbed the "Great Swamp" by settlers. It's the largest wetland-bog area of the state. The refuge totals 43,696 acres. The varied habitat includes oak savannas, sedge meadows, grasslands, and oak and pine forests; (608) 565-2551.

Rare species make their home at Necedah including endangered Karner blue butterflies and Blanding's turtle, state threatened massasauga rattlesnakes and black terns. Flights of the butterflies are best seen in mid-July to the first week in August.

Instead of an auto tour route, the refuge has six sites as viewing hotspots. It permits the picking of wild blueberries between July 1 and August 15. The Meadow Valley Wildlife Area is open for a number of public uses including primitive camping.

About 15 miles northwest lies the **Black River State Forest**, which encompasses 67,000 acres of pine and oak forest. The Black River and sandstone formations help provide a picturesque setting. Located just off I-94 in Jackson County. Nearby is Warrens, home of the annual cranberry festival held late September. Phone (715) 284-4103.

THE HIGHGROUND

Just north of the Black River State Forest along Highway 10 three miles west of Neillsville is the **Highground Veterans Memorial**, a solemn park overlooking a half-million acres of Wisconsin woodland and glacial moraine. Monuments to soldiers from American wars, including female veterans, MIAs, and Native Americans, are found on the premises. The 140-acre park is open to the public at no charge 24 hours a day, every day of the year; (715) 743-4424.

Korean War veterans are honored at a state memorial in Plover, just south of Stevens Point along I-39.

The Highground's mission statement maintains that the site is "a place of education, a place of healing and hope, a place of peace, serenity and beauty." The park accomplishes its mission in no uncertain terms. The Highground is best known for the **Vietnam Veterans Memorial**, but equally impressive are sculpted tributes to veterans of World War I, World War II, and women who have served in any military capacity; the National Native American Vietnam Veterans Memorial is another moving tribute.

The hillsides and lower park southwest of the plaza are the site of the **Earth Dove Effigy Mound**, which pays tribute to those who were or are prisoners of war and those who remain missing in action. East of the plaza is the Gold Star

Grove, dedicated to families who have lost loved ones. The Earth Dove Effigy Mound contains soil from all 72 counties as well as hundreds of locations throughout the United States. The Dove's wingspan measures 140 feet. Also in the lower park area are picnic shelters and tables, as well as a partially developed three-and-a-half-mile walking trail.

To maintain the reverent and patriotic mood, visit the state's **Korean War Memorial**, along I-39 in Plover, just south of Stevens Point; it's another impressive tribute to our war veterans in the general vicinity.

WAUSAU

Wausau could well be called central Wisconsin's most well-known but least-visited city. Motorists on Highway 51 cruise right along, anxious to get where they're going as quickly as possible, which means the North Woods if they're driving north and Illinois if they're headed south. But don't sell Wausau short. Stop and see what others are missing.

Dominating Wausau's horizon is **Rib Mountain**. It's not a mountain, in fact, it's not even the highest point in Wisconsin, but it provides downhill and cross-country skiing in the winter and camping year-round on it's large hillside. The billion-year-old hill is one of the oldest geologic formations on earth. A new owner recently bought Rib Mountain Ski Area, changed its name to **Granite Peak**, and embarked on a three-year plan to expand and upgrade the facilities; phone (715) 845-2846. Skiers will find the longest downhill run in the state (one mile) among a total of 51. There are four bunny hills, three intermediate hills, and four challenging runs. The DNR offers 40 campsites at the 1,172- acre **Rib Mountain State Park,** (715) 842-2522.

Downtown Wausau still has structures remaining from its sawdust days. A walking tour map is available at an information center, 300 Third Street. The **Andrew Warren Historic District** includes homes and carriage houses. The **Grand Theater**, 415 Fourth Street, is a Greek-Revival structure representing the golden age of performing arts (that means before TV). Originally opened in 1929, the Grand contains classic examples of colonnades, marble statues, and the original solid Indiana limestone façade. The schedule includes both touring productions and local entertainment. Phone (715) 842-0988 or (888) 239-0421.

The **Rosenberry Inn**, 511 Franklin Street, is a 1908 Prairie School-style home built for attorney Marvin Rosenberry, who later became chief justice of the Wisconsin Supreme Court. It's located in a downtown walking district. Phone (715) 842-5733.

The **Leigh Yawkey Woodson Art Museum**, Franklin and 12th Streets, is a blend of big-city style and small-town atmosphere; it contains a permanent collection of historic and contemporary paintings with an emphasis on birds. Gardens dotted with sculptures located on the grounds. It's free; (715) 845-7010.

One of the best attractions in the area is the **Dells of the Eau Claire County Park,** which features spectacular geological formations along a gorge formed by the Eau Claire River, plus hiking trails, 25 campsites, and other park facilities. It's located just off Eau Claire River Road, about 15 miles east of Wausau. Phone (715) 261-1550. Fifteen miles north of Wausau is **Council Grounds State Park**, which has 55 isolated sites along the Wisconsin River; (715) 536-4502.

STEVENS POINT

Downtown Stevens Point—what wasn't razed to build a homely mall—is redeemed by more than 60 original buildings along and near Main Street and the town square, which hosts the longest running farmer's market in the state on Saturday mornings. At one time, "Point" was among the most Polish towns in the nation. You can still see some the alphabet soup surnames on the old storefronts.

In the year 2000, Stevens Point and the neighboring community of Plover were named 2 of 141 "Dreamtowns" in the United States by Bizjournal.com. Some people joked that the computer-calculated ranking was a result of Y2K breakdowns.Yet the honor is justified by a balance of blue-collar and white-collar employment, the location of a state university, and Point's quaint reputation, which is boosted by a well-known local brewery.

It may be stretch to say that Point is "the Gateway to the Pineries" as the city slogan claims today (an accurate pitch . . . in 1850), but it can't be denied that Point is a green, tree-filled oasis in the sandy central Wisconsin flatlands. There are a number of impressive city parks, including one on the Wisconsin River. Main Street lies under a canopy of shade trees with the University of Wisconsin-Stevens Point administrative building, Old Main, providing a Midwest college town appearance.

The **Green Circle** is a collection of off-road and on-street routes looping around the city. The 24-mile route takes in views of the Wisconsin River, forest reserves hinting at the North Woods, and flat expanses typical of the sand

Old Main graces downtown Stevens Point and serves as the administration building for the University of Wisconsin–Stevens Point.

region. The trail is a mixture of asphalt pavement, packed gravel, and natural surfaces. The trail runs by the university's **Schmeekle Reserve**.

Established in 1857, the **Stevens Point Brewery** provided beer to troops during the Civil War, sparking a legend that continues to grow. When Prohibition and the Great Depression shut down most of the state's 80 breweries, the Point brewery managed to hang on due to the loyal, if not quite legal, patronage of the locals. Then, in 1973, Point Special was rated the top American beer in a taste test organized by the inimitable *Chicago Daily News* columnist Mike Royko. Still, the brewery did not sell it products far from Portage County, prompting the immortal T-shirt slogan: "When you're out of Point, you're out of town."

In 1990, for the first time in the 133-year history, Point was sold outside Wisconsin when it was introduced in Minneapolis. The brewery has continued to expand its horizon—to an extent. "We're a regional brewery," said brew master John Zappa, "and our beers are sold exclusively in the Midwest, specifically in Wisconsin and Illinois, as well as in parts of Minnesota and Iowa."

After a century and a half, the brewery produces six flavors, with its Point Special a consistent favorite for its full-bodied taste. And this regional brewer continues to rack up gold medals at international beer tasting events. Want to see how 52,000 barrels a year of this liquid gold are produced? Call (800) 369-4911 for tour information. The brewery is located at 2617 Water Street, at the corner of Beer and Water.

After the brewery tour, you may desire some relaxation. Downtown Stevens Point is home to two B&Bs that will be to your liking. **A Victorian Swan on Water**, 1716 Water Street, is a restored 19th-century home containing original woodworking and crown moldings; phone (715) 345-0595. **Dreams of Yesteryear**, 1100 Brawley Street, (715) 341-4525, is a three-story Queen Anne listed on the National Register of Historic Places. It contains the original brass and iron wood-burning fireplace; located on a quiet city street a few blocks from the downtown and the university. Owners Bonnie and Bill Maher are both from Stevens Point.

In addition, the usual chain motels and motor inns, including the aforementioned Holiday Inn, can be found in Point. The **Point Motel** on Division is the economical way to go.

Places to eat in Point include **Bill's Pizza** on Main Street and **Mickie's** Italian restaurant on Second Street. The fine dining place is **The Restaurant** in the SentryWorld (insurance) headquarters on North Point Drive, also home to the Sentry Theater and the highly regarded SentryWorld golf course. **Belt's Soft Serve** piles the ice cream high at 2140 Division Street. Look for the lines.

WHERE'S THE FISH FRY?

The Hilltop, on the east side of Stevens Point, at the Highway 10 and I-39 interchange, has a traditional Friday night fish fry and plenty of local memorabilia; (715) 341-3037. Just down the road at the **Silver Coach** you'll find potato-crusted walleye that's worth a couple or three visits. The Silver Coach harkens back to the day of fine dining aboard trains. The place looks deceptively small from the road, but additional seating is found in back, including an outdoor patio area, (715) 341-6588.

CHAIN O' LAKES ADVENTURES

Southeast of Point about 25 miles, in King, on the Waupaca Chain O' Lakes, is a popular spot for recreation called **Ding's Dock**. (How can you go wrong at a place named Ding's Dock?) Ding's is the outfitter for the famously fun Crystal River canoe trips. After a boat ride through two lakes along the Waupaca chain, canoeists are deposited in shallow water (2–3 feet deep) for a slightly wild and extremely wet three-hour ride down the Crystal River. Ages 6 and older will have a ball, but get ready: The canoes will get swamped, the fiberglass will make your skin crawl, and you will wonder if you'll ever feel dry again—and it's all part of good summer fun. Wear tennis shoes and a swimming suit or old clothes. Buses will shuttle you back to Ding's Dock; picnic area, snack stand, and gift shop are located lakeside.

The itchy fiberglass canoes are part of the famously fun Crystal River canoe trips departing from Ding's Dock.

Reservations for groups are strongly recommended. River trips are available daily from May 1 through September. Perfect outing for scouts, church groups, families. Ding's is located at E 1171 County Q, south of Highway 54, (715) 258-2612. If you like camping, Ding's is one mile from **Hartman's Creek State Park**. Rental cottages, private campgrounds, hotels, motels, and B&Bs can be found in the Waupaca area. The best-known lodging is the **Crystal River Inn B&B**, E1369 Rural Road, a riverside home four miles south of Waupaca. Phone (715) 258-5333. Also, the **Thomas Pipe Inn**, 11032 Pipe Road, is a historic inn located on a 19th-century state coach road. Phone (715) 824-3161.

IN AND NEAR WISCONSIN RAPIDS

The Wisconsin Rapids area is best known for helping Wisconsin supply the rest of the world with cranberries. The poor drainage of the central region, combined with an elaborate network of levees and canals, aids production of the fruit that turns a brilliant ruby red when ripe.

Cranberries aren't just another crop to Wisconsin. They are the state's number one agricultural export. Marshes produce 2.6 million barrels of harvested cranberries each year. One barrel equals 100 pounds, or 45,000 berries. Some marshes in the state have been successfully producing crops for more than a hundred years.

The annual harvest in mid-September and October is an opportunity to see a true Wisconsin spectacle, as the cranberry bogs run red with the glowing fruit. There's probably not a more spectacular sight in the state during the fall—and that's saying a lot. Of course, local folks celebrate the bounty with an annual festival (see the next page).

In Wisconsin Rapids, the local visitors bureau promotes self-guided auto tours, biking along the back roads, and offers limited tours of the cranberry marshes. Hotels offer special harvest time packages as well. If you want to see cranberry harvesting and processing, call Ocean Spray at (414) 421-5949.

Rapids is home to the **Alexander House**, a former paper executive's mansion along Wisconsin River Dr., now featuring an art gallery and historical museum. The 1907 mansion at 540 Third Street houses the collection of the **Wood County Historical Society**. A municipal **petting zoo** can be found at 1911 Gaynor Ave-nue, open from May to October. Contact the Wisconsin Rapids Area Convention and Visitors Bureau, www.visitwisrapids.com, (800) 554-4484.

The tiny town of Rudolph, eight miles north of Wisconsin Rapids, is home of the **Rudolph Grotto Garden and Wonder Caves**. Located behind Saint Phillip's Catholic Church, the grotto is the product of devotion by Father Philip Wagner, who worked on the shrines for 40 years after recovering from an illness. This is a place that would definitely appeal to the devoutly religious. Stations of the cross are depicted within giant stone frameworks. Religious monuments, statues, and fountains are spread out everywhere. A log chapel is suspended above walkways. The cave contains more of the same—tributes to Our Lady of

Lourdes that stretch for a quarter of a mile. The grotto is open year-round; covered pavilion, picnic tables, and restrooms on the grounds. Follow the signs from Highway 34 in Rudolph.

The annual **Cranberry Festival** in Warrens is big to-do, especially for craft sales. The event claims to be the largest cranberry fest in the world. Who's counting? And if they did count, what would they count—people or cranberries? There's "heapin' helpin's" of both come late September when Warrens, a little berry of a town 45 miles southwest of Rapids, holds its annual hoo-ha. One of the reasons the town plays host is that it seems to be the only dry ground in the middle of the largest concentration of cranberry marshes in the state. The celebration is a great opportunity to do some early Christmas shopping. In all, the festival brings in 1,000 booths of arts and crafts covering more than three lineal miles.

The festival culminates in a colossal cranberry weigh-in. Entries are weighed and measured, but don't underestimate the all-important presentation category. There are ten different classes of cranberries. The blue ribbon "Biggest of Show" cranberry has exceeded five grams. Parade, three miles of antique and flea markets lining Warrens, and cranberry bog tours are featured. For more information visit www.cranfest.com or call (608) 378-4200.

This chapel is elevated above the Rudolph Grotto Garden and Wonder Caves, a 40-year project of devotion by Father Philip Wagner.

If you missed the festival, the **Cranberry Expo** is great a way to learn about the crimson berry. This museum features a collection of machinery and other artifacts used in the cranberry industry over the years, plus educational tours and a gift shop. The museum is located a few miles east of Warrens, on County EW; open daily 10 a.m.–4 p.m., April 1–October 31; (608) 378-4290.

READ ALL ABOUT IT

The *Stevens Point Journal, Wausau Daily Herald,* and *Wisconsin Rapids Tribune* are three daily newspapers in central Wisconsin.

HAVE YOU HEARD?

WWSP, 89.9 FM, is the UW–Stevens Point college station that bills itself, rightly so, as central Wisconsin's "only alternative." WSPT, 1010 AM and 97.9 FM, offer talk and adult contemporary respectively; WYTE, 96.7 FM, is Point's country station; WKQH, 104.9 FM, is classic rock. WIZD, 99.9 FM, is the oldies station. WFHR, 1320 AM, in Wisconsin Rapids has local programming and news. WRIG, 1390 AM, Wausau, plays nostalgia, WSAU, 550 AM, has local news.

Double Take: Trivial Matters

It's the largest marathon of its kind: 12,000 people, 550-some teams, each team competing for 52 continuous hours.

The Beer Pigs will be there. So will Chilled Monkey Brains, Gene Autrey's Ninja Warriors, and Don't Pee on the Electric Fence. What exactly are these teams and others—Voices from the Microwave, Sotally Tober, and Burning Outhouses—doing?

They are participating in the world's largest pursuit of trivia . . . and fortifying themselves with string cheese and No Doze or cheese curds and Point beer, or sometimes, all of the above. They are trying to answer questions that in any other context would be irrelevant or useless. A typical question: Whose signature graces the baseball bat that Shelly Duvall used on Jack Nicholson in *The Shining*?

For more than three decades the University of Wisconsin–Stevens Point radio station, WWSP, 89.9 FM, has hosted a trivia contest that is anything but trivial. Players come from around the country and occasionally from other countries to play, though most participants are UW–SP alums or central Wisconsin residents—like the Nuts in Almond, for example. Area hotel rooms become temporary archives of pop culture. Garages become bunkers along the super information highway. Central Wisconsin gets a little strange.

The festivities commence the third weekend in April with a Trivia Parade that begins at 4 p.m. Friday and winds it way erratically through campus. Rain is scheduled every year. It's an anti-parade really, worthwhile if only to watch grown men and women act absurd, a highly contagious condition. A good time, with plenty of candy.

After the parade ends at about 6 p.m., when the snare drum crashes on Steppenwolf's "Born to be Wild," contestants begin vying for top honors by trying to answer eight trivia questions every hour until midnight on Sunday. That's 430 questions ranging from the local to the sublime, with loads of movie, music, and other pop culture in between. Sounds simple, doesn't it?

A better question would be: In the classic 1957 Coasters hit "Searchin'," there are a group of sleuths referred to in the lyrics; the vocalist at one point says that he is going to walk down the street just like which famous sleuth?

The first question changes every year, but the answer remains the same, such as: This Oscar-winning director and Hollywood leading man produced the 1988 film, *Milagro Bean Field War*.

The contest draws more UW–SP alumni to the city than the university's annual fall homecoming festivities. The atmosphere can be just as boisterous, though organizers have established relationships with area high schools and Portage County youth organizations to give parents assistance in hosting age-appropriate trivia parties. At the end of the weekend, the top three winning teams are awarded "big" trophies, according to organizers. The fourth- through tenth-place teams receive something less than "big" trophies donated by a local carpet company.

The long weekend encompasses forced insomnia, caffeine, aspirin, Point Beer, pizza, and lots of jumping up and down until the correct answers are jarred loose from your gray matter. Most people are there to have fun, maybe answer some questions, and enjoy the camaraderie of this unique weekend in Point.

You don't have to bat like Carl Yastrzemski, or walk like Bulldog Drummond, or look like Robert Redford. You just have to go to central Wisconsin and turn on your radio.

CHAPTER SEVENTEEN

LA CROSSE
Oktoberfest and a Drive North

Start with the Lederhosen Luncheon. Don't miss the Maple Leaf Parade.

Dance the polka with ten thousand close friends. Listen to the

music of the Gemutlichkeits or the Ridgeland Dutchmen. Enjoy a beverage

brewed according to ancient German purity laws. Eat the best bratwurst of

your life (the sesame-seed bun is the key). Shake the hand of the Festmaster.

Be dazzled by the Torchlight Parade—then live the life of the contented,

knowing you were part of La Crosse's Oktoberfest USA celebration, perhaps

the grandest autumn festival this side of Munich.

La Crosse (population 51,000) isn't just another city with a fall festival.

La Crosse and Oktoberfest are synonymous, like Coke and cola. While

dozens of similar celebrations take place in German-influenced Wisconsin,

when Oktoberfest is mentioned in the upper Midwest, it seems

to go without saying that it's La Crosse.

The city carries its weight in every other respect, too: a river port steeped in history; a commercial center with a thriving downtown; a spunky college town. Add one more crucial element—geography, the nation's greatest river winding through awe-inspiring bluffs and valleys—and La Crosse easily defies conventional description.

God's Country, indeed.

Like most cities, La Crosse emerged from equal parts destiny and luck. Named for the ball-and-stick game that French explorers observed Native Americans playing, the fledgling trading post barely survived the failure of the La Crosse & Milwaukee railroad in 1857. When the Civil War closed river traffic on the Mississippi below the Ohio River, however, the town became a major transportation link with the East, thus ensuring its economic recovery.

La Crosse's multipurpose location at the confluence of the Mississippi, La Crosse, and Black Rivers facilitated the city's survival as a manufacturing center, transportation hub, and shipment point.

But location alone doesn't fully explain the allure of this place: It is impossible to visit La Crosse without being moved by its beauty. Although prehistoric glaciers leveled much of Wisconsin like a giant woodworker's plane, this area was spared. Now, towering bluffs and deep valleys stand in contrast to glaciated Wisconsin. "Coulee country" is another oft-used moniker, a homage to the region's steep-walled valleys. More than anything else, the city's location as a geological wonderland has been La Crosse's signature—and will continue to ensure viability for decades to come in the travel-and-tourism-heavy economy of the twenty-first century.

GETTING THE MOST FROM OKTOBERFEST

The original Oktoberfest—the European granddaddy of all the rest—was a wedding party for Bavarian Crown Prince Ludwig and Princess Therese in 1810 and served double-duty as a harvest celebration. Many harvest moons later, in 1960, La Crosse, Wisconsin, grappled with the idea of a community-wide event to fill the longstanding void left after winter carnival had been abandoned decades earlier. Leave it to two German-Americans working in the malt house of the G. Heileman brewery to brainstorm the idea. The rest, as they say, is history. The traditional German celebration was a perfect idea born in a perfect setting. The city even patented "Oktoberfest U.S.A." a year later.

Sadly, the House of Heileman, major player in La Crosse's industrial and civic life dating back to the 19th century, is gone now, a victim of corporate mergers and downsizing. A popular attraction was the "world's largest six-pack," six huge silos painted to resemble Old Style beer cans, which stood outside the brewery. The Heileman tourist center served as a museum, hospitality room, and departure point for daily brewery tours. The silos are blank now, and La Crosse is working hard to find uses for the brewery. In a way, Oktoberfest is G. Heileman's bittersweet legacy.

Prosit! La Crosse's Oktoberfest is arguably the grandest autumn festival this side of Munich.

Today, hundreds of volunteers with La Crosse Festivals, Inc. run the celebration with all the love of a fine-tuned Bavarian cuckoo clock. Oktoberfest U.S.A. is held during late September and early October. For decades, the festival started on a Saturday morning and ran six consecutive days and nights. Starting in 2000, Oktoberfest was spread across two, three-day weekends.

The celebration truly offers something for everyone, beginning with pre-festival activities like the Miss La Crosse Oktoberfest reception and the Festmaster's Ball. A bike tour and race, auto show, golf tournament, recreational run/walk, photo contest, food extravaganza, community heritage night, and needlework show are among the obligatory activities.

After the impressive **Maple Leaf Parade**—with more than 225 units and 50,000 onlookers—everybody heads en masse to the festival grounds. Two festival areas play host to balance out the celebration, and more than 130,000 people jockey between the north grounds at **Copeland Park** and the south facilities near **Riverside Park** during the week. The midways have their share of rides, but the biggest draw is live music, heavy on oompah bands, naturally, with some of the best groups coming directly from Germany. Locals and families tend to frequent the north grounds, while the south grounds have come to personify the Oktoberfest experience—it's the area most traveled by visitors, a polka-frenzied place where things can get, well, wild.

The **Torchlight Parade**, which once served as the closing ceremony, now kicks off the festival's second weekend on Thursday night. Though torches are no longer used, just about every other type of illuminating device is; the parade is a rare and wonderful spectacle. Fireworks conclude Oktoberfest on Saturday evening. Viewing is best at Riverside Park and the south grounds.

The festival headquarters are located at 1 Oktoberfest Strasse (where else?) at the south grounds' main entrance. First-timers hardly need directions—just follow the happy crowds. Free shuttles run frequently between the north and south grounds and area hotels. Lodgings will be full during the festival, so book accommodations well in advance. For more information call (608) 784-3378 or visit www.oktoberfestusa.com for an online tour.

Oktoberfest atmosphere is contagious, so you'll feel a part of the celebration anywhere in the city, but getting into the festival grounds requires an official button. The attractive buttons, good for the entire week, are available at most locations in La Crosse for a ridiculously nominal fee: $2.50 in advance, $3 at gate. Proceeds go to local non-profits. Wear it proudly. The button is your ticket to autumnal nirvana. Prosit!

LA CROSSE: FUN ANY TIME OF THE YEAR

La Crosse is no shrinking violet the other 51 weeks of the year. A good place to start any weekend visit to La Crosse, no matter what the season, begins at the city's most prominent feature: **Granddad Bluff,** two miles east on Main Street. Towering nearly more than 500 feet above the city, on a clear day the summit affords a great view of three states—Iowa, Wisconsin, and Minnesota. At night, the city lights lay sparkling before you. The bluff can be visited daily 6 a.m.–11 p.m. Driving the switchback road is an adventure in itself. The **Alpine Tavern** is a popular stopping point on the way up, or down.

La Crosse's other not-to-miss feature (unavoidable, really) is the Mississippi River. **Riverside Park** at the base of State Street, one block from the downtown, provides the most convenient setting to see Old Man River. Coin-operated field glasses are mounted along the river walk, and standing watch is a 25-foot carved wooden sculpture of Hiawatha. The park is the docking site for the *Delta Queen*, *American Queen*, and the *Mississippi Queen*, the only full-sized, overnight-passenger-carrying riverboats plying the mighty Mississippi today.

Throwbacks to the heyday of river boating, the Queens visit La Crosse regularly during the summer and fall. Like days of yore, unashamed gawkers still hurry down to the park to catch a glimpse. As a Queen emerges from the river bend, lucky spectators are transported back in time to the Mississippi River's golden age. The scene alone is worth a visit to La Crosse. One of the three river Queens typically makes stops in September and October, the latter being part of a fall foliage tour from Saint Louis to Saint Paul. Phone the Delta Queen Steamship Company at (800) 543-1949.

Local ships contribute to riverboat lore as well. The *La Crosse Queen* docks at the north end of Riverside Park, three blocks west of Highway 53 off State Street. The paddle wheeler offers a 90-minute narrated sightseeing cruise of the Mississippi. Weekend brunch, dinner, and lunch cruises are available.

Sightseeing cruises depart daily at 11 a.m., 1:30 and 3:30 p.m., June 13 through September 1. The popular fall color cruises depart at 11 a.m. and 1:30 p.m., Labor Day to mid-October. Sightseeing cruises cost $9.95; over 59, $9.45; ages 2–11, $4.95. Reservations required for dinner cruises. Phone (608) 784-8523.

The local *Julia Belle Swain* is one of only six steam-powered boats still operating on the Mississippi River. She offers lunch and dinner cruises, as well as one- or two-day trips with all-inclusive rates for meals and entertainment on board and sightseeing and lodging on-shore. Call (608) 784-4882 or (800) 815-1005. The *Island Girl* offers daily lunch, cocktail, and dinner cruises aboard a modern yacht; Sunday brunch and moonlight cruises offered. Call (608) 784-0556.

A river city on the mighty Mississippi, La Crosse can be enjoyed from the water, aboard the *Julia Belle Swain*, or atop the river valley's imposing bluffs.

Riverboat history is featured at the **Riverside Museum**, located at the park. An extensive collection of Native American artifacts and historic photos detailing La Crosse's history are on permanent display. Open daily 10 a.m.–5 p.m., Memorial Day weekend–Labor Day. Donations. Phone (608) 782-1980. Riverside Park is also home to the **La Crosse Area Convention and Visitors Bureau**, 410 E. Veterans Memorial Drive, phone (608) 782-2366 or (800) 658-9424.

DOWNTOWN LA CROSSE

La Crosse offers another rarity: an honest-to-goodness downtown. Visitors will find stores, restaurants, entertainment, a riverfront convention center, choice hotels, and no less than 110 historic buildings, most dating back to the late 19th century. Italianate style is prevalent among the old buildings, and plenty of decorative brickwork and windows can be found. Sightseeing is best done on foot. The heart of downtown is bordered roughly by Riverside Park/Front Street, Pearl Street, Fourth Street, and State Street. A slew of taverns frequented by the local college crowd lights up the downtown streets at night, keeping the old town young. Bar-hoppers rank La Crosse among the worthiest in the state.

The Museum of Modern Technology at the corner of Sixth and King provides a glimpse into such diverse subjects as the atomic age, space exploration, and American cycling history. Kids will love the children's room and gift shop, which offers science kits, books, and toys, including items found only at the unique museum. Open Tuesday through Sunday, admission is $3 for adults, less for seniors and kids. Phone (608) 785-2340.

The Pump House, a block west of Highway 53 at 119 King Street, is just that—a former waterworks pump house built in Romanesque Revival style. Now serving as a regional arts center, the building hosts galleries dedicated to local and regional artists. Concerts are scheduled as well. Open Tuesday–Friday, noon–5 p.m., Saturday, 10 a.m.–3 p.m. Donations. Phone (608) 785-1434.

A self-guided walking tour devoted to buildings of architectural and historical significance can be found at the **Hixon House and Museum**, 429 N. Seventh Street. The mid-19th-century Italianate house contains original furnishings, including rugs, ceramics, and furniture of the Victorian period. Guided museum tours are available daily 1–5 p.m., Memorial Day–Labor Day. Admission $4; senior citizens $3; under 12, $2; family rate $10. Phone (608) 782-1980.

Much of the La Crosse's youthful exuberance can be attributed to the 9,000-plus students attending the **University of Wisconsin–La Crosse**, located east of the downtown area. Campus tours are available on weekends from spring through fall; phone (608) 785-8067. The university's art gallery exhibits prominent artists September through May. Cultural events also take place at Viterbo College.

LODGING AND DINING

La Crosse has a wide offering of lodgings and restaurants from which to choose. At least 21 hotels or motels are located in the vicinity, including the usual national chains. Downtown hotels are popular (and more expensive of course), only a few economy motels are centrally located.

Unique accommodations include the **Martindale House Bed and Breakfast**, 237 S. Tenth Street, an 1850s Italianate home listed on the National Register of Historic Places. Phone (608) 782-4224. The grandiose **Chateau La Crosse**, also on the National Register, offers luxury accommodations downtown at 410 Cass Street. Phone (608) 796-1090.

Those determined to do something different when it comes to an overnight stay may want to consider renting a houseboat. La Crosse, after all, is a river city. After minimal training, you'll captain your own cruise on a deluxe houseboat equipped with all the amenities. Three-day, four-day, and weeklong rentals offered. Sailing north of La Crosse offers sand beaches, islands, and the best scenery. Call **Fun 'n The Sun Houseboat Vacations**, (608) 783-7326, or **Huck's Houseboat Vacations**, (800) 359-3055.

La Crosse has a plethora of restaurants, but three have reputations reaching far and wide: **Piggy's**, 328 S. Front Street, is well-known for its barbecued baby back ribs and other pork and beef dishes; (608) 784-4877. And they a great slogan: "We overlook nothing but the Mississippi." **The Freight House**, 107 Vine, is located in a former Chicago Milwaukee & Saint Paul railroad freight house and

La Crosse's vibrant downtown features 110 historic buildings with plenty of shops and restaurants.

specializes in steaks and seafood, especially Alaskan king crab; the expansive bar has a good wine and beer selection (and a fireplace), and there's no lack of authentic railroad memorabilia in this intriguing setting; (608) 784-6211. In nearby Onalaska, **Traditions Restaurant**, located in a former bank building at 201 Main Street, draws rave reviews; (608) 783-0200.

THE GREAT OUTDOORS

Getting on the water, whether it's by sightseeing cruise, houseboat, power-boat, or canoe, is a good way to get a feel for the region. Likewise, traveling by auto, bicycle or foot, brings a deeper appreciation for the wonders of "Coulee Country" (so nicknamed because of the French word coulee, which describes the steep-sided valleys of this region).

The **Great River State Trail** runs 24 miles from Onalaska, outside of La Crosse, to the town of Marshland. The trail name is a bit deceiving since the route does not always parallel the Mississippi River but it's a scenic wonder nev-ertheless. Bicyclists will be treated to bottomlands—wetlands and deltas remi-niscent of the bayous found at the southern end of the Mississippi—and grassy prairies. No less than 18 bridges, scores of beautiful white oak trees, and any number of fauna can be seen along the way. Like other state rail-to-trail routes, the grade is easy (three percent maximum) and groomed with packed, crushed gravel; it's well suited to the weekend cyclist. A popular section is Onalaska to Trempealeau, a 15-mile stretch one-way. The **Great River Walk** is held here on the trail in September. The event offers shuttles, snacks, and refreshments; routes are 4, 9, or 15 miles in length. Call (608) 791-6872. The La Crosse River State Trail runs 23 miles east, from Onalaska to Sparta, by way of Medary, West Salem, Bangor, and Rockland. Both trails are multiuse, meaning the fun doesn't end when the snow flies. Daily or annual trail passes are required for individuals ages 16 and older and are available at trailheads.

NORTH ALONG THE GREAT RIVER ROAD

After doing it up right in La Crosse, it's time to take a spin up north on Highway 35, also called **Great River Road**, which parallels the Mississippi. The Wisconsin section of the road, distinguished by green signs bearing a riverboat wheelhouse, runs for 250 miles from Dickeyville in the south to Prescott in the north. Sorry, but hyperbole is inevitable here: this section of the Great River Road is one of the great scenic treasures in America. Imposing bluffs, soaring eagles, sleepy little towns—all this and more are found in abundance along the mighty Mississippi. But even superlatives fail to do justice to the region. Simply put, traveling this road can be an experience never to be forgotten.

One of the first of many places to take in the scenery is the village of **Trempealeau**, about 20 miles north of La Crosse. The village was a lumber port in the mid-1800s. When the lumber industry ebbed, Trempealeau turned to grain milling. In turn, the decline of wheat led to a decline for Trempealeau's mills and population. Equally devastating was a fire in 1881 that took all but six buildings. Trempealeau today makes its living from recreation. The half-dozen buildings not lost to the fire are on the National Register of Historic Places.

No visit would be complete without a stop—and consider an overnight stay—at the **Trempealeau Hotel**, 150 Main Street. This is one of the pearls of the River Road, a lodging nearly untouched by time. The hotel, constructed in 1891, has seven small rooms upstairs (shared bathroom) with prices starting at $30. A cottage is available on the grounds. This local lady is best known, however, for kicking up her heels. The hotel bar/restaurant plays host to a regular schedule of local and nationally known musicians; annual outdoor reggae and blues festivals draw big crowds. Diversity is spoken here. Locals, bikers, tourist families, alternative folks of all stripes, boaters, and bicyclists can be found mixing easily. The atmosphere is tops, no doubt, but it's the food that ultimately brings 'em back for more. Ask for a recommendation and you'll be directed to the walnut burger—and you won't regret it. Soups, salads, sandwiches, and dinners are available. The Friday night special, grilled bluegill, is worth a trip. One note to overnighters: the Trempealeau Hotel is a popular watering hole; things might not quiet down until after last call. Phone (608) 534-6898.

The Trempealeau Hotel has been a must-stop on the Mississippi for more than a century, first for steamboat passengers, now for hungry tourists craving the hotel's famous walnut burger.

Bikes and canoes can be rented at the hotel. Recreational-minded folks will inevitably head to the state park next door. Named for early French explorer and fur trader Nicolas Perrot, the 1,400-acre **Perrot State Park** beautifully highlights woodland, prairie, and river bottom. It's impossible to miss the 400-foot-high Trempealeau Mountain (a bluff-island, really) in the Mississippi. Called *la montagnes qui trempe à l'eau* by the French, *Hay-nee-ah-chah*, or "Soaring Mountain," by the Ho-Chunk, and Minnechonkaha, or "Bluff in the Water," by the Ojibwe, the bluff serves as an obvious navigational guide for river traffic. The park contains elaborate burial mounds, and is an important Hopewell Middle Woodland Site. Put on your hiking shoes. Two trails ascend the 520-foot Brady's Bluff, one of four bluffs in the park, the payoff being a magnificent vista. It's a mile-and-a-half-hike to 507-foot Perrot Ridge.

Heading north from Trempealeau, you'll encounter an uneventful off-the-river drive for 15 miles until **Fountain City**. Here you'll find Eagle Bluff, the highest point on the Mississippi River, 550 feet, roughly the same height as the Washington Monument in our nation's capital. Fountain City is the site of one of the strangest roadside attractions in Wisconsin, the **House with the Rock in It**, as it's unofficially called. In 1995, a 50-ton boulder awoke from a long sleep and rolled off the bluff. It rests for good, hopefully, in the house that broke its fall. And it's available for viewing.

From Fountain City, the rolling river road dazzles all the way to Prescott. Quintessential river towns (some are nothing more than crossroads, others are a mile long and a block wide) offer any number of excuses to stop: antiques shops, galleries, taverns, cafés, B&Bs, historical markers, lock and dams, pick-your-own farms, fishing, bird watching, or scenic overlooks.

Alma is a town designated as a National Historic District with a stairway cut into the bluff and a unique terraced cemetery; three miles north is **Rieck's Lake Park**, where wildlife watchers make the trek during mid–late October to view migrating tundra swans. The enormous snow-white birds (20 pounds, four feet long, seven-foot wingspan) fly in from breeding grounds on the Arctic Circle. After a layover, they'll continue to Chesapeake Bay. The park has a viewing platform with spotting scopes and is staffed by volunteers daily during swan season. Other good swan-watching venues include Frontenac State Park and Weaver Dunes Preserve on the Minnesota side. After Alma, you'll encounter a couple of other villages that demand mention—and a stop. One prominent early traveler said one of them, **Pepin**, "ought to be visited in the summer by every painter and poet in the land." The Swedish-settled town of **Stockholm** has a thriving art community.

Farther north up the road is **Maiden Rock**. The town was supposedly named for a young Dakota woman who, after an arranged marriage, jumped to her death in despair of having lost her true love. The story is suspiciously familiar to legends that Europeans brought to the area and used to promote the Upper Mississippi as America's Rhineland.

Our final destination, **Prescott**, was an important sawmill town and port (sound familiar?). When a land boom sent costs skyrocketing, residents moved 20 miles up the Mississippi River to Dayton's Bluff—better known today as Saint Paul. Prescott's early settlers had a taste for Greek Revival and Gothic Revival homes. Many remain.

READ ALL ABOUT IT

The *La Crosse Tribune* delivers daily to more than 35,000 readers in coulee country.

HAVE YOU HEARD?

WIZM, 1410 AM and 93.3 FM, is one of the stalwarts of La Crosse radio, while WLSU, 88.9 FM, is UW–La Crosse's student-run station. WRQT, 95.7 FM, features "Active Rock" and WKBH, 100.1 FM, offers an alternative format.

Double Take: A Trek into Minnesota

For those feeling the need for a side trip into Minnesota, a popular 90-mile loop tour will take you across the Mississippi and then back to La Crosse. At Hager City, 17 miles south of Prescott, take the Highway 63 bridge over to Minnesota. There, you'll be greeted immediately by the charming town of **Red Wing**, namesake of footwear and pottery. It's a convenient overnight destination for travelers looping their way around the river valley but stopping short of the Twin Cities. Red Wing has a thriving arts and shopping district. Information and brochures for a driving or walking tour of the historic sites are available at area hotels and the town information center. **The Pottery Place**, 2000 W. Main Street, features 52 factory outlets and specialty shops. The restored Victorian **Saint James Hotel** on Main Street contains boutiques, shops, and the **Port of Red Wing** restaurant. Each room in the charming, four-story hotel contains Victorian antiques and decor. Rooms range from compact to spacious. The **Treasure Island Resort and Casino** is located three miles north on County Highway 18. For more information, the **Red Wing Convention and Visitors Bureau** is located at 418 Levee Street, (800) 498-3444. Red Wing hosts its share of fall events: the NAWA Fishing Tournament in late September, the Red Wing Arts Festival and woodcarvers show in mid-October, and a fall craft show in early November.

Heading southbound on marvelously scenic Highway 61 will take you along the river through Lake City, Wabasha (Minnesota's oldest city), Kellogg, Weaver, Minneiska, Minnesota City, Winona, and La Crescent, most of which, like their neighbors across the river, provide ample opportunities for itinerant travelers to stop and take a look. The **Johnny Appleseed Days** festival is held in Lake City in October. Kellogg holds a **watermelon festival** in September and a "volksmarch" along the river in October. La Crescent holds its **Apple Festival** on the third weekend in September. Apple Blossom Scenic Drive is a nice side trip any time, providing spectacular views from the bluff tops. Follow Highway 29. Apple orchards on the south loop add a special character to the scenery, with many varieties of premier Minnesota apples available at fruit stands along the way.

CHIPPEWA VALLEY
God's Country

In the back of our minds there is a small, old-fashioned town that

existed long ago, before World War I, where Victorian homes graced

elm-lined streets and big-rimmed bicycles were the only pneumatic-tired

vehicles on the streets. The boys wore knickers, the girls wore pristine white

dresses, women carried parasols, and men wore overcoats (even in July) and

smoked five-cent cigars. Everybody wore a hat. Nobody locked the doors.

No matter that none of us were alive then, or that the Good Old Days

may not have been as good as the romanticized version, we recognize the

homes and lanes and the shade trees as the home of our vision,

the birthplace of our collective nostalgia.

If the Good Old Days and Small Town U.S.A. did exist, then it had to occur when the prosperity of white pine merged seamlessly with the Victorian age in the Chippewa River Valley. For our purposes, it may come as a pleasant surprise to discover that Eau Claire and other area towns provide some of the most attractive walking tours in the state. And so, the Chippewa Valley is an ideal place for a Classic Wisconsin Weekend that presents a glimpse into trappings of late-19th-century life.

EAU CLAIRE

To begin, take any Eau Claire exit from the Interstate and follow the signs downtown. In the area of the Summit Avenue and Lake Street bridges you'll start to notice many of the University of Wisconsin–Eau Claire students walking out of necessity since the campus is linked by a footbridge across the Chippewa River. (Built on both sides of the Chippewa, UW–Eau Claire is arguably the prettiest campus in the UW system.)

Visitors, like the students, are best served on foot. Anybody with the slightest regard for architecture or somnolent, tree-lined, Old Money neighborhoods should take a mandatory stroll. Do yourself a favor. Park the car. (Owen Park off Water Street is good starting point.) Put on your walking shoes, and just go.

To say that lumber was king, that Eau Claire was known as "the sawdust city," is too subdued a statement. Lumber barons and bankers spared no expense in their personal lives. The central streets of Eau Claire are lined with one example after another of high living from a bygone era. You realize—standing at the corner of Lake and Third, looking at the four mansions on each corner, one of which looks like an antebellum plantation house replete with colonnades and two balconies—that money did grow on trees.

Eau Claire was a boomtown waiting to happen, positioned perfectly as the gateway to the northern pineries, with the Chippewa and Eau Claire rivers serving as natural highways for moving all that lumber. Sawmills started going up in 1845. For 50 years the good times rolled.

Today, in three downtown historic districts, every shape and size of home gussied up with every architectural bell and whistle imaginable remains like so much eye candy. There is but one likely response when seeing Eau Claire's painted ladies up close for the first time. Wow.

For starters there's the **Randall Park Neighborhood**. Architectural styles here include Georgian Revival, Greek Revival, Queen Anne, Gothic Revival, Second Empire, Italianate, Prairie School, Colonial Revival, Classical Revival. The district alone has more than 25 buildings registered as local or national landmarks. The **State Street Neighborhood**, on the other side of the Chippewa, has its share too, most notably four incredible Queen Annes, located on Oakwood Place near State and Summit. The **Emery Street Bungalow District** contains 60 houses built for the middle class between 1915 and 1930.

And the town has alleys. Not dark, dank alleys depicted in gangster movies, but quaint narrow lanes from yesteryear overgrown with shrubbery and offering rare views of old neighborhoods. The Randall Park area is honeycombed with alleys.

Most of the smaller (a relative word here) 19th-century Victorian homes built by those on a slightly lower economic rung (carpenters, accountants, millwrights) are no less attractive. Many an undergrad in Eau Claire has been lucky to live in some of the old abodes.

Eau Claire's Randall Park neighborhood contains dozens of Victorian homes from the town's golden age of lumber. This Colonial Revival beauty is one of four located at the corner of Third and Lake Streets.

Fortunately, Eau Claire had a diversified economy to support the people who lived in (or aspired to live in) the grand homes of Eau Claire after the lumber industry collapsed. The homes stand today, thank goodness, lost in time yet looking better every year. So take a step back in time. For a preview, look at the Randall Park Neighborhood Association's Web site, www.randallpark.com and have yourself a virtual walking tour.

If walking through time free of charge isn't cool enough, Eau Claire boasts the finest city park found in Wisconsin. Forget about the usual one-square-block green space with a gazebo and bubbler (water fountain). **Carson Park** is A 130 acres peninsula jutting into Half Moon Lake, a setting that draws easy comparison to Wisconsin State Parks and surpasses a few at that. This park is ac-cessed from Lake Street or Menomonie Streets. Facilities include a football and baseball stadium, three lighted tennis courts, 18 lighted horseshoe courts, two softball diamonds, and three museums. There are also four pavilions, which can be reserved: Oak, Birch, Pine, and Brauns's Bay. Braun's Bay pavilion features a barrier-free fishing pier and handicap-accessible restrooms. Fishing and boating on

Half Moon Lake is allowed, however, gasoline outboard motors are prohibited. Carson Park offers historic attractions as well: the Chippewa Valley Museum, the Paul Bunyan Logging Camp, and its fine baseball stadium.

It was at **Carson Park Stadium** that a nervous, 18-year old shortstop wearing number 6 made his professional baseball debut with the Eau Claire Bears, a class-C, minor-league team. On June 14, 1952, in his first two at-bats, the rookie hit two run-scoring singles. By the end of the season, Hank Aaron was named Northern League Rookie of the Year. A bronze statue of "Hammerin' Hank" stands in front of the stadium.

The **Chippewa Valley Museum** displays exhibits on Native American life and the region's logging industry and fur trade, (715) 834-7871. It also contains a turn-of-the-century ice cream parlor, eight-foot dollhouse with 21 rooms, and a museum library containing more than 10,000 historic photographs. The library is open to the public Tuesday through Friday, 1 to 5 p.m. and by appointment. The **Paul Bunyan Logging Camp** re-creates life in an 1890s logging camp. Built in 1930, the camp has a very good interpretive center; (715) 835-6200. Also present are period re-creations of the 1880s one-room **Sunnyview School** and the 1860 **Anderson Log House**, both open seasonally, (715) 834-7871. Lars and his wife raised 10 children in the two-story home. On Sundays from Memorial Day through Labor Day, the **Chippewa Valley Railroad Association** provides a scenic train ride, albeit a one-half mile train ride, on a narrow gauge loop in the park. Cost is $1, children 50 cents.

Eau Claire's longtime commercial district and hot spot, **Water Street**, today owes its prosperity to thirsty college students. As a result, the fun is skewed decidedly toward monumental weekend drinking binges. For the UW students who live it up as only UW students can, Water Street ranks with the hottest bar scenes in the state. **The Pioneer, Nasty Habit**, and **Brat Cabin** are old standbys, a slew of other bars can be found behind the venerable storefronts. The **Camaraderie**, a bar-restaurant since 1971 and a Water Street landmark building since 1876, was destroyed by fire in January 2001, breaking the hearts of countless patrons who had frequented "the Cam" over the years. A new face on the block is **Mona Lisa's** restaurant, a refreshing departure from the beer pens and fast food places nearby. Try the Bourbon Scallops. Of all the haunts along Water Street, however, one stands out from the rest —**The Joynt.** (See the accompanying sidebar.)

Double Take: The Joynt

An Eau Claire tavern called The Joynt has the misfortune of being lumped together with the cacophonous UW–Eau Claire bars crowding Water Street. That's too bad, because this is more than just another college watering hole.

An ancient saloon measuring just 22 feet wide and 65 feet long and containing a decor best described as Lumberjack Revival, the Joynt, 322 Water Street, defies easy description. That's exactly the way longtime owner Bill Nolte wants it. "This place will never be a destination," he says, drawing a distinction between his establishment and a universe of bars that frame their own news clips and offer "a ridiculous number of beers on tap."

There are other telltale indications that this is no ordinary bar: no neon signs hanging in the windows, no light beer sold, a jukebox selection that ranges from Bessie Smith to the Beastie Boys to pop crooners from India—and beyond.

The music is important. From 1974 to 1989, this little venue played host to the best jazz and blues artists performing as they made their way between Chicago and Minneapolis—their portraits hang all over the place. The live music has ended, but Nolte, who believes "music is the great democratizer," has instilled his philosophy in the jukebox. "If you don't like what's playing, take out a dollar and play what you want."

The Joynt offers a dizzying array of CDs. "If there's a better selection in the world, I want to see it," Nolte challenges. Don't try looking. And the songs that are played least remain on the jukebox.

Beside the music, you'll find a barber's chair, a beer can collection exceeding 700 artifacts, thousands of postcards from lonely Joynt fans stranded around the world, 8 oz. tap beers (Point, Grain Belt, Leinie's, Berghoff . . . no light), wood floors, bright lighting, a pool table, and a dog.

Nolte did break down and have a neon sign designed to hang above the cash register. It says No Light Beer. "Show me a bar that does not sell light beer," Nolte implores.

Is the Joynt a saloon? A beatnik bar? A pool room? A juke joint? A North Woods neighborhood tavern? The answer is yes. This patron ranks the one-and-only Joynt as the state's top tavern, bar or joint.

Winding along the Chippewa River through the heart of Eau Claire and the UW campus is a scenic multi-use trail that eventually becomes **Chippewa River State Bike Trail**. The first eight miles are paved and frequented by walkers, joggers, in-line skaters and bikers; there's beautiful scenery along the chiseled banks of the Chippewa River—might be the prettiest urban trail in the state. The city

An impressive railroad trestle links the Red Cedar State Trail and the Chippewa Valley State Trail 14 miles south of Menomonie.

path evolves into the hard-packed gravel of the bike trail, with trailheads at Carson Park and the Highway 85 wayside. The route traces the quiet countryside and meanders with the Chippewa River until it connects with the **Red Cedar State Trail** at an impressive railroad trestle south of Downsville. The bike trail is 23 miles to the Red Cedar link including the eight miles in the city. Daily fees or annual State Trail Pass required for ages 16 and over on the bike trail section.

Interestingly, even with all those Victorian homes, Eau Claire does not have a downtown B&B. But Chippewa Falls and Menomonie do.

CHIPPEWA FALLS

Chippewa Falls has won well-deserved awards for its downtown preservation efforts. The crowning achievement came in 2000 when the community was named one of a dozen "Distinctive Destinations" by the National Trust for Historic Preservation. The town got the award because it saved several sites from the wrecking ball: **Moyer's Clock Service**, 29 West Spring, is the oldest building and the only remaining wooden structure. The **Marsh Rainbow Bridge Arch Bridge**, which survived the flood of 1934, and the **Chippewa Shoe Building**, at Bay and River Streets, are on the National Register. There are 12 historic structures total, including the Union Block, 123 North Bridge Street.

There is, of course, Leinie's. In 1867, Jacob Leinenkugel discovered the spring water that would be the key ingredient in his beer. Thousands of faithful Leinie's consumers visit each year to see brewing operation and browse the gift shop for memorabilia adorned with the Indian maiden logo at the **Leinenkugel Brewing Company**, 1 Jefferson Avenue Highway 124, Chippewa Falls, (715) 723-5557. Tour reservations suggested, admission free. Gift shop open Monday through Friday, 11 a.m.–4 p.m., Saturday 9:30 a.m.–3 p.m., Sunday 11 a.m.–3 p.m.

Irvine Park in Chippewa Falls contains a free zoo, but also on the grounds are the Glen Loch Dam and Overlook, a museum, and old school house. The park is free.

Outside of town, you can walk off some of the Leine's on the **Old Abe State Trail**, the 17.4 mile paved route following the Chippewa River from **Lake Wissota State Park** to **Brunet Island State Park** near Cornell. Lake Wissota park has 81 well-spaced campsites, some secluded, and a sandy beach. The park also rents canoes and has a permanent pier for fishing and a public access to the lake; (715) 726-7880. Brunet Island State Park has 69 campsites on 1,225 acres; (888) 523-3866.

McGilvray's Victorian Bed & Breakfast, 312 W. Columbia Street, is a century old home located in a quiet Chippewa Falls neighborhood. Its front entrance has a Georgian Revival portico featuring two-story columns. Guests can relax on one of three screened porches. Phone (715) 720-1600. **Pleasant View Bed & Breakfast**, 16649 96th Avenue, is a quiet country setting on Lake Wissota, (715) 382-4401.

MENOMONIE

Another example of Victorian-age architecture and design at its best is the **Mabel Tainter Memorial Theater**, 205 Main Street, Menomonie, about 25 miles west of Eau Claire. The lavish interior contains hand-stenciled walls and ceilings, carved mahogany, a marble staircase, and bronze opera seats. The theater presents a full calendar of modern performing arts. Seats 313 patrons. Phone (715) 235-0001. Guided tours given hourly every day at 1–4 p.m.; $5 adults, $4 seniors, children $3.

Other 19th-century attractions downtown include the 1868 John Holly Knapp House and the 1846 Wilson place. **Wilson Place**, a museum today, was the estate of Senator James Stout, founder of the University of Wisconsin–Stout. The **Rassbach Heritage Museum**, 1820 Wakanda Street, contains an underwear exhibit from the days when Victoria's Secret was secret; (715) 232-8685.

Winding south from Menomonie, the **Red Cedar State Trail** is the local rails-to-trails project providing bikers with a quiet 15-mile route south through

The opulent Mabel Tainter Memorial Theater in Menomonie, built in 1890, still hosts a full calendar of events.

Irvington and Downsville. At Downsville, you might want to take a peek at the **Empire in Pine Lumber Museum,** the remaining buildings of what was one of the largest lumber camps in the Chippewa Valley. An old iron trestle bridge links the route with the Chippewa River Trail from Eau Claire. (Nearby ruins are all that's left of Dunnville, once the county seat and busy steamboat stop.) The two trails form a 37-mile route between Menomonie and Eau Claire.

There are a couple of places to spend the night that evoke the Menomonie's past. **Hansen Heritage House Bed & Breakfast Inn,** 919 13th Street Southeast, was built by Torger Hansen during the peak of 19th-century logging industry. Its slogan: "Capture the moment . . . Recapture an era!" Phone (715) 235-0119. **Oaklawn Bed & Breakfast,** 423 Technology Drive East, was once the farmhouse of a lumber baron. Phone (715) 235-6155.

WHERE'S THE FISH FRY?

Lake Wissota is home to the popular **Water's Edge** on County S, (715) 723-0161. In Chippewa Falls, it's **Randy's,** 12 E. Spring Street. **Wally's,** 1505 N. Clairmont, Eau Claire, (715) 832-0880, has been the fish fry palace for 50 years. The **Old 400 Depot Café,** Menomonie, is a reconstruction of the Menomonie Junction depot that witnessed one of the great train feats of its day: the Chicago & Northwestern's 400 Line rolled through here on the way to Minneapolis, setting speed records for traveling 400 miles in 400 minutes and shaving over three hours off the previous time. Steam and whistles are long gone, but the food is making a name for itself. Located at 2616 Hills Court; (715) 235-1993. Also, Menomonie locals flock to the **Bolo Inn** supper club, 207 Pine Street, on the north side of town, (715) 235-5596.

READ ALL ABOUT IT

The weekly *Country Today,* published in Eau Claire, reports rural and agricultural news to more than 31,000 readers in the region, making it one of the most widely read weekly newspapers in the state (second only to the *Packer Report*). The *Chippewa Herald* publishes daily except Sundays to 7,200 area residents, the *Eau Claire Leader Telegram* is the largest daily newspaper in the region and issues a Sunday edition. Pick up the weekly *Bloomer Advance, Cadott Sentinel,* the *Cornell & Lake Holcombe Courier,* or the *Stanley Republican,* each with a circulation of a couple thousand readers, for small-town flavor.

HAVE YOU HEARD?

WCFW in Chippewa Falls, 105.7 on the FM dial, has the middle-of-the-road format traditionally found on AM stations: that's a mix of music, local news, talk, and polka coming through in stereo! Eau Claire has 13 radio stations; WAXX, 104.5 FM, and WAYY, 790 AM, are the old standbys with country music and news/talk formats respectively. WBIZ, 1400 AM and 100.7 FM, has sports and contemporary hits.

ST. CROIX RIVER VALLEY
Sparkling Waters

The St. Croix River holds a number of singular distinctions: It was included in the National Park Service's first list of National Wild and Scenic Rivers in 1968; it's the only river in the world protected from development for its entire length; and it was an obvious location for Wisconsin's first state park in 1900.

For centuries, the river has been an important link between the Mississippi River and Lake Superior, first for Chippewa Indians and French fur traders, then as the carrier of huge rafts of white pine logs, now as Land of Oz for recreationalists.

Today, Hudson, located at the intersections of Highway 35 and I-94, is the unofficial hub of the river valley. Just a short drive south is Prescott, at the confluence of the St. Croix and Mississippi. North from Hudson is Osceola, St. Croix Falls, and the secluded upper reaches of the river. Communities with a fair share of character remaining from the white pine days are found on both sides of the river in Wisconsin and Minnesota. With the still-pristine river, miles of scenic wonders, and many picturesque villages, the St. Croix River Valley makes for a terrific Classic Wisconsin Weekend.

THE ST. CROIX

The **St. Croix National Scenic Riverway** begins at its namesake flowage near Solon Springs, about 25 miles south of Superior, where the Brule River ends. At Gordon Dam it starts as stream winding through forests, marshes, and wide valleys. At Riverside, the river becomes wider, deeper, and slower, making the area popular for small powerboats and canoes. The last segment below St. Croix Falls becomes wider yet and more civilized, marked by pleasant towns and numerous pleasure craft.

The upper reaches of the St. Croix are great for canoeing and primitive camping. A few rapids are located here but none are considered whitewater. Outfitters can be found in nearby towns. Along the Wisconsin-Minnesota border are state forests, notably Governor Knowles State Forest, and state and county parks offering developed campsites, hiking, and cross-country skiing.

Bass and muskie can be found along the entire riverway. Anglers favor the northern reaches. Otters and birds such as osprey compete for fish. The presence of these and other animals and waterfowl draw both birdwatchers and hunters.

The **St. Croix Chippewa Reservation** consists of 11 separate communities in a four-county area. Reservation boundaries include some 3,000 acres of forested land throughout Barron, Burnett, Polk, and Washburn Counties in Wisconsin and in Pine County in east-central Minnesota. The **St. Croix Wild Rice Powwow** has been an annual event for more than 20 years. The three-day celebration takes place at the Tribal Center in Hertel in late August. For more information, call (800) 236-2195.

ST. CROIX FALLS

The hub for outdoor recreation in this scenic valley and the northernmost community on this tour is the town of St. Croix Falls. The proximity to Minneapolis and the river's width and calm surface make the lower reaches below the St. Croix Falls popular for boaters and water skiers. For more information about the area, contact the St. Croix Scenic Riverway, P.O. Box 708, St. Croix Falls, WI 54024; phone (715) 483-3284.

Interstate State Park, located in St. Croix Falls near the junction of Highways 8 and 35, is Wisconsin's oldest state park. It's not hard to see why this was the obvious place to initiate the state park system. An early visitor called it "one of God's beauteous spots on earth." The park is located on the east side of the **Dalles of the St. Croix River**, a scenic gorge cut out of the bedrock by glacial activity. The canyon walls rise 200 feet above the river. Scenic overlooks and strange rock formations with the requisite campy names (Old Man of the Dalles) are found in the park. Hiking trails, swimming beach, and a bathhouse are located within the 1,300-acre park, along with 85 campsites. Phone (715) 483-3747.

The Dalles of the St. Croix River, the reason the area was selected as Wisconsin's first state park in 1900.

Boat trips through the Dalles leave Taylor Falls, on the Minnesota side by the Highway 8 bridge, daily from May 1 to mid-October. Half-hour and 80-minute sightseeing cruises are offered aboard double-decker paddle wheelers. Dinner cruises also are available. Fares start at $6.50 for the 3-minute trip, $8.50 for the longer one. Phone (800) 447-4958.

The **St. Croix Visitor Center** in St. Croix Falls, at the intersection of Hamilton and Massachusetts Avenues, serves as park headquarters. Local history and multimedia presentations about the river are offered daily. Phone (715) 483-3284. Near the tourist information center (intersection of Highways 35 and 8) is the **Gandy Dancer State Trail**, a 47-mile bike trail running north to Danbury. (For the hardcore biker, another 51-mile leg continues north to Superior, crossing into Minnesota and back again.) The trail takes its name from the Gandy Tool Company. In the 19th century, its equipment helped build railroad lines, and so railroad workers in general became known as Gandy Dancers.

OSCEOLA

Charming little Osceola, seven miles south of St. Croix Falls, is located on top of the bluffs along the St. Croix River Valley. Once a popular tourist stop for excursion boats, tourists would follow a boardwalk to **Cascade Falls**, located at 104 North Cascade Street, where Osceola Creek drops 108 feet on its way to the St. Croix River. The 25-foot falls can be observed from an observation deck and below is **Wilkie Glen**. Osceola has 10 historic buildings, including the former courthouse and the only barrel-shaped art deco Mobil gas station remaining in Wisconsin, located at 202 N. Cascade.

Follow the boardwalk to Cascade Falls, located in Wilkie Glen just below Osceola's quaint downtown.

The **Osceola & St. Croix Valley Railway** departs from the former Soo Line depot and offers 50- or 90-minute narrated excursions aboard restored trains along the river valley. Tickets can be purchased in the fully restored (circa 1916) depot. Trips depart Saturday and Sunday at 11 a.m., 1:00, and 2:30 p.m., Memorial Day to October 31. Fare is $10–13; over 62, $9–12; ages 5–15, $5–7. Family rates available. Phone (715) 755-3570 or (800) 711-2591.

HUDSON

About 25 miles south of Osceola, Hudson has become one of Wisconsin's fastest growing communities. Just 20 minutes east of the Twin Cities along I-94, the town is populated by many people who work in Minnesota but who prefer to reside in Hudson to maintain their peace of mind. And who can blame them? Like other towns in the St. Croix and Chippewa Valleys, Hudson maintains a palpable connection to its past. Vestiges of its boom years remain in the downtown and residential areas, especially among the houses along Third and Vine. There are four historic districts, and it's a good walking town.

Among the town's featured homes is the **Octagon House**, 1004 Third Street, a unique eight-sided dwelling built in 1855. It was home to Judge John Moffat who came to Hudson from New York. (Hudson's name comes from Yankees who were reminded of the Hudson River Valley back home.) The county historical society owns the home, which is a museum complex including the gardens and carriage house. It's open May through October and for holiday tours. Contact (715) 386-2654.

With Interstate State Park in St. Croix Falls, Willow River State Park just north of Hudson, and Kinnickinnic State Park just south of Hudson, the area has become a state park mecca. **Willow River State Park**—3,155 acres of forests, lakes, waterfalls, and panoramic river scenery—is one of the most popular attractions in the Hudson area. The park includes campsites, hiking trails, and two lakes for fishing, sailing, and canoeing. Contact (715) 386-5931. The area was once called Buena Vista, or "beautiful view."

Kinnickinnic State Park features 1,242 acres of open prairie and hardwood forest. Parking and a picnic area are located near the river's gorge. The park also includes a wide, sandy river delta available to river travelers for overnight camping. It's south of Hudson on County F, (715) 425-1129.

Lakefront Park in Hudson is one of many local places along the river to fish, feed the ducks, or just enjoy the river. There is a beach too, staffed with a lifeguard from noon to 7 p.m. daily, June through mid-August. The park also features a playground, boat launch, trailer parking area, band shell, and picnic area. Docking facilities are available for a fee. Then enjoy the mile walk across the Old Toll Bridge to Minnesota.

For an overnight stay in this romantic river town, travelers can choose from the economical to the unapologetically luxurious. The former is found at the **Royal Inn**, a clean, 30-unit motel with prices starting at $41. The latter can be found in the restored **Jefferson-Day House**, an 1857 Italianate home listed on the National Register of Historic Places. Located at 1109 Third Street, (715) 386-7111, it's a short walk from Hudson's downtown shops and restaurants. And you'll want to do some walking—a four-course gourmet breakfast is served daily in the dining room.

Fond of B&Bs? Besides the Jefferson-Day House, there are at least four good ones in Hudson. One of them, the **Phipps Inn**, 1005 Third Street, (715)

385-9002, is the grande dame of Queen Anne houses, a Victorian dating back to 1884. All of the guest rooms have fireplaces, double whirlpools, private baths, and queen-sized beds. The Phipps Inn was named Wisconsin Innkeepers Association's 1994 Pro-perty of the Year and has appeared on the cover of several magazines. Other B&Bs include the **Baker Brewster Victorian Inn**, (715) 381-2895; **Escape by the Lake**, (715) 381-2871; and **Grapevine Inn Bed & Breakfast**, (715) 386-1989.

SOUTH TO RIVER FALLS AND PRESCOTT

Named after the falls on the Kinnickinnic River, River Falls is home to a UW campus and at least 12 downtown buildings of historic significance. **Veterans Park**, at the corner of Main and Elm, is connected to **Heritage Park** by a footbridge spanning the Kinnickinnic. Try to find the city's old fire bell, in service until 1957, now resting quietly in Heritage Park. South from the park is a pathway that was once a railroad spur line.

Walking along the banks of the "Kinni" on any warm summer evening will reveal anglers prospecting the Class I trout stream for hatches. (Up to 6,000 trout per mile are present in some parts of the river.) Originating from springs three miles north of I-94 in the center of St. Croix County, the river flows 23 miles southwest before meeting the St. Croix River. River Falls is located at the river's midpoint and is the only city on the river. The stretch from its origin to River Falls consists of 12 miles of prime trout fishing featuring native brook trout; below River Falls brown trout predominate.

The **Kinni Creek Lodge & Outfitters** caters to both travelers and anglers. Fishing guides are available through Kinni Creek if you're looking to land some trout. The place is located along 180 feet of trout stream. You can practically fly-fish right outside the door! This is not a fancy destination, but it provides good comfortable lodging, 545 N. Main Street, River Falls, (715) 425-REST (7378) or (877) 504-9705.

To the southwest of River Falls, Prescott is one of the oldest towns on the Mississippi River, dating to 1839, when soldier and fur trader Philander Prescott built a cabin here. Prescott later operated the first ferry across the mouth of the St. Croix, married the daughter of a Sioux Indian chief, and sired nine children. Ironically, he was killed in 1862 during an Indian uprising.

The town is situated at the junction of the St. Croix and the Mississippi Rivers in Pierce County. Today, visitors can clearly see the line where the blue waters of the St. Croix join the dark waters of the Mississippi. Be sure to visit the overlook located downtown in **Mercord Mill Park**.

In the mid-19th century, Prescott was a prosperous river town, but it suffered hard times when steamboats were replaced by railroads. In recent decades, tourism has saved the day, with visitors lured by the scenery of the St. Croix and Mississippi. Still, Prescott maintains its small-town charm with a population of 3,550 people. The town also marks the northern end of the Great River Road in

Wisconsin. Visitor information is available at 237 Broad Street North, 54021, (715) 262-3284.

WHERE'S THE FISH FRY?

According to Paige Olson at the Kinni Creek Lodge & Outfitters (if they can tell you where to catch fish, they must know where to eat it), "Popular fish fries in and around River Falls are at the River Falls Country Club, Joe's Valley between River Falls and Prescott, and the West Wind Supper Club. Most other restaurants also have Friday fish."

READ ALL ABOUT IT

Weekly papers are the *Amery Free Press, County Ledger Press* in Balsam Lake, *Baldwin Bulletin, Tribune Press Reporter* in Glenwood City, the *Central St. Croix News* in Hammond, the *New Richmond News,* the tiny *Woodville Leader* (circulation 520), the *Dunn County News, Hudson Star Observer, Frederick Inter-County Leader,* and the *Osceola Sun.*

HAVE YOU HEARD?

Minneapolis radio stations will come through loud and clear in the St. Croix Valley, but for local flavor try WDGY, 630 AM, Hudson, and WWLC, 104.9 FM, Milltown; classic country is heard from WIXK, 1590 AM and 107.1 FM, New Richmond; and WXCE, 1260 AM, in Amery, plays oldies.

CHAPTER TWENTY

HAYWARD AND CABLE

Lumberjacks and Big Fish

In lumberjack lingo it's called the "boom run." Starting from a sprinter's position on a dock, competitors dash across eight floating logs extended end-to-end—about 30 yards—before leaping onto the opposing dock, spinning around, and high-tailing it back.

Most of us break a sweat just thinking about sprinting 60 yards. In Hayward, lumberjacks and lumberjills have little trouble running across logs that are bobbing and spinning in the water, but even the best boom runners find themselves in the pond now and again.

Welcome to Hayward, and the hundreds of square miles surrounding it, where they grow trees, muskies, and lumberjacks. And nothing says Classic Wisconsin Weekend more than a few days spent in the North Woods amid tall timber as far as the eye can see and ornery fish defying you to haul them in. If you go to Hayward at the right time, you can experience the scent of pine and sawdust, the crack of axes on tree trunks echoing from the "Lumberjack Bowl," and folks turning out in droves to support local boom runners and pole climbers who just happen to be the best in the world.

The sawdust is flying at Hayward's Lumberjack Bowl, a former holding pond for a lumber company.

The region begs your participation whatever the season. The vast green expanses host the world's best-known cross-country ski race and an exceptional system of off-road bicycle trails. Canoeing the shallow waters of the local rivers began centuries before anybody knew what "weekend getaway" meant. World-record fish have been reeled in from area lakes.

And intertwined with the area's natural history is the story of how people have tried to tame its wilderness. Tales of Indians, missionaries, voyageurs, loggers and bootleggers still linger. All this human history and natural beauty make Hayward and Chequamegon National Forest one of the state's must-visit areas.

Your first stop in Hayward should be **Scheer's Lumberjack Shows**. Fred Scheer, it's worth noting, is a four-time world logrolling champion. And his prowess is shared by other family members. His sister, Judy Hoeschler, is the women's multiple logrolling champion; brother Robert Scheer, is two-time speed climbing champion; sister "Timber" Tina is a title holder who makes a living in timber sports entertainment; nephew Cassidy is the 1999 boom run champion; niece Carly is starting in professional competition; then there are the four Hoeschler kids who are emerging on the scene. Some kids dream of being quarterbacks or cheerleaders. In Hayward, when a baby takes those first tentative steps it means one thing: get the logrolling shoes.

Scheer's lumberjack shows run the gamut of events that are becoming extremely popular on ESPN. After seeing the show, you'll be able to tell the difference between a single and double buck, a hot saw and an underhand chop, a standing chop and tree topping. As well, the clown acts taking place atop 90-foot poles are as funny as they are startling.

And all this takes place in, what else, the **Lumberjack Bowl**, the old holding pond for the Weyerhauser North Lumber Company. There is plenty of bleacher seating and parking available. The rustic **Lake Café**, a popular and scenic dining spot in its own right, is located pond-side, allowing visitors to enjoy a hearty meal (lumberjack-style, naturally) and watch the show from the deck.

Shows are held rain or shine at the bowl (on County B in Hayward) from Memorial Day to Labor Day. Call (715) 634- 6923. A series of craft and gift shops are on the bowl grounds. Admission $7.95 for adults, $5.95 for kids, under 4 free.

THE BEST LUMBERJACKS IN THE WORLD

To take in timber sports at their finest, be sure to head to these parts in late July, when the sawdust really flies. That's when the Lumberjack Bowl plays host to a three-day gathering of the best jacks and jills in timber sports at the **Lumberjack World Championships** (LWC). True to its name, the event draws competitors from the around the globe. Canada, New Zealand, and Australia send their best representatives, tremendous athletes all. When LWC convenes, however, it's worth the trip north to cheer our home-state competitors . . . our world champions.

One of them could be Sean Duffy, a prosecutor in the Ashland County district attorney's office. Growing up in Hayward, he started log rolling at age 5 and speed climbing (sprinting up 60 and 90 foot poles) at 13. He holds two speed climbing titles. Sean's older brother, Brian, holds five logrolling titles. Their niece, Taylor, was the 1998 women's boom run champion. One of the reasons that Sean is so good is that he went to logrolling school to learn his skills. Kids here take lessons much the same as other youngsters would take soccer lessons and swimming lessons in other communities.

The LWC was established to perpetuate logging history in northwestern Wisconsin. It succeeds. Logging culture is as thick as the forests around here, in part because of the annual gathering. The roster of competitors reads like a local phone book. All told, better than a quarter of the competitors in LWC are Wisconsin natives, nearly all having ties to Hayward. Several families have three or four members competing and holding titles.

The LWC is a leader as well in the recognition and support of the women's events in the timber sports arena. In recent years, the women's events have proven to be some of the most popular crowd-pleasers, as some incredible female athletes compete in the boom run or logrolling.

Roughly 12,000 spectators attend the LWC, but the crowds never become overwhelming in the cozy Lumberjack Bowl. You should, however, book your lodging accommodations early. General admission to the LWC is $11 per adult per day or $25 for a 3-day pass; less for seniors and kids. Reserved seats are $13–$30. Call (715) 634-2484 or log onto www.lumberjackworldchampionships.com.

The top timber sports athletes in the world compete every July at the Lumberjack World Championships.

Once a dying art, timber sports are alive and growing today thanks to Hayward. Be it Fred Scheer's Lumberjack Shows or the Lumberjack World Championships, this is great family fun for observers . . . and participants.

ATTACK OF THE GIANT MUSKIE

Ever stick yourself with a fishhook? Congratulations, you're eligible for induction into the **National Freshwater Fishing Hall of Fame and Museum**. Fishhooks that have caught more than bluegills are exhibited in fine fashion at this facility. The perpetrating hook, victim, hometown, date of poke, and location are actually documented by doctors who contribute to the museum as much as they contribute to the health and well-being of anglers everywhere. Booster shots not included.

The hall is best known for the giant muskie out front. Granted, we're proud of our well-stocked lakes, but this—this is a four-story, fiberglass muskie that looks like it was lying around the back lot of a science fiction movie. Rodan's Fish Fry! The muskie's mouth is a scenic overlook to more gigantic fiberglass fish at ground level. Inside you'll find the aforementioned exhibit—"When Hooks

Attack"—with an impressive collection of outboard motors, rods and reels and tackle boxes. Look there's grandpa's slop bucket. The exhibit called "Poor Taxidermy" is a real hoot. The hall serves as the repository for freshwater fishing records as well.

Hayward is proud of its big fish, obviously. These surreal catches are the found at the National Freshwater Fishing Hall of Fame.

The Hall of Fame and Museum is located in downtown Hayward at the junction of Highway 27 and County B. It's open April 15 to November 1, 10 a.m.–4:30 p.m. (5 p.m. summer). Phone (715) 634-4440.

If you haven't had your fill of strange animal exhibits, stop by the Moccasin Bar. This place has poker-playing raccoons. Some of the world's largest muskies, truly huge fish (one is 67 pounds) are here, preserved under glass, although Louis Spray's world record holder at 69-plus pounds is on display at the hall of fame. There are two Moccasin Bars: one located in downtown Hayward, another containing a museum next to the Lumberjack Bowl.

BIKING THE CAMBA SYSTEM

When you arrive in the Hayward area, you'll think that you've died and gone to mountain bike (or cross-country skiing) heaven. The region, which includes the town of Cable about 20 miles north, is best known for the world's largest cross-country ski race, the **American Birkebiner**, held every February. It's the largest such event in North America, the Boston Marathon of cross-country skiing. More than 6,000 skiers glide 51 kilometers over the hilly terrain between Hay-ward and Cable.

But during the more temperate months, mountain biking is the thing to do along the same trails used by the Birkie and along hundreds of miles of other trails. The vast expanse of tracks, combined with the natural atmosphere, deservedly places the **Cable Area Mountain Bike Association (CAMBA)** system among the best in North America. We're not talking about recreation suited only to Generation X daredevils who like to hammer their way through woodlands—although it's perfect for that. No, cyclists of all abilities, from families to extreme riders, can find a favorite path among the system's 300 miles, which cover more than a million acres. These are among the most beautiful trails ever cut, routes rolling through a wilderness of striking beauty.

Biking the CAMBA system is the best way to immerse yourself in the beauty of the North Woods and do so at a level suited to your ability. After all, area cyclists created the CAMBA system in and around the Chequamegon National Forest (as well as Bayfield and Sawyer counties) to make this vast area available to everyone.

The cost is free (except for a $3 parking fee at some Forest Service trailheads), and the system is user-friendly. Routes are mapped and marked. Markers include frequent "You Are Here" posts with a number corresponding to the map, signboards with more maps, and map dispensers at each trailhead. The routes follow a variety of paths, including logging roads, fire lanes, snowmobile trails, and ski trails (single and double tracks). There are no paved bike paths. The landscape consists of rolling terrain with lakes, rivers, streams, ridges, and meadows. The entire system is heavily wooded. You'll see deer and bald eagles, maybe some black bears, and any number of other forest animals. Fall colors begin in early September and peak in early October, a time of gold aspen and red maple leaves.

The system is divided into six clusters, each with one or more trailheads. Trail clusters are located in the communities of Cable, Delta, Drummond, Hayward, Namekagon, and Seeley. The Drummond cluster has easy trails for families and beginners, while most trails are intermediate in difficulty. Bike shops in the area can direct you to riding that best suits your ability. Log on to http://cambatrails.org for more information. One other bicycle event is worth noting. In the summer, the **Chequamegon Fat Tire Festival** uses the Birkie routes for the largest off-road bike race in the United States.

CHEQUAMEGON NATIONAL FOREST

If Nicolet National Forest in northeast Wisconsin is immense, then Chequamegon National Forest to the west is, well, even bigger. There are small nations that hope to be as big as the Chequamegon.

Chequamegon (which comes from an Ojibwe word, *sho-wah-ma-gon*, that means "place of shallow water") is remote and has few visitors, making it ideal for wilderness adventures. Its lakes are famed for the size and number of the fish that anglers haul in, and its many waterways offer exciting opportunities for canoe enthusiasts of all skill levels. Chequamegon's recreation possibilities are boundless, including about 800 lakes located within its 856,938 acres.

CHEQUAMEGON BY AUTO

The Chequamegon's main auto route is Highway 77, which is designated as the **Great Divide National Scenic Highway**. This picturesque 60-mile road can be breathtaking at dawn or dusk, after new-fallen snow or on a bright autumn day. It passes through the heart of the Forest from the town of Glidden in the east to Lost Lake in the west. There are thousands of miles of other (paved and gravel) roads to enjoy as well.

Areas of interest within the forest that are easily accessed by motor vehicles include the **Penokee Overlook** located in the Glidden Ranger District just west of the town of Mellen. There are two unique timber bridges found in the forest —**Smith Rapids Covered Bridge** and **Teal River Bridge**. In the Marengo River Valley, three historic Swedish settlement sites are open for self-guided tours.

The **Round Lake** log-driving dam, the last remaining structure of its type in Wisconsin, can be found 16 miles east of Fifield just north of Highway 70. The dam was built around 1880 by Frederick Weyerhauser to help move winter timber harvests downstream.

In the Glidden Ranger District 12 miles west of Mellen, **St. Peter's Dome** and **Morgan Falls** stand above the surrounding landscape at 1,710 feet above sea level, the second-highest point in Wisconsin. Morgan Falls tumbles 80 feet over black granite as it rolls through the valley.

CHEQUAMEGON BY FOOT, PEDAL, AND HOOF

Two hundred miles of developed trails in the Chequamegon are open to hiking, horseback riding, and, in many cases, mountain biking. Winding through the forest are segments of two trials that are part of the National Scenic Trail System. The **North Country Trail** winds for 60 miles through the forest's glacial terrain and scenic beauty. The **Ice Age Trail** stretches across Wisconsin; the 42-mile section passing through the Chequamegon follows the cusp of the final glacial advance and is highlighted with scenic vistas of glacial wetlands. In addition, the **Rock Lake National Recreation Trail** provides more opportunities for viewing the glacial landscape and pristine lakes.

For the truly remote outdoor experience, there are nearly 11,000 acres of rugged and serene beauty in two wilderness areas reserved for foot travel only. And they are located close to one another. The **Rainbow Lake Wilderness** is about five miles north of the town of Drummond, while the **Porcupine Lake Wilderness** is about the same distance to the southeast. Only the loons will break the silence. For more information about Chequamegon call (715) 362-1300, or log onto the forest service Web site at www.fs.fed.us.

ON THE WATER

One of the most popular activities in the Chequamegon is canoeing on the 632 miles of rivers and streams—especially the Chippewa, Jump, Yellow, Flambeau, Bad, and Namekagon Rivers, which served as the major routes of travel in the 19th century. The Namekagon is a National Wild and Scenic River with Class II and Class III rapids.

Boaters can find easy access (and few people) on the abundant lakes within the forest. Lakes and streams are thick with muskie, northern pike, bass, walleye, panfish, and trout. For good fishing tips, stop at any of the ranger districts: Park Falls, Medford, Hayward, Washburn, or Glidden. Local sporting goods stores can also be helpful.

CAMPING

Campsites are available on a first-come, first-served basis. For information call (715) 762-2461 or write 1170 Fourth Avenue S, Park Falls, 54552. The Drummond area contains sites on Perch Lake and Two Lakes. Namekagon Lake near Cable is a popular camping area. In the Clam Lake vicinity, Day Lake, East Twin Lake, and Moose Lake offer campsites.

CHIPPEWA FLOWAGE

If you love fishing, the **Chippewa Flowage** is the place—and that says something in Wisconsin's lake country where good fishing may be as close as the next boat landing. Also called Lake Chippewa Flowage, or more commonly "the Big Chip," this watery gem is Wisconsin's third-largest lake, and it remains in a pristine state: 15,000 acres of water, 140 islands, and more than 200 miles of undeveloped shoreline, a veritable universe of angling. Muskie, walleye, crappie, smallmouth and largemouth bass, perch, panfish are all here. No less an authority than *Muskie* magazine called this flowage "a Muskie Factory." The world record muskie, at 69 lb. 11 oz., was caught here in 1949. Take a virtual tour at www.chippewaflowage.com.

The Big Chip caters to avid fishermen to canoeists and kayakers who can move quietly along undeveloped shorelines. Camping at one of the several island campsites is as secluded as you can get.

In general, the angling opportunities, according to the Department of Natural Resources, range from "abundant" for walleye, crappie, perch, and bluegills; "common" for muskie, northern, and bass. Minnows, carp, suckers, and bullheads can be found, even sturgeon. Catch varies by year, season, weather, food conditions, and fish population cycles, but catch-rates and sizes compare favorably with statewide and regional averages.

Camping is allowed at no charge on a first-come, first-served basis at 16 island sites accessible by water only. There is a 10-day limit on camping at all state campsites within the Chippewa Flowage. The DNR regularly checks campsites and visitors may not leave unattended camping equipment to hold the site. You may camp at any of the existing campsites designated on DNR maps. You cannot establish new campsites. Other experiences from rustic campsites to full hook-up facilities are available at private facilities on the flowage.

Those in the know say that winter is one of the best times to visit the area. That's when the local power company lowers the lake 12 feet to generate power, exposing sand and rock bars that provide picture-perfect winter scenes.

THE HIDEOUT

The Hideout in Couderay, 17 miles southeast of Hayward, was Al Capone's weekend "cottage" to which he retreated when presiding over a vast mob empire in Chicago became burdensome. Built from native fieldstone, the cottage includes a massive fireplace, mahogany spiral staircases, stained-glass window . . . and a machine gun tower. Depression-era stories abound of smugglers' airplanes landing on nearby Pike Lake and Big Al visiting the local barbershop. (Imagine handling a straight-edged razor on Al Capone's neck under the watchful eyes of his entourage.) The Hideout has been on the auction block, so call (715) 945-2746 to make sure it's open.

ACCOMMODATIONS

There is no lack of accommodations in and around Hayward—hotels, motels, cabins, campgrounds, and North Woods resorts—plenty of choices to suit your style. Advance reservations are a necessity during the peak months of July and August. The **Best Western Northern Pine Inn**, the **Edelweiss Motel**, **Americinn**, and the **Super 8** are reliable standbys; the **Grand Pines Resort** and **Ross's Teal Lake Lodge** (cottages) are good accommodations outside of Hayward. The **Lumberjack Mansion Inn** is an 1887 Queen Anne Victorian close to the shops and restaurants in Hayward.

A departure from the many Victorian B&Bs in the state, **Stout Trout Bed & Breakfast**, W4244 County F, Springbrook, about 13 miles southwest of Hayward, is a 1920s fishing lodge with a private bay, 40 acres of neighboring rolling farmland, and large tracts of public forests. Phone (715) 466-2790. **Connors Bed & Breakfast** is a "country estate" in Cable, north of Hayward. It's within walking distance of the Birkebeiner ski trails, CAMBA mountain biking trails, and four area lakes. Phone (715) 798-3661.

WHERE'S THE FISH FRY?

Ask a dozen people and you'll get a dozen different answers. The best response came from the folks at the LWC who simply said, "Take your pick." Walleye is found on practically every menu in this neck of the woods. Family restaurants tend to go with cod. Ask locals where their favorite supper club is located. You'll probably have to drive, but that's a part of the super club experience. **Club 77**, **Tally-Ho**, **The Fireside**, **The Beach Club**, and **Maximilian Inn** are just a few.

READ ALL ABOUT IT

The *Sawyer County Record* circulates to more than 6,600 readers in the area.

HAVE YOU HEARD?

WHSM, 101.1 FM, keeps the busy summer months moving with adult contemporary and offers sentimental favorites on 910 AM. For variety, try WOJB at 88.9 FM, featuring everything from Native American music to National Public Radio.

CHAPTER TWENTY-ONE

LAKE SUPERIOR
South Shore Serenade

I should come as no surprise that an ideal time to visit Lake Superior's south shore is summer and fall. Sure, you say, anybody with half a brain and a lot of people from Minnesota know that. But do you know two terrific reasons why (other than the mild weather and snow-free roads)? They're the Big Top Chautauqua and the Bayfield Apple Festival. And they're perfect attractions for a Classic Wisconsin Weekend spent in the far northern reaches of the state.

THE BIG TOP AND BIG FUN

The entertainment mish-mash known as **Big Top Chautauqua** presents, arguably, the best live show north of Highway 29. Nestled at the foot of Mount Ashwabay's ski hill, a couple or three miles south of Bayfield, the circus tent plays host to an impressive slate of recording artists and musical/historical reviews. Most people come to sing along with Warren Nelson's infectious tunes and hear the crackerjack house band. In the spirit of old-time American entertainment—with modern amenities like large-screen projection and digital sound to boot—Nelson has been orchestrating the "Carnegie Hall of Tent Shows" since 1986. His shows are the Big Top's bread and butter, broadcast every week on public radio stations across the country.

High noon of a Classic Wisconsin Weekend: the apple-peeling contest at Bayfield's Applefest. The Big Top Chautauqua's house band provides the musical entertainment.

Big Top Chautauqua serves a greater purpose as well. Those who have attended a show know it captures the essence of Lake Superior's south shore. Indeed, Big Top Chautauqua has become the voice of the region, as integral to the area as the Madeline Island ferry or Highway 13. This is a must-see for anyone looking to embrace the south shore experience.

Big Top's season runs from early June to early September. Visitors can look for signs near Washburn. The tent seats about 800 people and parking is free. Concessions and a gift shop (CDs and cassettes in-stock) are located on the grounds. Admission fees vary per act. "Riding The Wind," Big Top's flagship production, costs $18 for reserved seating, $12 general admission; children 12 and under, $8 reserved, $4 general. For more information, write Big Top Chautauqua, 101 West Bayfield Street, P.O. Box 455, Washburn, WI 54891; phone (888) 244-8368; or log on to www.bigtop.org.

If you make the trek north in late September when fall colors are peaking, the circus tent will be taken down for the season. Fear not, for you can get a dose of the house show in the only setting that equals the one in the Big Top, the **Bayfield Apple Festival**.

Here you can join the revelers, who may number 35,000—more than three times the population of Bayfield—in celebrating everybody's favorite fruit. Out on Rittenhouse Avenue, happy folks partake of apple bratwurst, apple wine, apple pie, apple cider, apple fritters, caramel apples, all the while carrying 10-pound bags of fresh-as-the-morning-dew MacIntosh, Cortland, Beacon, Wolf River, Duchess, Wealthy, Fireside, Macoun, Dudley, or Hume apples.

Or you can join a thousand toe-tapping folks who take in a free concert while six lucky contestants are seated in front of a flatbed truck waiting to do their thing. On the truck, the Big Top Chautauqua's house band hits its stride amidst mercurial autumn weather that produces both sunshine and snow showers in this postcard-perfect Lake Superior village. On the six folding chairs sandwiched between the stage and the crowd, the contestants are setting new standards for concentration. This is high noon of the festival: the apple-peeling contest. The rules are deceptively simple. The longest unbroken peel wins.

Locals Know

apple with a fine blade (razor or knife). The narrower the width of skin between the incisions, the better chances the contestants have to produce the longest peel. About $1/18$th of an inch is pro-league cutting. Once the incision has been made, start at the top again, but hold the blade (or the apple) at a 45-degree angle to separate the skin from the fruit. Participants have one hour.

BAYFIELD

Once named the best small town in the Midwest by the *Chicago Tribune* after a lengthy search, Bayfield is a great town for poking around and a great place to visit any time of the year, winter included. The tiny fishing village contains a museum, docks for the Apostle Island cruises, shops, fish mongers, cafés, lodgings, taverns—enough excuses to easily fritter the day away, though it can get busy during high season.

The **Bayfield Maritime Museum** is managed by volunteers whose yarns are worth the price of admission. The gleaming new facility, opened in 2000, is located on 1st Street across from the marina; (715) 779-9919. Shipwrecks, boat building, lighthouses, and other important facets of the region's maritime heritage are presented in fine exhibits. Admission is $5 for adults, less for children.

Sprawling across hills behind Bayfield are the orchards that produce both the fruits of the apple festival and breathtaking views: rolling orchards and farms, islands in the distance.

Bayfield has several fine restaurants, but for a true taste of Lake Superior, you have to sample the cuisine at Greunke's **First Street Inn**. This old standby lays claims to having pioneered a delicacy with—get ready—whitefish livers. Whitefish livers had been enjoyed by local fisherman for ages when Victor Greunke began serving them to patrons in his restaurant in the 1940s. The livers are prepared fried or sautéed with peppers and onions. People who have tried the dish are sold. Greunke's also serves walnut-breaded trout and trout Hemingway (pan-fried with sesame seeds and lemon sauce) that was featured in the 1983 *Bon Appetite Cookbook*. Hearty breakfasts served until 1 p.m. everyday. Lots of Americana nailed to the walls. Greunke's rents twelve rooms, six with private baths, ranging from $52 to $105 a night. Celebrity visitors have included Merle Haggard, Garrison Keillor, Billy Bob Thornton, Brad Pitt and Jennifer Aniston, and John F. Kennedy Jr.—but not all at once. Phone (715) 779-5480.

APOSTLE ISLANDS

Fixed in Lake Superior's brilliant blue water just off Bayfield County are the state and national treasures known as the Apostle Islands. Those that live here revere the lake and the islands. They are so grand in scope that detailing the islands and their many attractions is worthy of a separate book. (Think Grand Canyon or Yellowstone—their status as the **Apostle Islands National Lakeshore** speaks to the order of magnitude as national treasures.)

Sailing, fishing, camping, kayaking, hiking, biking, sightseeing, snowmobiling, snowshoeing, skiing—it's all here except swimming (usually too cold). The following is a cursory introduction for weekend visitors. For the straight dope, write the Apostle Islands National Lakeshore, Route 1, Box 4, Bayfield, WI 54814; phone (715) 779-3397. The headquarters is located at Fourth and Washington Streets in Bayfield's brownstone county courthouse.

The **Apostle Island Cruise Service** runs sightseeing excursions, a good initiation, from the Bayfield dock. The Grand Tour is a popular narrated trip around the islands. You'll see lighthouses at Raspberry Island and Devil's Island and the Devil's Island Sea Caves. No stops. Other tours feature visits to Manitou and Stockton Islands or lighthouse tours. The Grand Tour runs 3 hours for

$22.95; ages 6–12, $11.95. Reservations recommended. Phone (715) 779-3925 or (800) 323-7619.

Early Jesuit missionaries christened these islands the Apostle Islands after counting 12 landforms, but the actual number is 22. The islands range in size from three acres to 14,000 acres. In 1970 the islands (except Madeline) and a 12-mile stretch of the Bayfield County were recognized as the Apostle Islands National Lakeshore, one of only four such designations in the country.

Like so many natural features in Wisconsin, the Apostles are the result of a glacial retreat that carved channels into the bedrock, leaving piles of debris. The lake's handiwork is evident in the cliffs, caves, hollows, and rock formations around the sandstone islands, especially the **Devil's Island Cliffs State Natural Area**. There are no bluffs. The islands were scraped flat.

Fur trading began early, in the seventeenth century, and the islands became the westernmost post along the fabled "Voyageur Highway." The Big Top Chautauqua folks can perform some of those robust French voyageur songs as if they just stepped out of a canoe.

Later, sandstone and lumber were harvested in quantity, the former becoming the brownstone seen in many prominent buildings near and far. The local quarries are credited with helping rebuild Chicago after that city's great fire. Look at Ashland's courthouse and Washburn's museum, a former bank, for fine local examples. But the common denominator has been fish. Commercial fishing continues today. Recreational fishing is as good as it gets. Salmon, whitefish, trout, chub, perch . . . it's all here.

Stockton Island, the largest island at more than 10,000 acres, has docks, a beach, campgrounds, a ranger station, an extensive trail system (15 miles), and regular shuttle service. A visitor center is open daily late May to early September. **Raspberry Island** is popular for its 1860s lighthouse. **Devil's Island** is the northernmost island, the farthest point north in Wisconsin; it takes a beating during storm season. The results are five acres of giant pockmarks and caves exposed above the sandstone waterline. Tour boats circle the island for photo ops but no regular stops are scheduled.

Eighteen of the Apostle Islands have free camping at primitive sites. Dispersed camping allowed as well. Sites can be reserved by registering no more than one day in advance at the Apostle Islands headquarters in Bayfield.

THE BIG ISLAND

What about **Madeline Island**, the best known of the Apostles? It looms an easy two miles, or a 20-minute boat ride, from the Bayfield dock. It's excluded from national lakeshore designation because it contains a permanent settlement —a year-round population of 180. Check out the **Burned Down Tavern**, considered by some to be one of the most unique taverns in the state.

Ferry service from the Bayfield dock to Madeline's village of La Pointe is scheduled until the channel freezes. Wind sleds are used for transportation once ice forms. When the ice is thick enough, motorists drive on a path marked by discarded Christmas trees. This path becomes an official road, County H, for the winter season.

Madeline Island ferries stop operating when the ice forms and resume when it breaks up. One-way base rate is $4 per adult, $2 per child ($1.75 to carry a bicycle to $9.25 for a trailer and hitch). Bicycles and mopeds can be rented in La Pointe. Two-hour bus tours run June through September.

Attractions on the island include: **Ojibway Memorial Park**; the one-room **Lake View School Museum**, circa 1904, filled with authentic furnishings; and **Madeline Island Historical Museum**, operated by the Wisconsin Historical Society with collections spanning three centuries. Contact the Madeline Island Chamber of Commerce at (715) 798-3833.

Madeline Island is home to **Big Bay State Park**. Located seven miles from the landing, the park contains three wonderful trails, 55 sites, and a pristine half-moon, white-sand beach. Camping on the edge of the inland sea otherwise known as Lake Superior is an awesome experience. The park is open all year long, and camping is available on a first-come, first-served basis. Phone (715) 779-4020.

Double Take: Asaph Whittlesey

The persevering, we-laugh-at-snow-and-wind citizens of the Lake Superior's south shore region are cut from the cloth of Asaph Whittlesey. Make that buckskin.

In 1854, Whittlesey built a cabin in what was to become Ashland on the southern edge of the deepwater harbor known today as Chequamegon Bay. The pioneer began negotiating for a railroad line from Chicago. He got it 23 years later, making Ashland a transportation hub for iron ore, lumber, and fish. But Whittlesey's legacy was frozen in time in January 1860 when, in order to take a seat in the Wisconsin Legislature, the determined frontiersman traveled from Superior to Madison—on snowshoes.

Along the way one frigid night, Whittlesey came upon a tavern in Sparta, some 250 miles south of Ashland and the location of the nearest train depot. Wearing buckskins and homemade eye goggles, he carried a knapsack, tin cup, and snowshoes that one observer said were crafted from fishing nets. The men in the tavern were so taken with Whittlesey that they contributed a suit of clothes for his inauguration. He left the snowshoes in Sparta (for the return home, perhaps) and was soon petitioning the governor to establish a new county called Ashland. Who could have turned him down?

Yep, these are stouthearted folks up here. The Alberta Clippers storm systems swing like an axe from Canada, slicing across the big lake with abandon. It snows in September. It snows in May. And it piles up anywhere from 80 to 120 inches every year. The gale winds can cut a man's skin and sink the greatest of Great Lake ships.

Having said that, the weather is not all bad here. Lake Superior has a moderating effect as well, keeping temperatures pleasant in summer and somewhat milder (hence, snowy) in winter. The windchill is the witch. And we know from Bayfield Apple Festival that the climate in Bayfield County, a peninsula, is perfect for growing fruit, much like another Wisconsin peninsula, Door County.

The **Asaph Whittlesey Snowshoe Race** is held in February with a 5K and 10K race through the hills of Bayfield. It's one of several winter events, including a sled dog race around the islands, a 5-mile run on the ice road from Bayfield to Madeline Island, and the Blue Moon Ball.

Ashland's colorful history is depicted in equally colorful murals throughout town.

SOUTH OF BAYFIELD

Let's turn our attention to more land-locked matters and begin to venture inland. The first stop is Washburn, a no-stop-sign village located on Highway 13 about 12 miles south of Bayfield. The brownstone bank building located on the main drag (can't miss it) is home to the **Washburn Historical Museum and Cultural Center**, which houses two floors of exhibits and a gift shop; the cultural center has ongoing art exhibits as well. Phone (715) 373-5591.

Eight miles south of Washburn, on the west edge of the city of Ashland where Highways 13 and 2 intersect, is the **Great Lakes Visitor Center**, a state-of-the-art facility built to replicate a lighthouse. One of the reasons that it's more than a garden-variety tourist center is the great interactive displays. Push the button to illuminate Great Lake shipwreck sites for a real eye-opener. Mounted fish and wildlife are featured, including a timber wolf, and the region's history from the Ice Age to the present is detailed in fine fashion. Phone (715) 685-9983.

ASHLAND

Ashland (population 8,700) rests opposite Washburn on Chequamegon Bay's south edge. The evening lights from either vantage point are pretty. It's impossible to miss the city's 800-foot ore dock. It's so big it's scary. Five impressive murals painted on downtown buildings salute local pioneers and serve as unique attractions.

Ashland is still feeling the effects of a fire that gutted the old Soo Line Depot in April 2000. The beautiful brownstone building had been the center of Ashland's heritage since the 19th century and was a popular gathering spot for travelers and locals alike after being converted into a micro brewery/restaurant. The façade remains standing . . . a heart-breaking sight. An organization called Friends of the Depot hopes to restore the building.

For some local fare, fish eaters have relied on the top-notch yet reasonably

207

priced **Hotel Chequamegon**, a longstanding favorite in its own right for planked whitefish. Wood planks have been used for centuries to prepare delicate foods, especially fish. The waterlogged planks heat the food without subjecting the fish to direct flames and add a subtle, smoky flavor. Salmon is still commonly prepared on planks in the Pacific Northwest. The Hotel Chequamegon takes the technique to another level. The exquisite dinner of whitefish, vegetables, and garlic mashed potatoes is prepared and served on the thick maple plank. It's the hotel specialty for good reason. Don't pass on the North Coast chowder either! A standard fish fry is offered on Friday nights. Dinners are served in the restaurant and Molly Cooper's Pub, named after the Ashland resident who distinguished herself in the world's oldest profession. Great pictures of local pioneers and early athletic clubs line the hallway outside the restaurant—some of those folks probably knew Molly better than others. Located on Highway 2; (715) 682-9095.

ALONG THE SHORE

To enhance your south shore experience, don't confine it to the Chequamegon Bay area. Head northwest from Bayfield on Highway 13 as it winds through quaint fishing villages that have, among other charms, great views of Lake Superior that are worth a long, lingering look. Red Cliff is the center of the Red Cliff Indian Reservation. Between the town and Cornucopia, lies the **Hokeson Historic Site**, a water-to-dinner-plate interpretation of commercial fishing located at Little Sand Bay; several buildings are open to tour. Phone (715) 779-3397. Cornucopia is a commercial fishing center and is Wisconsin's northernmost village. Two other villages along the way, Herbster and Port Wing, provide even the most reluctant shutterbug with numerous nautical photo ops.

SUPERIOR

To begin to appreciate **Superior**, 100 miles west of Bayfield, it's important to understand the city's relationship with Duluth, its cross-river Minnesota cousin.

Cousin? Well, Superior is more like a stepchild. Duluth has the bluffs, the Victorian homes on the hillside, the morning sun warming the cockles of her downtown. In contrast, Superior lies in backwater flats, her coal piles and grain elevators the only things remotely resembling bluffs. Railroad cars bang and rattle. Drizzle and fog were invented here. And so Duluthians look down on Superior—literally and figuratively. If all this weren't hard enough, Superior was once billed as "the Pittsburgh of the West." Thanks a lot.

Superior need not shrink from her detractors, however. Beauty is in the eye of the beholder, so behold an industrial, working-class port of international proportions, the workhorse of the Great Lakes with cargoes departing for destinations around the globe. Along the 28 miles of shoreline are shipyards, grain elevators, heavy industry, and some huge docks. Three Burlington Northern ore docks are the largest in the world—80 feet tall and 22 football fields long; the concrete and steel giants can hold 100,000 tons of payload. Untold tons of ore have

As one of the nation's busiest ports, Superior welcomes ships from around the globe.

been shipped from these docks. Incidentally, it was from the Burlington Northern docks that the *Edmund Fitzgerald*, a lake-going bulk carrier loaded with 26,116 tons of iron ore pellets, departed on its doomed voyage on November 10, 1975.

Superior's preeminence as a port is aided by the longest freshwater sandbar in the world, a 3,000-year-old peninsula running parallel to the shore for 10 miles. The sandbar's west side belongs to Minnesota; Wisconsin Point on the east side features a lighthouse.

Superior's most overlooked and underrated attraction is its **municipal forest**. It's the second largest city-owned forest in the country, a 4,500-acre retreat featuring 17 miles of hiking and cross-country skiing trails. Challenging terrain and views of Lake Superior are offered. Cross-country trails are at least 18 feet wide to accommodate both track and skate skiing; considered some of Wisconsin's best. Fee. The trailhead is at the corner of 28th Street and Wyoming Avenue.

For more information, contact the Superior/Douglas County Chamber of Commerce and Convention and Visitors Bureau, 305 Harbor View Parkway, Superior, WI 54880, phone (715) 392-2773 or (800) 942-5313.

Barker's Island, set along Highway 2/53 in the downtown harbor area, combines a marina, shopping village, miniature golf, and picnic areas. The featured attraction is the **SS *Meteor* Maritime Museum**. The *Meteor* is a whaleback, an unusual, if not revolutionary, wide-bottomed ship designed to carry bulk materials on the Great Lakes. Thirty-nine whalebacks were built in Superior-Duluth in the late 1800s. The *Meteor* is the lone survivor, once described, accurately, as "pig nosed." Open Memorial Day to October, (715) 392-5742. Overlooking Barker's Island is the grand **Fairlawn Mansion and Museum**, a 42-room Victorian mansion styled after a French chateau, built by lumber and mining

Big Manitou Falls, the state's largest waterfall, never fails to impress visitors at Pattison State Park.

baron Martin Pattison in 1890. Open daily except holidays. Admission $7; seniors and students, $6; ages 5–12, $5; families, $20. Phone (715) 392-5742.

For the best views of Superior (and Duluth) **Vista Fleet** operates sightseeing tours from Barker's Island. You'll see up close those world-class grain elevators, freighters, and docks, and the famous Aerial Lift Bridge. Lunch, dinner, and moonlight cruises are available aboard the *Vista Star* from Duluth's DECC Dock. Sightseeing cruises $9; ages 3–11, $4.50. Phone (715) 394-6846 or (218) 722-6218.

PARKS AND WATERFALLS

Two nearby state parks are worthy of visits. **Amnicon Falls State Park** is located ten miles southeast of Superior. Open May through October; phone (715) 398-3000. The mandatory park visit is **Pattison State Park**, 10 miles south on Highway 35. Pattison contains the tallest waterfall in the state. At 165 feet, the waters of Big Manitou Falls crash down the craggy canyon with a resounding cascade. Big Manitou is a good as it gets in Wisconsin as far as a single waterfall is concerned. Impressive. Scenic overlooks provide optimum photo opportunities. The park contains 62 campsites; (715) 399-3101.

READ ALL ABOUT IT

The *Daily Telegram* in Superior delivers news daily except Sundays, likewise the *Ashland Daily Press*. The *Bayfield County Journal* delivers weekly.

HAVE YOU HEARD?

When in or around Superior: KDAL, 610 AM, news; KRBR, 102.5 FM, modern rock; KTCO, 98.9 FM, country. KUWS, 91.3 FM, presents a unique blend of jazz, R&B, and alternative music from independent labels, along with public radio programs. In Washburn, WEGZ, 105.9 FM, plays country; in Ashland, WATW, 1400 AM, plays standards; WBSZ, 93.3 FM, country; WJJH, 96.7 FM, classic rock. One of the hippest stations around, KVMD, 103.3 FM, broadcasts from Duluth, Minnesota.

THE NORTH WOODS
Never Far from the Past

This Classic Wisconsin Weekend reveals that the North Woods region has

two feet firmly planted in the snow. But they willingly straddle the line

between the mythic past and the all-too-real present. Wherever you travel

in the area, you'll find that you can never quite escape its colorful past,

and that's a good thing. While the North Woods designation extends to

other parts of northern Wisconsin, this weekend focuses on the

recreation-intensive area bordered by Rhinelander, Eagle River, and Hurley.

SNOWMOBILE HEAVEN

If we have to start somewhere, we'll start with the northern Wisconsin winters. They are the stuff of legend, an almost mythic backdrop for stories of farmers and timber workers battling the elements, of awe-inspiring beauty and treacherous crossings, of ingenuity laughing in the face of crushing solitude. Where else can you find organized cootie races?

In the dead of one such winter about 80 years ago, Carl Eliason was working in the garage behind his family's general store in Saynor, a venison-belt crossroads about 15 miles south of Michigan's Upper Peninsula. Eliason loved to hunt and fish and trap as much as the next guy in Vilas County, but a bum foot hampered treks through deep snow in pursuit of his hobbies. In January 1924, he hammered two skis, a 2.5-horsepower boat engine, and some spare bicycle parts onto a toboggan. A couple of upgrades later, the young inventor thought his homemade contraption worked well enough to file a patent.

He called his machine the Eliason Motor Toboggan, and later descendants of it became popular far beyond anything the North Woods tinkerer ever imagined. Eliason's story should be put in the file marked only-in-the-USA, necessity-is-the-mother-of-invention, right-time-right-place. The U.S. Army purchased 150 motor toboggans for use in the defense of Alaska during World War II. (A group of Russians also visited to test-drive the toboggans on the Pigeon River. They borrowed a machine gun from the local library, mounted it on the hood, and fired imaginary bullets up and down the riverbank.)

By the mid-1950s, the final line of motor toboggans had directly influenced Polaris, Arctic Cat, Ski-Doo and other fledgling companies as they produced snowmobiles to meet growing popular demand. Motor tobogganing had become a new recreation, a new sport, a new industry—all because Carl Eliason wanted to beat his buddies to the best ice-fishing hole.

Some of Eliason's original toboggans can be viewed at the **Vilas County Historical Museum** in Saynor. The museum is open every day in the summer (funny time to see a snowmobile). Otherwise, stop by **Eliason Hardware**, operated by Carl's grandson, to see some of the early models. Visit eliasonsnowmobile.com for history, photos and blueprints.

Indeed, Wisconsin is the birthplace of the snowmobile and a snow-covered Oz encompassing the most extensive trail system in the nation: 25,000 miles. That's the equivalent of riding from here to Seattle and back . . . five times. Wisconsin Trail Number 13 (there are 45) traverses the state from north to south, making it possible to leave the Bucksnort Cafe in Land O' Lakes, on the Wisconsin/Michigan border, and arrive at Big Dog's Tap & Bowl in Sharon, on the Illinois border.

Everywhere throughout the North Woods, there are signs that this indeed is snowmobile country. At the Amoco station in Eagle River, motorists will have to wait in line behind sleds clamoring around the pumps before getting their own tank topped off.

At the Friday night fish fry at the Honey Bear in St. Germain, the parking lot will be filled with Ski-Doo's and Arctic Cats, not sports-utility vehicles or pickup trucks. And "Welcome Snowmobilers" appears on the marquee of every lodging establishment north of Highway 29—at least every establishment hoping to keep the lights on another year. Ditto for restaurants and taverns. It's sublime.

Most enthusiasts are members of one of the 600 riding clubs in the state and nearly all are conscientious folks who look after themselves and the trails. Tavern hopping is a tradition, certainly, as a means to warm up, maybe get a heaping bowl of chili (topped with cheese), and play a hand or two of sheepshead with friends. To the typical snowmobiler there is nothing better. Who can argue with that? Not I.

SNOWMOBILE HALL OF FAME

If this area saw the birth of the snowmobile, it should come as no surprise that it's also home to the **Snowmobile Hall of Fame**. Yes, in addition to the homage paid to Eliason's ingenuity at the Vilas County Historical Museum and Eliason Hardware, the Hall of Fame celebrates the sport that Carl built: "Dedicated to preserving and showcasing the rich and exciting history of snowmobiling at both the recreational and competitive levels through the operation of a museum, hall of fame and library for the sport."

And I thought it was a place to see 25 cool racing sleds, plus a lot of historic photos, trophies, and other memorabilia. It's located about between Minocqua and Eagle River on Highway 70; and it's open all year long. Call (715) 542-4488 for times and more information.

Machines racing at breakneck speed draw more than 30,000 spectators annually to Eagle River's World Championship Snowmobile Derby.

For a taste of the irresistible adrenaline rush that occurs when cranking the accelerator, plan on witnessing the **Valvoline World Snowmobile Derby**, held every year in Eagle River. Thirty-thousand spectators standing in single-digit temperatures must know something. Watch one race—speeds reach 100 mph—and you'll be hooked. The event has all the hoopla and excitement of a NASCAR race.

Roughly 300 racers compete for trophies, prizes and cash awards of more than $100,000. Derby queens are crowned. Semifrozen beer is drunk. The state-of-the-art venue includes the half-mile track ringed with three-story viewing boxes and private suites containing bar and restroom facilities. Stadium lighting makes nighttime races especially popular.

RHINELANDER

Rhinelander, 25 miles south of Eagle River, is the unofficial capitol of the far northeast corner of Wisconsin. Although the town has a number of appealing North Woods attractions, it is most famous for being the birthplace of the **Hodag**, a mythical creature created in the 1890s as practical joke on the community. Rhinelander's good citizens made the most out of being hoodwinked, however, gradually transforming the beast into a civic mascot that now adorns all manner of paraphernalia; you'll see the horned critter everywhere, even on top of taverns. To get your own personal Hodag, visit the Pioneer Park gift shop. (See below.)

A more conventional Rhinelander attraction is the **Oneida County Courthouse**. It's listed on the National Register of Historic Places and contains the obligatory murals depicting pioneer life, but the best thing is seeing the Tiffany glass in the dome. Take a gander.

Also evoking the area's North Woods past, **Pioneer Park** is home to several historic sites that have been moved here from their original locations and nicely restored, including the **Rhinelander School Museum** and an 1892 Soo Line railroad depot that had been in service for nearly a hundred years. The star of the show is the **Rhinelander Logging Museum**, a complex of three buildings that show what life was like in 19th-century logging camps. Inside each are housed numerous logging tools and artifacts. The legend of the Hodag is discussed in detail. And there's a souvenir shop featuring items made by senior citizens who work at the museum; lots of Hodags on display and for sale.

WHERE'S THE FISH FRY?

Water, water everywhere and so many fish to fry. Lot's of choices in the land of lakes and knotty pine supper clubs. Near Rhinelander, you'll find **Al-Gen's Supper Club**, the **Rhinelander Café & Pub**, and **Three Coins** at Holiday Acres Resort. Our resource at the Best Western swears that the hotel restaurant has some of best food in Rhinelander. The Rhinelander Café has been in business since 1911; there's counter service on one side, bar service on the other, and enough mounted firearms to invade the Upper Peninsula.

THE MINOCQUA-WOODRUFF AREA

Minocqua and Woodruff, located right next to each other on Highway 51, are set dead center in the middle of northern Wisconsin, in the region containing more lakes than there are names for lakes. This is an area that many visitors use as their point of departure for venturing into the nearby lush state forests and other natural delights.

Minocqua has become the nerve center of north-central Wisconsin, the place where tourists fill the many hotels/motels and shop at the kind of mega marts that are more typical of suburbs back home. Expect to see just as many minivans in the parking lot as back home.

That's because surrounding Minocqua and Woodruff are 3,200 lakes, the Northern Highland American Legion State Forest, the Willow Flowage, and the Turtle-Flambeau Flowage. The lakes comprise the largest concentration of freshwater bodies in the world. Wisconsin boasts a total of about 15,000 lakes, and it wouldn't be far from the truth to say that most of them are concentrated in this north-central region. As you can guess, boating and fishing are the dual draws, wildlife areas are everywhere, and hunting and snowmobiling are hugely popular. Entertainment ranging from casinos and horseback riding to water skiing shows and miniature golf provide as many other diversions as tourists could want.

Abandoned railroads and a network of old logging roads provide a strong trail system for year-round use. Anywhere from 80 to 95 percent of the land in the towns of Woodruff and Arbor Vitae is owned by the federal, state, or county governments and is not available for private sale. Outdoor recreationists love it. An average of 65 inches of snow falls in the winter for snowmobilers and cross-country skiers. For hikers and bikers, the **Bearskin Trail** is well known and well used, a rail-trail project running between Minocqua and Tomahawk. The Madeline, McNaughton, and Lumberjack trails are former logging roads with grass and dirt surfaces ranging from easy to moderate in difficulty.

When in Minocqua, the local institution that merits more than a glimpse is **Bosacki's Boat House**, located on the north end of the Highway 51 bridge, (715)

You know you're in Minocqua when you see Bosacki's at the bridge and snowmobiles parked at the restaurant's docks.

356-5292. During winter, more snowmobiles will be parked out back on the frozen lake than vehicles in the parking lot. That's the kind of place you want to visit. Best thing is that Bosacki's has a full service restaurant serving food from 11 a.m. to midnight seven days a week. The fish fry is one the biggest in the area and no reservations are taken.

The Lakeside Bar & Restaurant has casual dining for lunch and dinner and a good walleye fish fry, 7855 Leary Road. For lumberjack-sized portions in a lumberjack setting, where else but **Paul Bunyan's Cook Shanty**. Look for (who else?) Paul and Babe standing out front. Located on the main drag, Highway 51, **The Thirsty Whale**, 453 Park Street, (715) 356-7108, has been the tavern of choice for more than a hundred years.

The Minocqua area has roughly 16 hotels or motels ranging from mom-and-pop places with seven rooms to chain hotels with 70 units. Then there are the resorts. Some are truly well-appointed resorts, with condominiums, spas, and a myriad of amenities. Others are musty trailers. Most offer the in-between North Woods experience with lakeside cabins, a boat landing, and a small beach. Lodging guides will list 50 or more resorts. Private homes and cottages offer more choices, and there are plenty of private campgrounds, too.

If you aren't floating your own boat, the most enjoyable way to enjoy the beauty of the local Willow Flowage is through **Wilderness Cruises** in Hazelhurst. The 76-foot *Wilderness Queen* runs late May to October. Sunset dinner cruises, champagne brunches, and general sightseeing cruises are offered. Phone (715) 453-3310 or (800) 472-1516.

LAC DU FLAMBEAU

After enjoying the creature comforts of Minocqua and Woodruff and getting a feel for the North Woods, it's time to find out more about the first residents of this vast tract of forest. And the huge **Lac du Flambeau Indian Reservation** is the place to go. Located just northwest of Minocqua and Woodruff and bisected by Highway 47, this huge expanse contains a traditional Ojibwe village, cultural center, and various business enterprises, including the Lake of the Torches Casino. For more information about the reservation, call (715) 588-3333 or 588-9052.

The Lake Superior Chippewa (Ojibwe) Indians settled the area in 1745 under the leadership of Chief Keeshkemun (Sharpened Stone). Fish were taken by the light of a flaming torch, thus providing the name of Lake of the Torches, or Lac du Flambeau.

The centerpiece of the region is **Wa-swa-goning**. This complex was a recipient of the 1999 Wisconsin Trust for Historic Preservation award for it authentic recreation of an Ojibwe settlement. The site is a great place for field trips and group retreats. What makes Wa-swa-goning so unique is its authenticity. Where else can you spend a night in a real tepee? The tepee rental fee is only $25 per night. Supplied are one free bundle of wood, access to the outdoor kitchen and campfire area, a solar shower, and a dollar discount on a village tour. It's an unforgettable experience. Tepees are available mid-May through September. Imagine a fire inside your tepee on a cool evening, smoke rising through the top, stars twinkling through the smoke hole. Wa-swa-goning is located at the intersection of Highway 47 and County H, 8 miles northwest of Woodruff; phone (715) 588-3560. It's open Memorial Day through Labor Day.

The **George W. Brown, Jr., Ojibwe Museum and Cultural Center** in downtown Lac du Flambeau features a huge collection of Ojibwe artifacts and holds classes in the traditional Ojibwe language and in the making of birch bark baskets, beaded tobacco bags, and fish decoys. You could learn to construct a birch bark basket that will last for years; it's so waterproof that you can boil water in it. The building is not bad looking either; it's located in downtown Lac du Flambeau, (715) 588-3333.

TURTLE FLAMBEAU FLOWAGE

The **Turtle Flambeau Flowage** is yet another northern Wisconsin Valhalla for anglers. Located in Iron County, west of the Northern Highland-American Legion State Forest and the La du Flambeau Reservation, this huge expanse of water was designated as a protected wilderness area in 1992. There are nearly 19,000 pollution-free acres to use and enjoy in a variety of ways—but fishing for walleye, muskie, bass, or panfish will be the drawing card. Area streams attract trout devotees. There are several ways to access the flowage but the most convenient is to take County FF west from Mercer or east from Butternut.

Speaking of Mercer, this self-proclaimed loon capital of the world has (what else?) a big loon sitting along the roadside, while the real loons are on the hundreds of nearby lakes. The **Mercer Depot and Historical Society** is located

Mercer takes great pride in billing itself as "the loon capitol of the world." The real loons are found on hundreds of nearby lakes.

in the only remaining wooden rail depot in Iron County. The town can be easily accessed from Woodruff on Highway 51 and from Lac du Flambeau via Highway 47, then 51.

HOME ON THE RANGE

The northernmost community on this tour (and one of the northernmost in the state) is **Hurley**. Nowadays the town greets visitors like a jaded old madam leaning in the bawdy house door: she has one helluva reputation preceding her, but cold, hard reality stares you in the face.

The metaphor is appropriate. For years "Cumberland, Hayward, Hurley, and Hell" was the rallying cry of fevered lumberjacks and miners who turned the Iron Range into a vice playground of epic proportions. What a playground it was. At its frothy pinnacle, 75 bars were crammed onto Hurley's Silver Street, many with gambling dens in the basement and hourly room rentals upstairs. An estimated 7,000 pent-up miners from surrounding camps sowed their wild oats on any given weekend in Hurley.

The town's wild times are long gone. Today Hurley survives—barely—on the reputation of days gone by. Timber and mining, the two legs supporting the local economy, gave out decades ago, leaving Hurley with double-digit unemployment. Iron County is still tops in unemployment among the state's 72 counties, recent boom times have passed the county by. Silver Street has a few bars and the notorious "lower block" is home to a handful of strip joints. Things pick up a little when the nearby ski hills are busy in winter. More often than not, you'll find newspapers swirling along the streets before you find tourists doing the same.

The former Iron County Courthouse at 303 Iron Street, which houses the **Iron County Museum**, will help you imagine. Within this huge, cavernous building everything *and* the kitchen sink is on display. This is not a state-of-art museum full of track lighting and computer displays. A friendly museum volunteer will give you a handwritten tour outline and you're on your own to turn on the lights (really, you turn on the lights) in room after room of artifacts. Interactive? Sure, pick up anything you want and take a closer look. The big courtroom is nice, the clockworks in the tower interesting. The basement is downright creepy; among the winding rooms you'll pass an alcove decked out like a tiny funeral parlor, tin casket and all—right out of *Wisconsin Death Trip*. Open Monday, Wednesday, Saturday, and Sunday, 10 a.m.–2 p.m.; (715) 561-2244.

The **Plummer Mine Headframe** southwest of Hurley is the last mining headframe standing in the state, an 80-foot steel skeleton (which looks bigger) that served as a giant pulley to deliver and retrieve miners and ore cars from the bowels of the earth. At the peak of iron mining in early 1900s, head frames like the Plummer lined the horizon. Opened in 1904 by the Oliver Mining Company, the Plummer frame angled 60 degrees downward into the earth for 23 floors, a depth of 2,367 feet. Keep your eyes peeled for the small sign on Highway 77 that points to the attraction. The headframe is just a half-mile or so down dirt roads,

roads that remain rust colored from iron.

Also along Highway 77 is **Montreal**, a beautifully preserved company town built in 1921 by the Oglebay-Norton Mining Company. Recognizing that happy workers were productive workers, the company provided all the amenities of daily life, including housing, entertainment, and recreation. Take a stroll down the main drag to admire the charming white frame houses and explore grounds of the huge machine-works building, now adandoned, at the north end of town. Next to the warehouse, nearly hidden by overgrown brush, are the remnants of the Hamilton Club, the company social center where families enjoyed movies, billiards, and a soda fountain. Around the bend is the superstructure of another abandoned warehouse along with rusted equipment. All it takes is some minor exploration to see these stark, ghostly artifacts from the days of ore.

Iron County lays claim to more than 50 waterfalls, supposedly the highest concentration in the Midwest. Most are located in remote areas. Some are of the roadside variety, others require a walk. The Superior and Potato River Falls are the highest, both at 90 feet.

Eagle Bluff Scenic Overlook is a spectacular vista with views of two states and Lake Superior. It's located south of Highway 2 on County D at the Eagle Bluff Golf Club, one mile west of Hurley.

READ ALL ABOUT IT

The *Rhinelander Daily News* is the daily newspaper in this part of Wisconsin; the *Vilas County News-Review* and the *Three Lakes News* are two of the weekly papers. Farther north, the *Lakeland Times* in Minocqua, *Iron County Miner*, *Park Falls Herald*, and *Phillips Bee* are well-read weekly newspapers.

HAVE YOU HEARD?

In Rhinelander, one of the prominent stations is WHDG, 97.5 FM; in Eagle River, it's WRJO 94.5 FM, for oldies and the snowmobile races. One of the coolest radio stations in the North Woods is WXPR, 91.7 FM, in Rhinelander, with a translator at 100.9 FM in the Hurley/Ironwood area and a repeater station at 91.9 FM in Wausau. WXPR is an independent, listener-supported public radio station, not be confused with Wisconsin Public Radio, which is supported by state tax dollars. Broadcasting to the hinterlands, the station would not be viable if it specialized in a single genre, so listeners get an eight-music format: big band, classical, folk, blues, new age, bluegrass, polka, and jazz.

Nostalgia and pop standards are the sounds of the Lakeland at WLKD, 1570 AM, and WNBI, 980 AM.

Double Take: Little Bohemia

In the 1980s, a popular slogan invited travelers to "Escape to Wisconsin." Fifty years earlier, escaping to Wisconsin was a necessity for the kind of travelers who carried loaded violin cases for luggage. Wisconsin's remote North Woods

provided rest, relaxation—and deep cover—when things got a little, er, "hot," in Chicago. Al Capone made his summer home in Couderay, near Hayward. And John Dillinger spent an epic weekend in Manitowish Waters at a lodge called **Little Bohemia**, which preserves the Dillinger mystique to this day.

In April 1934, Dillinger checked into the lodge with his full accompaniment of well-dressed associates: Homer Van Meter, John "Three Fingered Jack" Hamilton, Tommy Carroll, and the killer's killer himself, Lester "Baby Face Nelson" Gillis. Little Bohemia's owner recognized the outlaws; he also recognized that each man had bulging armpits, not a fashion statement but the result of carrying .45 caliber handguns in shoulder holsters. By smuggling messages written in matchbook covers, Little Bohemia's owner secretly notified relatives, who contacted the Chicago bureau of the federal Justice Department.

Government agents, the legendary G-men, converged on Little Bohemia. Chaos erupted in the freezing, pitch-black woods as agents opened fire on three Civilian Conservation Corps workers leaving the lodge bar, killing one of the men and injuring the others. Alerted to the ambush, the gang returned fire, escaped through back windows and vanished into the woods.

A quintessential North Woods gathering spot today, Little Bohemia in Manitowish Waters was the site of an infamous shootout between federal agents and John Dillinger's gang in 1934. The lodge still bears the scars of that fateful night.

Virtually every corner of the globe was soon talking about the shoot-out and the gang's escape. The debacle resulted in Dillinger being named "America's Public Enemy No. 1." In the decades since, the incident has been dramatized countless times in books, television, and movies.

Visitors who happen upon Little Bohemia today are welcomed in a decidedly more pleasant manner. The lodge serves up history and North Woods charm in equal measure. A canopy of pine trees towers over the long driveway, veiling the building from the road. (Not hard to see why the secluded resort was appealing to outlaws seeking a low profile.) Placid, sparkling-blue Little Star Lake provides a scenic backdrop.

Little Bohemia still bears the scars of that fateful night. The walls are riddled with bullet holes, shattered windows are preserved for posterity. Vintage newspaper headlines cover the vestibule walls. Though no longer a lodge, Little Bohemia is a popular supper club where diners can enjoy exquisite walleye or roast duck and gaze at personal items left behind by gang's hasty departure. The lodge bar, with its big stone fireplace, mounted animals and hardwood paneling, is a quintessential northern Wisconsin gathering spot.

Little Bohemia is located on Highway 51 in Manitowish Waters, south of Mercer. Closed off-season (January to April), the restaurant does brisk dinner business the rest of year and serves lunches in July and August. Phone (715) 543-8433 for reservations.

NORTHEAST WISCONSIN
Big Pines and Whitewater

For anyone who's spent time in the North Woods, there comes the inevitable moment, and it's a little unsettling. It can happen anytime, but it usually occurs when you're lost on an old logging road, standing amidst a 600,000-acre primeval forest, or searching your rearview mirror for any sign of human life. That's when you get the feeling that you are unquestionably, absolutely, oh-so-all alone. Your mind might start to race. Did I leave the stove on? What if my car breaks down? Bigfoot is a fake, right?

Stop right there. Relax. It's part of the North Woods experience. This minor epiphany, a result of pure solitude, will likely remain etched in your memory forever. That's a priceless souvenir, but it doesn't cost a dime. Solitude is such a rare commodity. It's important to know that tranquility still exists, that another paradigm for everyday life is out there, and that Wisconsin lays it at your feet for little cost and effort.

Look at it this way, monks spend a lifetime in seclusion searching for true peace. You might find it on an old logging road in the Nicolet National Forest or beside a cascading waterfall in Florence County. (No offense to monks, who brew great beer.) And, by the way, if you don't find enough seclusion and tranquility among the area's natural surroundings, Nicolet even one-ups Mother Nature and provides a natural place of devotion for such purposes, the Cathedral of Pines near Mountain.

Finally, if you somehow tire of all the serenity and hanker for wide-open excitement, try a trip down one of the area's rivers on a raft, canoe, or kayak. Adventures await during all seasons. Spring and summer are ideal for fishing or canoeing, mountain biking, or whitewater rafting; the fall and winter provide opportunities for fishing or hunting, cross-country skiing, or snowmobiling. It almost goes without saying that northeastern Wisconsin offers all the right ingredients of a Classic Wisconsin Weekend for outdoor people, even for indoor people who crave a big dose of the outdoors.

NICOLET NATIONAL FOREST

To give you an idea of the size of the Nicolet National Forest, compare a map of Wisconsin with one of Rhode Island. If you look closely (and the maps are in the same scale), Rhode Island will barely cover Wisconsin's northeast corner, much of which is occupied by the Nicolet. In the north, the forest starts at the border with Michigan's Upper Peninsula and extends south approximately 65 miles to just north of the Menominee Indian Reservation.

The national forest, maintained by the U.S. Department of Agriculture, is divided into four districts: Eagle River, Florence, Laona, and Lakewood. If you are driving north of Highway 29 and east of Highway 51, you'll be in or very close to some portion of the Nicolet. Highways 8, 32, 55, 70, and 139 are the main roads though major portions of the forest.

By the numbers, the Nicolet covers 661,200 acres of this marvelous lake and recreation region. Within the forest's confines are part or all of seven large counties, 1,200 lakes, 1,100 miles of streams, 400 spring ponds, 800 miles of snowmobile trails (marked and groomed), and 300 miles of hiking, biking, and walking trails. Twenty-two campgrounds are all located on lakes or streams.

NICOLET ACTIVITIES

Hunting is permitted for deer, bear, and upland game in season. Anglers can expect to find trout, pike, bass, muskellunge, walleye, perch, and bluegill in abundance. The Peshtigo and Wolf Rivers are noted trout streams within the Nicolet, stocked with rainbow, brown, and brook trout. Many tributaries enter these rivers along their way.

In winter, Nicolet becomes a paradise for cross-country skiers and snowmobilers. The **Anvil Ski Trail** is one of the oldest and most popular cross-country trails in the state. Trails are groomed for traditional skiing as well as ski skating.

Several loops are available over varied terrain, ranging from easy to difficult. Originally constructed in the 1930s by the Civilian Conservation Corps, the system has been expanded and was made part of the National Recreational Trail System in 1978. Trail length is 19 miles with any number of loops, and the terrain is suitable for all skill levels; it connects to the Nicolet North Ski Trail, another popular route.

The serenity of Nicolet National Forest beckons visitors throughout the year.

The Anvil Trail is found nine miles east of Eagle River on Highway 70 at the northwestern edge of the Nicolet. Marked by its winding passage beneath deep hardwood and pine, the Anvil Trail serves double-duty as a popular mountain biking path in the summer.

NICOLET CAMPING

The Nicolet offers more than 600 individual campsites. Each site has a fire ring, picnic table, and parking. Drinking water and toilets are also provided. Campsites can accommodate RVs up to 30 feet long. Swimming is offered at most of the campground lakes. Unlike state parks, campsites are offered on a first-come, first-served basis. (Reservations can be made at two campgrounds only.) Fee information is posted at each campground pay station, the going rate is $10 to $12 a night, plus a park sticker for $10.

In addition, camping is permitted just about anywhere throughout the forest; there is no fee. Just keep your vehicle off the road, take out what you carry in, and keep one eye on the campfire and the other eye on uninvited guests, like bears. Use common sense and hang your trash out of reach of animals. Camping is most popular from Memorial Day through Labor Day, with holiday weekends pushing capacity. For the most part, you can find somewhere to camp if you are willing to be flexible. Boulder Lake campground near the Wolf River is probably the most popular.

As if this isn't enough, Nicolet has 33,000 acres of designated wilderness that are designed for a more remote experience; hundreds of dispersed campsites are available at no fee. These sites do not have toilet facilities or drinking water. Wilderness trails wind through three areas: Whisker Lake, eight miles west of Florence on Highway 70, an area that includes Riley and Whisker Lakes; Blackjack Springs Wilderness Area, eight miles east of Eagle River on Highway 70, containing spring ponds; and the 22,000-acre Headwaters Wilderness Area, eight miles east of Three Lakes on Highway 32 and Forest Road 2183. The Forest Service asks that you fill out a destination card at the trailheads before embarking on any trip.

For more information about camping and campsites, contact the Forest Supervisor, Nicolet National Forest, 68 S. Stevens Street, Rhinelander, WI 54501; phone (715) 362-1300, Monday–Friday, 8 a.m.–4:30 p.m.; www.fs.fed.us

SCENIC BYWAYS

The quintessential Nicolet driving route is the stretch of Highway 32 running north–south between Mountain and Laona. There are more than a dozen natural or historical points of interest along the way, all numbered. But the unsung route is Highway 55 through the Menominee Indian Reservation, which contains forestland as pure as any you'll find and contains natural attractions that include rapids and dells along the Wolf River. The far northern leg of Highway 55 is an official **Heritage Drive Scenic Byway** that stretches from Argonne to Alvin. However, you can't go wrong with any of the roads through the Nicolet: they're all scenic byways.

Mountain is home to an ancient and well-preserved general store, a fire tower that is great for the vista but not for the weak-kneed or faint-of-heart, and the nearby Cathedral of Pines. The 100-foot lookout tower is the only one still standing out of 20 that were built by the Works Progress Administration in the 1930s. It's creaky, wide open to gusting winds, and well worth the adventure. If climbing to the top seems daunting, you can still admire the view of the area from the tree line.

Off County W east of Mountain is the **Waupee Flowage** and the **Logging Camp**, the ghostly remains of a 19th-century camp; both secluded sites are worth the bit of extra effort needed to find them. West of Mountain off County 55 is the **Boulder Lake Campground**, Nicolet's largest such facility with 89 secluded sites, 24 of which are reservable and lakeside! North of Lakewood is the **Cathedral of Pines**, a group of trees that are among the oldest in the forest, surviving from as far back as the late 19th century. Imagine that years ago much of the state was blanketed with pine such as this.

Located about 30 miles north of Mountain at the junction of Highways 8 and 32, Laona is famous for **Camp Five**, a complex of historical and natural sites. Its main draw is the *Lumberjack Special*, a train with a steam-powered 1916 Vulcan locomotive that takes riders from the Laona Depot to Camp Five. There, visitors can tour the logging museum filled with artifacts from the late 1800s. The complex also contains a farm corral, country store, and nature center. Pontoon rides through a wild rice marsh and bird sanctuary are available. Train runs June–August and for two weekends in the fall. Train and museum, $14; ages 13–17, $9; ages 4–12, $4.75; family rate, $38. Phone (800) 744-3414; or visit www.camp5museum.org.

MENOMINEE NATION

Adjacent to the southern edge of the Nicolet Forest is Menominee County, home of the Menominee nation. The Menominee, or "wild rice people," have lived in Wisconsin for as many as 5,000 years. The tribe lost their lands after Green Bay's Fort Howard was built in 1816 but avoided relocation to other territories due to the leadership of Chief Oshkosh.

In 1854 the Menominee founded a reservation north of Shawano. It was Oshkosh who instituted forest management practices among his people that are hailed throughout the world today. By harvesting timber slowly from different sections of the forest, Oshkosh taught, the forest would have time to replenish itself. The reservation's timberland currently contains more board feet of lumber than in 1854, despite the fact that it supports one of the busiest timber industries in the region.

The Menominee reservation also offers wonderful recreational opportunities. It is bisected by 24 gorgeous miles of the Wolf River, a nationally designated Wild and Scenic River on which rafting is popular. Waterfalls and dells are abundant.

And Highway 55, which parallels the twists and turns of the nearby Wolf, makes for a scenic auto tour through the area. Especially look for the signs to the **Wolf River Dells**, located three miles west of Highway 55 near the County M intersection. A hiking trail will take you along the rocks high above the dells for a spectacular sight. Farther south, at Keshena Falls, the **Menominee Logging Camp and Museum** features more than 20,000 artifacts in seven log buildings, making it one of the largest and most comprehensive museums of its kind in the world. It's located at just west of Highway 55, at the intersection of Highway 47 and County VV. Phone (715) 799-5258.

The Menominees hold powwows on Memorial Day weekend and New Year's Eve. A powwow contest is held the first week in August. Call (715) 799-5217. Discover more at www.menominee.nsn.us

WHITEWATER FUN

Parallel to the Nicolet Forest's eastern edge are Marinette and Florence Counties, home to both wild and tame rivers that have become a mecca for waterfall spotters, whitewater rafters, and canoeists. If you didn't get your fill of whitewater fun from the Wolf, this is an area that will provide as much as you can handle.

Marinette County bills itself as the "waterfall capital of Wisconsin." Eleven scenic waterfalls can be enjoyed as part of the county's fine park system. Some falls are found easily near Highway 141, others take a little exploring.

Long Slide Falls may be best of the bunch. To get there, take Highway 141 north from Pembine for about five miles, turn east on Morgan Park Road, and follow the signs. From the parking lot it's a quarter-mile hike on a path to the falls, which are on the North Branch of the Pemebonwon River. The falls drop 50 feet, as the rushing water courses over and through the rocks, making for a gorgeous scene anytime of the year. You can then hike about a mile and a half back to Smalley Falls (you will have passed the entrance to **Smalley Falls** on your way to Long Slide). You can then travel a couple of miles east to **Morgan Park** for camping, swimming, and picnicking.

Dave's Falls County Park boasts two scenic waterfalls, Bull Falls and Dave's Falls, on the Pike River. In addition to the scenic falls and rock formations, the park offers playground and restroom facilities. The falls are located on Highway 141, a half-mile south of Amberg, which is 8 miles south of Pembine.

Two dollars a day is the cost of admission to Marinette County's network of parks, which should not be overlooked for camping (seven parks allow camping). For further information, contact the Marinette County Tourism Office, 1926 Hall Avenue, Marinette, WI 54143, (800) 236-6681.

For you adventure hounds, whitewater rafting is also popular on the Brule, Wolf, Peshtigo, Menominee, Popple, Pike, and Pine Rivers. Known for having reliable water levels throughout the season, the Brule River provides canoe routes even through dry summer periods—it's been called a canoeist's dream. The best time for running the Peshtigo is during spring run-off. It's a Class II trout stream stocked with rainbow and brown trout. Many Class I and II tributaries enter the river along the route; the Peshtigo's a good river to fish while floating.

The Menominee, Peshtigo, and Wolf are best known for whitewater rafting, with a range of challenges from Class I to IV. Whitewater outfitters or charters are found near the towns of White Lake and Athelstane. Northeast Wisconsin's rivers are fed by springs, rainwater, and melting snow. That means warmer water temperatures than on most midwestern rivers, which are fed, generally, by melting glaciers.

GOVERNOR THOMPSON CENTENNIAL PARK

When Wisconsin's Natural Resources Board took a look at where it would locate the newest state park to celebrate the park system's centennial in the year 2000, the obvious choice was Marinette County, dead-center in a region where few state parks existed. (One of them, Copper Culture State Park is 480-acre, day-use-only park located near Oconto.) The new park is being developed adjacent to the Caldron Falls Reservoir near Athelstane. The park was named in honor of former Governor Tommy Thompson, who helped preserve 225,000 acres of Wis-consin wilderness during his 14-year tenure. The 2,187-acre park opened in 2001.

PESHTIGO

For those of you who may be water logged from all the falls and rapids, there's some relief waiting, but be warned, it involves fire. You have probably heard of the horrible conflagration that consumed much of Peshtigo and its environs on October 8, 1871. Fate, however, would have it that Chicago was ablaze the same day, forever obscuring the far more severe Peshtigo fire in the annals of American folklore.

Peshtigo, located on Highway 41 north of Green Bay and the easternmost location on this tour, is home to the **Peshtigo Fire Museum**. The museum occupies one of the first buildings, a church, constructed after what has become known as the Peshtigo Fire. The blaze still stands as the worst disaster of its kind in the United States, taking a total of 1,500 lives, 800 in Peshtigo alone. Severe heat conspired with the remains of indiscriminate lumbering to set 2,400 acres of land on fire that fateful day. Flames and cinders wafted across Green Bay and ignited blazes in Door County miles away.

It's hard to imagine the hell that the fire caused, but the museum is a sobering reminder. Small, poignant artifacts—a charred pocket Bible open to the book of Psalms, uncovered in 1995—can be viewed. Hundreds of everyday items recovered from the remains are on display on the first floor and in the basement.

Photographs taken following the fire are a heartbreaking testimonial, as is the cemetery adjacent to the museum where several hundred victims were laid to rest in a mass grave. The museum is located one block off the highway on Oconto Avenue; phone (715) 582-3244. Open daily June through October 8 (the fire's anniversary), 9 a.m.–5 p.m. Free.

AREA LODGING

As you would imagine, cottages, cabins, trailers, and woodsy resorts are ubiquitous in Wisconsin's wild northeast. Marinette (population 11,800) has the usual prospects if you're looking for a hotel in addition to a few B&Bs. In Mountain, the **WinterGreen Inn** is a small four-season inn with modern amenities overlooking a small lake. Phone (715) 276-6885.

In Florence, the **Lakeside Bed & Breakfast** is located on Fisher Lake near the border with the Upper Peninsula, but the owners claim that "Lakeside exists in a state all of its own." Phone (715) 528-3259. Breakfast is served by candlelight.

A legendary establishment in the area is **Jesse's Historic Wolf River Lodge**, a classic log retreat overlooking the Wolf River just north of Langlade; it also of-fers cabins. Phone (715) 882-2182. In Crandon, the **Courthouse Square Bed & Breakfast** on Polk Street is located in a turn-of-the-century home where owner Bess usually has something delicious baking in the kitchen. Phone (715) 478-2549.

READ ALL ABOUT IT

The *Marinette Eagle Herald* is the daily newspaper in region. The *Florence Mining News*, *Niagara Journal*, *Peshtigo Times*, *Three Lakes News*, and *Forest County Republican* are a few of the weekly papers, some with circulations of less than 800 people.

HAVE YOU HEARD?

WMAM, 570 AM, broadcasts sports and talk from Marinette. WRLO, 105.3 FM, has classic rock from Antigo.

Double Take: Mickey-Lu's

The mandatory stop in northeast Wisconsin is Mickey-Lu's Bar-B-Que in Marinette, home of flame-grilled hamburgers and thick-as-mud malts. Look for the vintage neon EAT sign on Highway 41 near the south side of town.

The delicious burgers are the draw—charcoal-cooked to order and served on specially baked hard rolls with a pat of butter. The meat is ground and patted daily, and onions are chopped by hand.

The atmosphere is just as irresistible. Not much has changed since Mickey-Lu's opened in 1942. Scratch that—*nothing* has changed since Mickey-Lu's opened in 1942. The signs are original. The little jukeboxes on the counters are original. Even the recipe for the hard rolls is original . . . it was written into the sale transaction through three owners.

Have a seat at the counter and say hello to owner Chuck Finnessy as he manages to turn a dozen burgers over the dancing flames. The place is diminutive, distinctive, authentic—you'll be hard-pressed to find a truer burger joint in the state. Worth stopping if just for a cup o' Joe . . . but get a malt, too.

INDEX